*When Are You
Coming Home?*

## Critical Issues in Crime and Society

RAYMOND J. MICHALOWSKI AND LUIS A. FERNANDEZ, SERIES EDITORS

Critical Issues in Crime and Society is oriented toward critical analysis of contemporary problems in crime and justice. The series is open to a broad range of topics including specific types of crime, wrongful behavior by economically or politically powerful actors, controversies over justice system practices, and issues related to the intersection of identity, crime, and justice. It is committed to offering thoughtful works that will be accessible to scholars and professional criminologists, general readers, and students.

For a list of titles in the series, see the last page of the book.

# When Are You Coming Home?

## HOW YOUNG CHILDREN COPE WHEN PARENTS GO TO JAIL

HILARY CUTHRELL
LUKE MUENTNER
JULIE POEHLMANN

RUTGERS UNIVERSITY PRESS
*New Brunswick, Camden, and Newark, New Jersey*
*London and Oxford*

Rutgers University Press is a department of Rutgers, The State University of New Jersey, one of the leading public research universities in the nation. By publishing worldwide, it furthers the University's mission of dedication to excellence in teaching, scholarship, research, and clinical care.

Library of Congress Cataloging-in-Publication Data

Names: Cuthrell, Hilary, author. | Muentner, Luke, author. | Poehlmann, Julie, author.
Title: When are you coming home? : how young children cope when parents go to jail / Hilary Cuthrell, Luke Muentner, Julie Poehlmann.
Description: New Brunswick, NJ : Rutgers University Press, [2023] | Series: Critical issues in crime and society | Includes bibliographical references and index.
Identifiers: LCCN 2022019248 | ISBN 9781978825703 (paperback) | ISBN 9781978825710 (hardback) | ISBN 9781978825727 (epub) | ISBN 9781978825741 (pdf)
Subjects: LCSH: Children of prisoners—United States. | Prisoners—United States—Family. | Prisoners—United States. | Child welfare—United States.
Classification: LCC HV8886.U5 C867 2023 | DDC 362.82/950973—dc23/ eng/20220825
LC record available at https://lccn.loc.gov/2022019248

A British Cataloging-in-Publication record for this book is available from the British Library.

rutgersuniversitypress.org

*For the millions of U.S. children who have had a parent go to jail or prison.*

# Contents

# FOREWORD

CREATING THIS BOOK has been a team effort—of course for Hilary, Luke, and Julie—but also with the larger team of many, many undergraduate and graduate students and postdoctoral fellows at the University of Wisconsin-Madison (UW-Madison), professionals in the communities in which we work, leaders and staff at the jails, and colleagues across the nation and world. Most notably, we want to thank the children, parents, and caregivers in our study for opening their lives and hearts to us, for sharing so much about themselves and their past and present circumstances, and their hopes for the future. We spent many hours talking with, observing, and learning from the families. Their stories are the cornerstone for this book and we are incredibly grateful for their time and patience as we strive to learn and often create new methods for capturing all of the rich facets of their lives and children's development in the context of parental incarceration. We have done our best to amplify their voices in this book.

From Hilary: I would like to thank all of the families that bravely agreed to share their stories with us in this endeavor. My hope is that the experiences they have shared will help influence policies and practices that support children and families of the incarcerated. I want to acknowledge and show deep appreciation to Dr. Cynthia Burnson and Dr. Lindsay Weymouth, who both spent countless days over multiple years working in the field, conducting interviews, completing observations, training lab members, and analyzing data pertaining to this work. Your dedication to the families and the integrity of this project is unparalleled. I would also like to thank my brothers, Colin and Byrnes, with whom I so closely experienced childhood and for whom I have endless admiration, and my imperfect parents, Ellen, Allen, and Jan, who showed me there is beauty in the process of parenting. Thank you to the informal caregivers that greatly influenced my childhood (Ruby, Debbie, Ann, and Beth); to my husband, Benjamin, for his endless support and sacrifice; to Katherine, Emily, Shelby, Cera, Catherine, Bonnie, Misha, Chase, Mikey, Mac, and Tammy for the unending encouragement; to Luke Muentner whom I have watched become an incredible scholar over the last decade—the sky's the limit, my dear friend; and, lastly, a big thank you to Julie Poehlmann, my former advisor. Your knowledge and innovative approaches to this work are incredibly influential and inspiring to the field at large!

**From Luke**: I would like to thank the families in this study and all others with loved ones caught up in the criminal (in)justice system; may this book shed light on the humanity of those living in the shadows of the system. I express gratitude to my mom whose resilience and humanity energizes me to pursue this work; my dad who instills in me values of empathy and understanding in the pursuit of knowledge; my sister whose goodness keeps me grounded; and all my dearest friends whose love and support never waver. My contribution to this work would also not be possible without my training under Dr. Pajarita Charles, Dr. Lonnie Berger, and all other faculty and colleagues at the UW-Madison Sandra Rosenbaum School of Social Work, as well as under Dr. Rebecca Shlafer and my Department of Pediatrics colleagues at the University of Minnesota. Additionally, I would like to thank my fellow students (turned friends from countless hours together in the lab) for making this study and project all that it was: Nikki, Anthony, Zoe, Lexi, Kaitlyn, Delaney, Missy, Kristen, Carly, Amy, Katie, and Brianna. And finally, an endless amount of thanks goes out to you, Julie and Hilary—I owe so much of who I am as a scholar and person to your mentorship and friendship. Working on this project with you two has been a dream come true.

**From Julie**: I would like to thank my children for their patience and encouragement all these years, as I have learned so much about child development and what it means to be a family from you. I also thank my father (who sadly died of COVID-19 in 2020) and my mother for their love and support, as well as my friends, who are like family to me. Special thanks are due, too, to former and current graduate and undergraduate students (in addition to Luke and Hilary), including Dr. Lindsay Weymouth, Dr. Cynthia Burnson, Kaitlyn Pritzl, Zoe Milavetz, Juliana Horowitz, and Dr. Kerrie Fanning, who have contributed much to this body of work. I am also grateful to the benefactors who have supported my career and made much of this work possible, especially UW-Madison distinguished alumna Dorothy O'Brien and her husband Richard Antoine. Special thanks are also due to my UW-Extension colleagues Mary Huser and Beverlee Baker, and to the corrections folks and policy makers across the Midwest and other areas of the country and world with whom I interact. I look forward to working together with all of you to make things better for more children who have incarcerated parents in the future, including reducing their numbers. I am deeply thankful to the families who opened their homes and hearts to us over the years. Finally I would like to dedicate this book to my dear friend D. Miller, who died last year before we could publish together.

# PREFACE

AT A PARK ABOUT 30 MINUTES from my home, the youngest of my three children, who was 14 at the time, watched me get handcuffed and arrested by two police officers. I was calm and talked directly to my son, reassuring him that it was a mistake—a weird mistake given I had worked with sheriff's deputies, corrections officers, jail and prison administrators, as well as incarcerated parents and their children for more than 20 years, and particularly weird given that I had done nothing wrong.

I was put into the back seat of the police car and driven to the county jail before I could make sure that my son got home okay, despite repeatedly telling the officers I was worried about him. When I arrived at the jail's intake center, I was strip searched, finger printed, dressed in a blue jail resident uniform, had a mug shot taken, and was escorted to a filthy holding cell, all the while given little to no information. Meanwhile, as a response to the fear and trauma my son experienced, his stress system kicked in and resulted in a flight reaction where he ran away from the officers on the scene and hid in the woods, even though he, too, had done nothing wrong.

Hours passed before an officer came to the cell and matter-of-factly told me that I could leave. It was a mistake. I was not charged with anything. But it was too little, too late—so much hurt had already been done. I changed into my own clothes, put my hair tie back in, collected my belongings, and walked out the door only to see my sons waiting for me with terrified looks on their faces that I will never forget. In the time that had passed, my youngest had snuck out of the woods not long before a different officer spotted him and let him use his phone to call his older siblings. My older son anxiously picked up his brother at the park, after which they immediately came to the jail to find me. I have never felt more concerned, ashamed, and distressed walking toward them that day. Once back at home, I gave them each so many hugs.

That day was traumatic for all of us. Even though my kids were older than those who are the focus of this book, they were still confused, distressed, afraid, and angry—particularly my youngest who saw me being handcuffed and driven away. Still, each of my children vividly remember that day. Over the years, though, we have engaged in therapy to help ease the trauma, talked about the events that transpired to process the feelings, and created a joint narrative that puts the events in a place in our lives where it cannot hurt us anymore. We are resilient.

We are resilient like so many of the children and families affected by the U.S. legal system, and like those whose coping is spotlighted in this book. In light of the challenges that these families face, every single one has their own story to tell—often one of hurt and hardship, but also one coupled with so much strength and resilience.

This experience, as negative, traumatic, and nonsensical as it was, invigorates the importance of the work that my colleagues and I do in trying to protect and help the millions of children whose parents come into contact with the system each year. Just like so much could have been done to minimize the trauma that my kids and I experienced that day, much more can be done to help the more than 10 million children who have ever had a parent go to jail or prison. My hope is that this book can help spread the word about what we can do, as individuals and as a society, to bolster resilience in children whose parents go to jail—be it for a day, a week, a month, or a year.

Julie Poehlmann, March 2022

*When Are You*
*Coming Home?*

# CHAPTER 1

# A National Tragedy

LINCOLN IS AS BUSY, CURIOUS, AND EAGER to explore as any five-year-old boy can be, evident from the second he greeted us at the door to his home. A thin White boy with olive skin and dark, short, wavy hair that sweeps over his eyes stands proudly in the entryway to welcome us into his home, wearing an oversized blue-and-orange-striped sweatshirt and baggy jeans, his barefoot toes poking out from underneath. As we set down our toy bag and begin to unpack, his interest piques at every item we remove, his head swiveling as he actively takes in all the newness in his surroundings. Eventually, his big blue eyes settle in on a set of dress-up items that our research team member removes from the bag. He exclaims to his mom, "A firefighter hat!" His mom, Haley, a 28-year-old White woman, slowly walks over to meet him in this pop-up toy area, sitting herself a bit at a distance from him on the thick-black-leather couch.

The room around them is bright, the sun shining through a wood-framed patio door at the end of the space. Across from the couch on which Haley sits is a boxed television set that has been playing a series of action movies since we walked in, a shelving unit with well over 50 DVDs placed in the corner next to it. Beige carpet spans the room, being greeted at each end by wooden baseboards that extend up to the off-white colored walls. The walls themselves are bare, with the exception of one framed decorative picture hung above the couch. Structurally, the living space is small but feels even tighter in actuality with Lincoln and his seven-year-old sister Aubrey boisterously exploring the space, demonstrating autonomy and ownership over this place that they call home.

After a few minutes of Lincoln rifling through the case of cars and then the container of blocks that we have brought with us, Haley slowly moves off of the leather couch to crouch on the floor, still a bit removed from her son. She awkwardly pulls her teal screen-printed T-shirt over her rhinestone-covered denim jeans as she attempts to situate herself somewhat comfortably

amidst the scattered toys. Her demeanor is reserved, and she does not readily involve herself in Lincoln's play until suddenly he comes to her with
concern, lifting a car to her eyes and lamenting, "Oh no, the big wheel is
broken!" Uneasily, she attempts to distract him by asking why he needed
to use that toy, directing his attention to the countless other cars he could
choose. Lincoln quickly becomes defensive and exclaims, "Because it's
my daddy's favorite! It's broke and he's going to be so sad." His remark is
emboldened by a fiery mix of frustration and passion, a response that may
be expressive of how he has been coping since his father has been in jail.
Then Lincoln somberly looks at his mom and asks, "Mommy, when's he
coming home?"

   His dad, David, a 29-year-old White man, is currently serving time in
the county jail for what he says must be at least the 15th time. During this
stint, he has been away for about three and a half weeks, but it is the fifth
time he has been separated from Lincoln within the past four years. David
has been devastated that he cannot play a more active role in Lincoln's and
his other two children's lives now that he is in jail. For some reason, this
incarceration feels different for David, and is proving to be especially difficult mentally. He tells us that he has slumped into a fairly serious depression
since he has been away. He blames part of this difficulty on Haley, saying
that she has been refusing to bring his children to visit and expressing dis-
taste that she has since moved in with her new boyfriend, Drew, with the
children in tow. In short, he conveys sincere concern over his kids' well-
being, wondering if they are doing okay.

   Drew's house, where Lincoln now lives with his mom, sister Aubrey, and
10-month-old brother Allen, has five rooms, counting the living space,
kitchen, bathroom, and two bedrooms. As Lincoln chases Aubrey around,
begging her to wear the other firefighter hat, the cramped space feels over-
taken by chaos. Subsequently, Allen begins to cry. Haley quickly seems
overwhelmed, which appears to devolve into visible insecurity and distress
as she seems unsure of how to gain control over the room and her children.
Yet, despite her reported depressive symptoms, she manages to make her way
across the room to comfort Allen while also attempting to involve herself
in joint play with Lincoln and Aubrey. Her presence is distracting to them,
with Lincoln's demeanor demonstrating that he sees her as more of an
annoyance to his imagination than an active player.

   Suddenly Lincoln has an idea. Grabbing the blocks, he excitedly yells,
"Let's make a parking lot for the cars!" to Aubrey. He runs further from his
mom and closer to where Aubrey is playing across the room, sitting gently
on the floor and moving the blocks into their prescribed places. He has his
legs crossed and is wiggling his toes as the sun shines through the patio
door, landing softly on his face to reveal rosy cheeks. His fingers move the

blocks deliberately into parallel parking stalls, precise extensions of his small hands, covered in green and orange marker, and his thin arms, covered lightly in freckles. He quite obviously finds friendship, comfort, and solace in his older sister, preferring to ask Aubrey for assistance in his construction rather than his mom, who is still seated nearby, appearing zoned-out while staring at the two siblings and still holding her youngest son. Later, Haley tells us that Lincoln has been repeating that same question about his father's return home (as he did while holding that toy car to her face) quite a bit lately. She shares that she never quite knows what to say in response and usually keeps it vague, with statements like "Not for a while, buddy," as she did this day too. After that brief conversation, we saw Lincoln soberly resort back to the haven he clearly finds in his sister. The two of them have an evident strong bond, sharing a mutual adoration of superheroes and motorcycles. In fact, it was an imaginary Spider-Man who drove the first car into the newly completed wooden block parking lot, notably the same three-wheeled vehicle concerningly, but admiringly, deemed to be their dad's favorite.

## When Parents Go to Jail

Regardless of where they fall on the continuum of coping and resilience, most young children with incarcerated parents ask, "When are you coming home?" From a young child's point of view, longing for the absent parent is typical, despite the challenging circumstances that often accompany parental incarceration. Although a small minority of children experience relief or improved well-being when parents are removed from the home and taken to jail or prison, especially when severe parental substance abuse or child maltreatment is involved (Wakefield & Powell, 2016; Wildeman, 2010), most of the research finds a host of negative associations between parental incarceration and children's well-being, even suggesting that parental incarceration harms children and further increases inequality (Poehlmann-Tynan & Turney, 2021; Wakefield & Wildeman, 2013). Given the millions of people who cycle in and out of jails and prisons in the United States each year (Zeng & Minton, 2021)—people who are most often parents of minor children (Glaze & Maruschak, 2008)—these findings should be viewed as a national tragedy. Although incarcerating fewer people is part of the solution, preventing the negative effects of parental incarceration on young children is urgently needed, especially when a parent is in jail (where the vast majority of incarceration occurs).

Our study of diverse young children and families with a parent who has gone to jail provides evidence to support this argument. Employing a unique mixed-method, multirespondent design, we collected data using a combination of qualitative and quantitative techniques including interviews, questionnaires, observations, and biological samples from children, their caregivers, and their parents who were in jail. Based on our research, we argue that preventing harm to and building resilience in young children with jailed parents should involve (1) protecting them when a parent is arrested; (2) supportively intervening with their caregivers during parental jail incarceration, especially in the areas of decreasing poverty and financial insecurity and improving mental health; (3) supporting children and their families so that they can have positive relationships during parental incarceration, including facilitating opportunities for ongoing, supported contact with the incarcerated parent and bolstering positive co-parenting experiences; and (4) supporting more optimal community reintegration and family reunification for incarcerated parents after their release from jail. As *When Are You Coming Home?* explores the breadth of how young children cope when parents go to jail, we unpack each of these calls to action by grounding them in the lived experiences of families with young children struggling to adjust to having a parent in jail. We also fold in commentary and research regarding racial and economic disparities as well as family and community risks that are all too pervasive—all through the eyes of young children. This chapter introduces our study, the details of which are expanded upon in appendix A, which focuses on our methods, and in appendix B, which lays out the various data collection measures described throughout the book. We also review the previous literature linking parental incarceration to children's well-being. This discussion, and all the findings discussed in the remainder of the book, are situated in a model of resilience, which is also introduced herein.

What becomes evident throughout *When Are You Coming Home?* is how parental jail incarceration undoubtedly increases children's risk for a number of deleterious outcomes. Increased risk is not equivalent to certainty, however. In other words, children with incarcerated parents may be twice as likely to develop behavior problems or five times as likely to experience other trauma than children who have not experienced parental incarceration (Poehlmann-Tynan & Turney, 2021; Turney, 2018)—however, many children develop competencies and thrive despite the risks. That is resilience. Each child and family unit engages with their own unique set of individual, family, and community strengths and challenges that may make them more or less at risk for instability, more or less adept at employing coping strategies, or some combination thereof. Recognizing and trying to understand the full range of coping with parental incarceration helps us learn from families who are doing well, so we can apply that knowledge to help children and families who may be struggling. This lens offers a personal perspective on how losing a parent to incarceration may affect individual children and their families, thereby creating space to understand nuances within systems-impacted families amidst more on-average research trends.

## Our Investigation into the Lives of Young Children with Jailed Parents

While studies examining the collateral consequences of incarceration for children are growing in number and quality, few studies have focused on young children (who are the most vulnerable to the negative effects of parental incarceration) with jailed parents (where the vast majority of incarceration in the United States occurs) (Poehlmann-Tynan & Turney, 2021). Even fewer studies have collected data directly from children affected by parental incarceration—and the studies that have done so generally focus on older children. The study presented in this book is both groundbreaking and innovative because it focuses on a group of children aged 2–6 years during parental jail incarceration and uses direct assessment and observation of those children in addition to interviews and assessments with their at-home caregivers and incarcerated parents. The assessments and observations occurred where the children lived and at the jails where their parents stayed, typically involving children who were interacting with their caregivers and jailed parents—playing and doing what children do. The multitiered, multi-method data collection strategy, which moves the needle of data collection in this area beyond parent-report survey responses used in prior research, allowed us to focus on a number of risk and protective factors as they occurred and played out over the course of the incarceration for each member of the family. We present our data collection and findings through a developmentally oriented resilience model that situates a parent's jail incarceration in the very real lived experiences and perspectives of young children. It is the resilience model based on ecological theory that is delineated and visually depicted in Poehlmann-Tynan and Eddy (2019, p. 359).

### Study Basics

The study was funded by the National Institutes of Health and conducted in three county jail facilities and across many family homes over the course of several years (2012–2016) in the Midwestern region of the United States—an area that consistently sees some of the highest racial disparities in incarceration rates in the entire nation. We talked with multiple people in each family, working to understand what life was really like for young children who were separated from their parents because of jail and how they were coping while their parents were away. For each family, we started the research process with the parent incarcerated in one of the three county jail systems that collaborated with us on this research. With the assistance of the jail administrators, we identified the parents who were currently incarcerated in each of their facilities. This was a difficult task because most corrections systems do not administratively, systematically, or routinely collect data about parental or dependency status during intake, which makes it difficult to know exactly how many children are being left behind. While we can estimate that well over half of those incarcerated are parents based on nationally representative samples of those incarcerated in state and federal prisons (see, e.g., Maruschak et al., 2021), or on data collected from state prisons in a single region (see, e.g., Shlafer et al., 2019), it is difficult to know precisely who these adults are and how their children are faring back home. After surveying who was in the jail and going through both the men's and women's housing units to present information about the study, we went through a screening process with anyone interested to determine eligibility. If the jailed parents were eligible, we began going through the consenting process, which explained our study to them in more detail to make sure they understood and agreed to help us answer the questions we sought to ask.

### Interviews with Jailed Parents

Once deemed eligible and after they had signed informed consent forms (approved by our university) and Certificates of Confidentiality (issued by the National Institutes of Health), we sat down with a total of 165 fathers and mothers (who had been incarcerated an average of two months at the time we met) to begin interviewing them about how their current time in jail has affected them, their family, and ultimately their children. Generally, we talked to them about how they "do" parenting while in jail, asking them to tell us as much as they felt comfortable sharing about their experiences as a parent, their thoughts and views of their child and the child's at-home caregiver, and their hopes and plans for release. Through this process, they told us about co-parenting approaches, experiences of visits, and about their personal history with the criminal legal system. Those in our study proved willing to be candid with us, sharing their experiences on often personal topics such as whether or not their child witnessed their arrest or crime, how they coped with being separated from their child, histories of trauma and mental health struggles, and how they talked to their child about their incarceration. Following each interview, we guided the jailed parents through a number of standardized assessments, like a vocabulary test and mental health screener, and asked them for permission to look up information in a public database regarding their convictions and outcomes related to potential arrests or convictions that may occur in the future (to determine future recidivism).

At the end of the interview, which typically lasted a couple of hours, the parent who was in jail signed a consent form for us to interview and assess their child who was between two and six years old and gave us the contact information of the child's at-home caregiver. If they had multiple children in this age range, we worked with them to select one at random. We then reached out to the child's caregiver to see if they would be willing to meet with us, including a home visit for a few hours while we conducted interviews, assessments, and observations.

*Home Visits with Caregivers and Children*

More than half of the caregivers with whom we were put in contact followed through with the home visit. In fact, 86 of them graciously opened their doors to us to help us better understand how the experience of parental incarceration plays out through the eyes of their young children. At the children's homes, we received additional written informed consent from the child's caregiver (usually the child's mom when the dad was incarcerated, and most often the child's grandmother when the mother was incarcerated). We also asked for verbal assent from the child and then immediately got down to playing with the kids and getting to know the family.

While we were there, our research team divided up to gather as much information about the family system as we could. One study member worked predominantly with the child's caregiver, asking about demographics, home environments, parenting strategies, co-parenting, stress and mental health, and children's well-being and behavior. Caregivers also shared their childhood experiences, challenges with their co-parent being in jail, any hardships or strengths of the family, as well as stories that spanned across medical, mental health, child welfare, childcare, and educational systems. Additionally, caregivers reflected back on the crime, arrest, and sentencing of the child's jailed parent, describing the situations to us, whether the child witnessed it, and how the child reacted. We then video recorded interactions between the child and caregiver playing with a bag of toys that we brought with us, and later we coded how this involvement and joint-play went. These adults, too, completed a few standardized assessments regarding themselves and a handful of parent-report measures about the children.

Meanwhile, another research team member worked directly with the child. All 86 focal children in our study ranged in age from two to six years; again, if a family had multiple children in this age span, one child was chosen at random to participate in the study. We weaved data collection with children in between building block towers, cooking make-believe meals, taking breaks for snacks or stickers, and having silly conversations with the children. We observed the child playing and naturally interacting with others in their homes and later completed attachment measures based on these observations. In between these playtimes, we completed both vocabulary tests and standardized cognitive assessments with children. On top of that, we also asked children aged three and up to complete play-based, family-oriented story stems, and video recorded them to later code and determine how they represented families in their play. We did this by enacting scenarios with the little dolls and miniature furniture that we brought with us, such as pretending that a child doll spilled juice while eating dinner, fell and hurt their knee while walking at the park, or became fearful when going to bed at night. After that, we laid out a collection of markers and asked children to draw us a picture of their family. We then took this back to our lab to assess for things like who was included in their depiction of "family" and the emotions that might have been expressed in the illustration. At the end of our time with the children, we asked (of course with written consent from the child's parent or legal guardian) if it would be okay if we cut a tiny piece of hair from their scalp—almost all agreed. Using a child-friendly protocol, we took a small scalp hair sample about the width of a pencil eraser that allowed us to analyze the biological stress hormone secretions within their hair that had accumulated over the past few months since their parent's arrest—one of the most innovative and important elements of our study.

While we were busy with caregivers and children, other research team members watched after any other children in the home if needed, spending many hours running around together in backyards, feeding snacks and bottles when asked by caregivers, and coloring pictures with siblings and cousins. Our home assessments ranged anywhere between three and five hours, and because of their nature, we sometimes needed to come back a second time if we could not complete it all in one visit. While all of the data collection elements (and the many human beings present) made for a lot of moving parts during these visits, the rapport built with children and caregivers allowed for rich data collection that has proven to be fundamental in better understanding the consequences for young children when a parent goes to jail.

### Observing Visits in Jail

Our data collection did not stop with the interviews with incarcerated parents in the jail or with the home visits. Following the jail interviews and after we met the families in their homes, we asked both adults if we could join them on one of their child's upcoming visits with the incarcerated parent at the jail. While not every family had visits at that time (for a number of financial, logistical, or relational reasons), about one-third (30) of the families invited us along to their upcoming visits, usually occurring in the following days or weeks. At each observed jail visit, we arrived early and watched the caregiver and child arriving, going through security, and waiting in the lobby. We then observed the child engaging in a visit with their incarcerated parent with the child's caregiver present, as was required by the jails. With jail-approved pens and papers, because audio and video recordings were not allowed in the facilities at that time, we created running records of our observations of children's behaviors and emotional reactions in the visiting spaces and documented the children's interactions with their incarcerated parents, caregivers, and correctional facility staff, writing furiously so we did not miss a thing. In the jail lobbies and visiting spaces, we completed a checklist capturing some of the characteristics of the correctional facilities and family interactions with correctional staff. We also recorded the observable emotional expressions and behaviors of children when they interacted with their caregivers and incarcerated parents in the jail setting. We completed developmental screenings of children while they waited for the visit to see if this matched with the home-based child assessments. This enabled us to determine if we could screen and refer young children with incarcerated parents to needed services while they waited for jail visits. Observing children's visits in correctional settings in these ways is yet another groundbreaking component of our work.

### Reports from Teachers and Childcare Providers

Lastly, we invited children's teachers and childcare providers to fill out questionnaires about children in an effort to gain additional insight into the development of each child in our study, as it occurred outside of the home and with others outside of the family system. When reaching out to them, we did not disclose that the study focused on children with incarcerated parents; rather, we said that the children were part of a more general study focusing on child development and family well-being. These early childhood education professionals provided nuanced detail on each child's social, emotional, and cognitive development in relation to the other children they interacted with on a frequent basis, providing rich context for our other forms of data collection.

### Longitudinal Data Collection

Toward the end of the study, we began looking up information about the incarcerated parents' convictions and the longitudinal outcomes of the convictions using a public database (with the parents' consent). For most incarcerated parents, we were able to determine if they had been released and if they had had any subsequent criminal legal involvement in the following year. In doing so, we could determine who was transferred to a prison and who was released to the community—some on supervision, some not. For those released, we followed along with any new criminal charges or potential revocations for those released on extended supervision. Some parents did not have any additional documented criminal involvement, suggesting that they made it through their first post release year without recidivating.

### Putting It All Together

Throughout this book, we synthesize the different parts of the study to create a picture of the child and whole family unit. Our multitiered data collection that paired observational data and standardized assessments with personal interviews and stories across the entire family created a rigorous and nuanced account of young children with jailed parents. Although we report on group findings, including some that have been previously published and others being presented here for the first time, the case studies of children and families presented in this book (like Lincoln's which opened this chapter) are meant to provide a deeper and richer understanding of children and their contexts of development. They help bring the families' stories to the forefront and provide light for us to see the children for who they are—real kids who are learning, growing, and exploring just like other kids, except that they have a parent who is in jail.

Each and every one of the children we met, including Lincoln and his siblings, was unique and showed us a multitude of strengths alongside the challenges they experienced. We chose the specific cases presented in each chapter of the book to illustrate the lived experiences of the families, although we have changed the names and aspects of the demographic information that may have identified them to protect the confidentiality of the children and families. Because of the strength, beauty, and aspects of resilience that we so vividly saw within each and every family, selecting a small sample of children to illustrate the wide range of experiences of children with jailed parents for this book was no easy task. We are endlessly grateful to all 165 jailed parents, and every one of the 86 children and caregivers whom we came to know over our time together. To better understand these children within the context of what is already known about children with incarcerated parents, we now turn to discussing current research about child well-being when a parent is in prison or jail.

### What We Know about Child Well-Being When a Parent Is Incarcerated

Our study comes at a time when children who were born in the last three decades in the United States are more likely to experience a parent being arrested and leaving for jail or prison than at any prior time in U.S. history (Sykes & Pettit, 2019). The United States incarcerates more individuals than any other country in the world, and most incarcerated individuals are parents of minor children (Glaze & Maruschak, 2008; Sawyer & Bertram, 2018). A recent report found that one in every two adults in the United States, or

113 million individuals, has experienced the incarceration of an immediate family member (Enns et al., 2019). Reasons for mass incarceration in the United States are the topic of much debate, but one fact is clear: mass incarceration did not happen in response to the ups and downs in crime that occur over time (e.g., Wakefield & Uggen, 2010). Rather, mass incarceration is the result of massive policy shifts beginning in the 1970s fueled by the War on Drugs and a shift toward "tough on crime" mentalities (see, e.g., National Research Council, 2014). Since that time, the country's jail and prison rates have increased fourfold. These "tough on crime" policies and associated actions in law enforcement and courts disproportionately targeted low-income communities of color more than affluent White communities. As a result, jails and prisons saw a rapid influx of Black and Latino men who overwhelmingly had low incomes and low levels of education (Western & Wildeman, 2008).

The incarceration of vast numbers of individuals in the past several decades has resulted in a nationwide crisis. Point-in-time statistics show that in 2016 alone, there were 6.7 million people supervised by U.S. adult correctional systems, with nearly 2.2 million incarcerated in local jails or state or federal prisons (Kaeble & Cowhig, 2018). The relatively short nature of jail stays makes point-in-time statistics misleading, however. For instance, statistics gathered in 2019 found that county and city jails held 734,500 individuals on any given day; however, the total number of local jail admissions (or the number of people who come through the doors) that same year was more than 10.3 million individuals (Zeng & Minton, 2021). Although the number of admissions is down from 2008, when there were 13.6 million admissions, the 2019 figure is still extremely high and means that more than 10 million people who are friends, neighbors, sons, daughters, and mothers or fathers are removed from their home communities. The reasons why someone finds themselves in these positions certainly vary but, in 2019, about 65 percent of those incarcerated in jails were waiting for court action on a current charge—meaning that they had not yet even been convicted— and the other 35 percent were serving their sentence in jail or awaiting a sentencing decision. Even though most incarcerated individuals are men, 2,879,000 of yearly jail admissions are for women, and 80 percent of these are mothers (Sawyer & Bertram, 2018). Additionally, what is left out of most jail population reports is how many times individuals have repeat admissions; in other words, the number of people who have been rearrested or reincarcerated and are spending another stint in jail is often missing in the reports. This begs us to ask what this "churning" process means for families repeatedly left void of a parental figure in the community.

But how many children experience parental incarceration? As mentioned, most corrections facilities and systems do not include parental status in their intake procedures, which makes this number systematically difficult to track. Recent findings from national datasets, where children or at-home caregivers are asked questions about parental incarceration, suggest that more than 5 million children, representing 7 percent of all children, have been separated from a parent that they lived with because of jail or prison by age 14 (Murphey & Cooper, 2015). This does not include the millions of children with a nonresident or noncustodial parent who has been incarcerated, even though we know that the incarceration of parents outside of the home can also have effects on children (Geller et al., 2009). It also does not account for how long parents were incarcerated and the proportion of their lives that children were left potentially missing or longing for their parents while they were away.

What we do know fairly certainly, though, is that young children seem to be the most at risk. Initial episodes of parental incarceration typically occur before children turn nine years old; among all U.S. children younger than six years, 5 percent will experience a resident parent leaving for jail or prison (Murphey & Cooper, 2015). Young children with incarcerated parents are also more likely to experience early adversity than older children with incarcerated parents (Turney, 2018). And several longitudinal studies—those that collect data on the same children multiple times as they grow older—have found that children who experience parental incarceration early in their lives are more vulnerable to the negative effects of the incarceration than children who experience parental incarceration when they are older (Poehlmann-Tynan & Turney, 2021). Such "age-graded" effects underscore the vulnerability of young children when a parent is incarcerated.

In addition to young children, children of color are disproportionately impacted by parental incarceration. Although likely an underestimate of disparities, Black children are seven times more likely to experience the incarceration of a parent than White children (Glaze & Maruschak, 2008). Children from low-income families are also at risk, with children from poor families experiencing three times the risk as children who come from families with higher incomes (Murphey & Cooper, 2015). Likewise, children whose parents have little education are 41 percent more likely to have experienced parental incarceration than are children with at least one parent who has some education beyond high school, and children living in rural areas are more likely to experience parental incarceration than those living in metropolitan areas (Murphey & Cooper, 2015).

So, how are children with incarcerated parents faring? Much of what researchers know about children with incarcerated parents in the United States comes from relatively recent analyses of large datasets that were designed to represent certain groups or populations in the United States, although additional smaller-scale studies have contributed to the literature as well. We present the datasets that are commonly used for these analyses in table 1.1.

TABLE 1.1

*Large datasets used to study children with incarcerated parents in the United States*

| Dataset | Sample size | Study information |
|---------|-------------|-------------------|
| Adolescent Brain Cognitive Development Study (ABCD) | 11,878 | **2015–ongoing** <br> The ABCD study consortium, funded and established by a number of institutes and centers within the National Institutes of Health and administered at 21 research sites across the United States, began to follow a cohort of over 10,000 children aged 9–10 years. Researchers use data from this study to track biological and behavioral development through adolescence and into young adulthood. <br><br> Recent waves of data include information about parental criminal justice involvement, including arrest and incarceration. <br><br> Garavan, H., Bartsch, H., Conway, K., Decastro, A., Goldstein, R. Z., Heeringa, S., Jernigan, T., Potter, A., Thompson, W., & Zahs, D. (2018). Recruiting the ABCD sample: Design considerations and procedures. *Developmental Cognitive Neuroscience, 32*, 16–22. |
| Fragile Families and Child Wellbeing Study (FFCWS) | 4,898 | **1998–ongoing** <br> The FFCWS follows a sample of children born to largely unmarried mothers in low-income families of color in large U.S. cities shortly after birth and again at ages 1, 3, 5, 9, 15, and 22. The study design includes interviews and assessments with mothers, fathers, primary caregivers, and a focal child in an effort to assess the conditions of raising children in what have been termed "fragile families" in a representative sample. <br><br> Interview waves include questions that inquire about justice-related experiences for parents between waves with the ability to triangulate between respondents. <br><br> Reichman, N. E., Teitler, J. O., Garfinkel, I., & McLanahan, S. S. (2001). Fragile families: Sample and design. *Children and Youth Services Review, 23*(4–5), 303–326. |

*(continued)*

TABLE I.I

*Large datasets used to study children with incarcerated parents in the United States (continued)*

| Dataset | Sample size | Study information |
| --- | --- | --- |
| Great Smoky Mountains Study (GSMS) | 1,420 | **1992–2003**<br>The GSMS focuses on the experiences of children in rural counties in western North Carolina where each age cohort reaches a given age in a different year. Assessments were completed with the child and the primary caregiver until age 16 and then with the participant again at ages 19, 21, 24–26, and 30. The study originally set out to examine health-related outcomes, including psychiatric disorders, mental health service use, and substance use.<br><br>The core data include demographic variables of the children and families, including indicators of previous and current justice involvement.<br><br>Costello, E. J., Angold, A., Burns, B. J., Stangl, D. K., Tweed, D. L., Erkanli, A., & Worthman, C. M. (1996). The Great Smoky Mountains Study of Youth: Goals, design, methods, and the prevalence of DSM-III-R disorders. *Archives of General Psychiatry, 53*(12), 1129–1136. |
| Linking the Interests of Families and Teachers (LIFT) | 671 | **1991–1994**<br>LIFT is a longitudinal randomized controlled school-based prevention trial using a population-based sample. The original study sampled fifth graders from what were deemed "at risk" neighborhoods and school districts in Eugene-Springfield, Oregon, and followed them into adulthood. The components of the prevention trial include (a) classroom-based child social and problem skills training, (b) playground-based behavior modification, and (c) group-delivered parent training.<br><br>The study includes a number of measures of defiance, delinquency, violence, and crime—both for the child and within the family/household.<br><br>Eddy, J. M., Reid, J. B., & Fetrow, R. A. (2000). An elementary school-based prevention program targeting modifiable antecedents of youth delinquency and violence: Linking the Interests of Families and Teachers (LIFT). *Journal of Emotional and Behavioral Disorders, 8*(3), 165–176. |

TABLE 1.1

*Large datasets used to study children with incarcerated parents in the United States (continued)*

| Dataset | Sample size | Study information |
| --- | --- | --- |
| Multi-site Family Study on Incarceration, Parenting, and Partnering (MFS-IP) | 1,991 | **2008–2014**<br>The MFS-IP is a multisite evaluation of programs meant to promote healthy relationships and strengthen families with incarcerated fathers. Conducted across five states, the study was funded to document program implementation and the impact of programming on relationship stability, parenting, financial well-being, and recidivism. Incarcerated men and their romantic or co-parenting partners were first interviewed during the father's incarceration and then again 9-, 18- and 34-months later.<br><br>Study topics include criminal history and behavior, incarceration experiences (including family contact during incarceration), program and service receipt, expectations for release, and experiences with reentry.<br><br>Lindquist, C., Steffey, D., McKay, T., Comfort, M., & Bir, A. (2018). The multisite family study on incarceration, partnering, and parenting: Design and sample. *Journal of Offender Rehabilitation*, 57(2), 83–95. |
| National Survey of Children's Health (NSCH) | Varies across years | **2003–ongoing**<br>The NSCH is comprised of cross-sectional telephone surveys representative of U.S. noninstitutionalized children from birth to age 17 (with surveys collected in 2003, 2007, 2011–2012, and then annually beginning in 2016). The data provide information on intersecting aspects of children's lives—including physical and mental health, access to quality health care, and the child's family, neighborhood, school, and social context.<br><br>The data include indicators for parental justice involvement at each time point.<br><br>Ghandour, R. M., Jones, J. R., Lebrun-Harris, L. A., Minnaert, J., Blumberg, S. J., Fields, J., Bethell, C., & Kogan, M. D. (2018). The design and implementation of the 2016 National Survey of Children's Health. *Maternal and Child Health Journal*, 22(8), 1093–1102. |

*(continued)*

Table 1.1

*Large datasets used to study children with incarcerated parents in the*
*United States (continued)*

| Dataset | Sample size | Study information |
|---|---|---|
| Panel Study of Income Dynamics (PSID) | >18,000 | **1968–ongoing** The PSID is the longest-running longitudinal household survey in the world and is composed of individuals living in 5,000 families across the United States. The study collects information on primary respondents and their descendants continually, including information on family formation, relationships, financial stability, and child development. The sample is nationally representative, and participants were followed annually through 1997 and biannually thereafter. Included in the survey are questions about family members criminality, including incarceration. McGonagle, K. A., Schoeni, R. F., Sastry, N., & Freedman, V. A. (2012). The Panel Study of Income Dynamics: Overview, recent innovations, and potential for life course research. *Longitudinal and Life Course Studies, 3*(2). |
| Pittsburgh Youth Study (PYS) | 3,436 | **1987–2001** The PYS sets out to document the development of antisocial and delinquent tendencies from childhood and into early adulthood in three samples of boys who were in the first, fourth, and seventh grades in Pittsburgh, Pennsylvania, public schools during the 1987–1988 academic year. Assessments were conducted semiannually and then annually with the boys, their parents, and their teachers. The study includes various measures of conduct problems, substance use/abuse, criminal behavior, and mental health—primarily for the children, but it includes items at the family level. Loeber, R., Farrington, D. P., & Stallings, R. (2011). The Pittsburgh Youth Study. In R. Loeber & D. P. Farrington, *Young homicide offenders and victims* (pp. 19–36). Springer. |

TABLE 1.1

*Large datasets used to study children with incarcerated parents in the United States (continued)*

| Dataset | Sample size | Study information |
| --- | --- | --- |
| Pregnancy Risk Assessment Monitoring System (PRAMS) | 1,000 to 3,000 per state | **1987–ongoing** The PRAMS is a state-based survey given yearly by the Centers for Disease Control and Prevention and state public health departments. The study uses a stratified random sample of women who have delivered a baby in each of the participating states and was originally designed to reduce infant morbidity and mortality by influencing maternal behaviors before, during, and immediately after pregnancy. Study tools include indicators of parental justice involvement. Shulman, H. B., D'Angelo, D. V., Harrison, L., Smith, R. A., & Warner, L. (2018). The Pregnancy Risk Assessment Monitoring System (PRAMS): Overview of design and methodology. *American Journal of Public Health, 108*(10), 1305–1313. |

One of the most popular datasets to analyze in the literature on children with incarcerated parents is the Fragile Families and Child Wellbeing Study (FFCWS). Analyses have consistently found that children who have ever experienced the incarceration of a father are more likely, on average, to exhibit externalizing behavior problems such as acting out, inattention, and aggression; academic challenges; and health concerns compared to children who have never experienced paternal incarceration, controlling for a host of "selection" factors or other observed risks or characteristics that may differentiate children and their families even before parental incarceration occurs (including factors that may have led to the incarceration) (Geller et al., 2012). Research using the FFCWS data has also found that children with incarcerated parents experience more family problems than other children, including more frequent moves, poverty, parental separation or divorce, domestic violence, and caregiver mental health problems (e.g., Craigie, 2011; Geller et al., 2009; Geller et al., 2012; Perry & Bright, 2012). For some children, such problems were evident even before the parent's incarceration, whereas for many other children, parental incarceration caused or exacerbated such problems.

The findings are less consistent when it comes to children with incarcerated mothers, however. Analyses of the FFCWS dataset have found that accumulated preincarceration risk factors—that often continue during the incarceration—may account for many of the problematic child outcomes that are seen during or following maternal incarceration (Turney & Haskins, 2019). In other words, it may not be exclusively the incarceration itself that leads to more poor outcomes for children; instead, accumulated disadvantages (like poverty, housing insecurity, low-quality early childhood education, maternal substance use) also contribute to such risk. Yet studies using other datasets, as described below, have found that sequelae of maternal incarceration can be substantial, as children show more internalizing behaviors (e.g., withdrawal, anxiety, or depression), adolescent risk behaviors (e.g., using alcohol or drugs, having sex at an early age), and less access to health care as young adults, even when controlling for many risk factors (e.g., Foster & Hagan, 2017; Wildeman & Turney, 2014).

In addition to the FFCWS, other datasets have measured parental incarceration and child and adolescent well-being, and some studies have followed children into adulthood. For example, the National Survey of Children's Health (NSCH) represents the whole population of U.S. children aged 0–17 years. Turney (2014b) analyzed 2011–2012 NSCH data and, controlling for confounders, found that parental incarceration related to children's developmental delays, learning disabilities, and speech/language problems, in addition to attention-deficit/hyperactivity disorder (ADHD) and conduct problems. However, no relations were found between parental incarceration and indices of children's health (overall health, depression, anxiety, asthma, obesity, activity limitations, and chronic school absence) after adjusting for these confounders.

In addition to the FFCWs and the NSCH, the Panel Study of Income Dynamics (PSID) is another population-based dataset with information about parental incarceration. In an analysis of the PSID dataset, R. C. Johnson (2009) found that children aged 3–17 were more likely to exhibit elevated externalizing behavior problems when their fathers had a history of incarceration. Both paternal and maternal incarceration were associated with elevated parent-reported internalizing behavior problems, controlling for other risk factors.

A number of studies have used the National Longitudinal Study of Adolescent to Adult Health (Add Health) to examine how parental incarceration relates to adolescent and young adult well-being. In their analyses, Foster and Hagan (2007, 2009) and Hagan and Foster (2012) found that children with incarcerated fathers had lower high school grade point averages and educational attainment, and that they were less likely to complete college compared to children whose fathers were never incarcerated. Foster and Hagan (2017) also found that young adult children with incarcerated mothers were less likely to receive needed health care, controlling for previous receipt of health care and other variables. In addition, Lee and colleagues

(2013) analyzed the association between parental incarceration and adult health outcomes (average age of 29 years). Parental incarceration was associated with 8 of 16 health conditions examined, including high cholesterol, asthma, migraines, HIV/AIDS, and poor or fair overall health.

Gifford and colleagues (2019) used data from the Great Smoky Mountains Study, a longitudinal population-based study of children from 11 rural counties in North Carolina. Parental incarceration was associated with higher prevalence of childhood psychiatric diagnoses, including depression, ADHD, and conduct disorder. After adjusting for childhood psychiatric diagnoses and exposure to other risks, parental incarceration was still associated with having an anxiety disorder, illegal drug use, being charged with a felony, being incarcerated, not completing high school, and becoming a parent early in adulthood.

Although analyses of large longitudinal population-based studies have been critical in moving the field forward to better understand the prevalence of parental incarceration and its consequences, one limitation is that few analyses focus on processes through which parental incarceration affects children or conditions under which these deleterious effects occur. Another limitation is that the studies were not designed to assess parental incarceration in relation to children's development. Thus, they are missing some of the most relevant and rich information regarding how children cope with parental incarceration, including whether or not the child witnessed the parent's crime or arrest; whether the children visit their parents in prison or jail and how the visits unfold; how families talk to children about the parent's incarceration; details about the crime and the incarceration; and the age(s) at which the children experience parental incarceration.

For example, most of the studies reviewed for this book did not distinguish between parental jail or prison incarceration, although prison and jail populations differ in important ways, such as crime severity, sentence length, involvement of alcohol and substances, and mental health concerns (see, e.g., Yi et al., 2017), which has both direct and indirect implications for their children. Prison and jail facilities differ in many ways as well; according to the Bureau of Justice Statistics (Zeng & Minton, 2021), jails are locally operated correctional facilities that can confine persons before or after sentencing. Those serving their sentences in jails are typically charged for one year or less (often for misdemeanor, low-level, and nonviolent offenses), whereas prison sentences are generally more than one year (more often for felonies or higher-level charges). As mentioned earlier, the majority of those in jail are not actually serving a sentence—they may be awaiting formal charges or are being held because they cannot post the money needed for bail. There are also many differences once inside these carceral settings, including the types of programming and direct services offered to incarcerated individuals, location of facilities, and visiting policies and practices. Because of key differences in the way corrections systems operate, there are likely differences in the types of effects seen for families and children.

On top of these differences by setting, many studies focusing on parental incarceration rely on dichotomous "ever" or "never" measures of parental incarceration that miss the challenges associated with churning in and out of the carceral system—which we know is all too common, especially in jails. In short, many of these nuances are missed in studies that either collapse parental imprisonment and jail time together or employ simplified, ever/never measures and measures that do not capture specific information about the age at which children experienced parental incarceration.

Despite their growing numbers and high-risk status, children with jailed parents are understudied and underserved (Turney & Conner, 2019). Jailed parents and their families are less likely to have services offered to them compared to imprisoned parents, in part because of the lack of programs in jail settings and the relatively short stays. Thus, information that is essential to understanding the development and well-being of children with jailed parents is largely missing from the literature, including the effects of trauma resulting from witnessing the parent's crime or arrest, reactions to separation from attachment figures, changes in family relationships, effects of parent-child visits in jail environments, and the process of developing resilience. We cover many of these gaps across the subsequent chapters of this book.

## RESILIENCE MODEL USED IN THIS BOOK

The study and overall structure of the book are guided by a systems model of resilience for children affected by family involvement in the criminal legal system. This conceptual framework takes a systems-level approach because understanding child development in the context of parental incarceration also requires understanding structural barriers and resilience processes of more distal contexts, including the community, culture, and larger society, in addition to knowledge of proximal contexts such as the family. As a strengths-based model for studying children affected by parental incarceration, it explores child development across multiple domains, including mental health and emotions, relationships and identity, language and communication, learning and development, safety and material well-being, and physical health. Although the incarceration of a parent has the potential to disrupt a child's development in any of these categories, within each domain is the opportunity for resilience processes that can enhance child adjustment in the face of adversity. Through this comprehensive framing, we can explore the ways in which the loss of a parent because of time in jail impacts children in both proximal and distal ways while also highlighting the areas of children's lives that can buffer some of these negative consequences.

Situated within three tiers (child-level, proximal contexts, and community and systems levels), the first level of the resilience model focuses on the microsystem, or the most immediate environment in which the child operates (Bronfenbrenner & Ceci, 1994). The resilience processes depicted here involve both individual-level characteristics as well as interactions with other individuals and systems that directly affect how a child lives and grows. For example, the physical health domain presents ways in which a child can be physically healthy, including getting adequate nutrition and sleep and optimal stimulation for brain development. These core individual-level processes are heavily influenced by contextual factors. Recognizing this, the relationships and identities sector discusses how the child reacts to other people in their microsystem. It captures important components of development such as attachment, sense of belonging, and identity development. Through this ecological approach, it becomes evident that it is a combination of both a child's particular characteristics (such as temperament) and supportive interactions (such as meeting the child's communication needs) that facilitates resilience processes in a child's most proximal environments, rather than one of these elements in a standalone fashion.

The next level in the model situates the proximal environment in a larger context. These realms of a children's environment encompass the interaction of the different microsystems in which children find themselves. For example, while it is clearly important that children have their basic needs met (such as access to adequate shelter, food, and clothing, as well as safe places to sleep, eat, and play), it is also important to understand, for example, whether the child's parents and teachers experience relatively low stress—factors associated with children's improved emotional well-being. Combined, these experiences in the safety and emotional domains can facilitate resilience processes for children's health, mental health, relationships, and physical well-being. In contrast, if a child experiences unsafe environments as well as interactions with parents or teachers who are experiencing high levels of stress, this may negatively affect a child's development in several domains.

The final tier in the conceptual model refers to community and systems factors, including cultural patterns and values, dominant beliefs and ideas, and societal trends and pressures that affect a child indirectly. One can imagine how employment and education opportunities for the adults in their lives, perceptions of racial or ethnic identity, or access to community health centers are mechanisms outside of the child's immediate control that indirectly affect their adjustment. Of paramount importance for the children in our study is how legislation and social policies, as well as criminal legal factors and trends in mass incarceration, set the stage structurally for how children can cope when a parent is incarcerated.

The subsequent chapters focus on the sections and tiers in the resilience model, helping to build the argument that preventing the negative effects of parental incarceration on young children is needed—and urgently so—especially when a parent is incarcerated in jail. Indeed, exploring children's family relationships, behavioral and intellectual development, health, poverty, caregiver stress and coparenting, trauma, visiting and other forms of contact, and reentry and recidivism is necessary in order to understand what helps children develop when a parent is incarcerated and prevent harm. As stated, while reducing the number of children with incarcerated parents is of utter importance, learning how to best support children and families being impacted right now, in the interim, is the purpose of this study and the goal of this book.

CHAPTER 2

# "Is Daddy Getting Taken Away?"

## PARENTAL ARREST AND FAMILY SEPARATION

OUR RESEARCH TEAM ARRIVES at Louise's apartment late in the afternoon on a cold day in January. We ring the buzzer to the duplex on the outskirts of town at the same time that the exterior door buzzes to unlock loudly. As we climb the dimly lit wooden stairs to the second-floor unit, the apartment door at the top of the stairs swings open, and we hear giggles and the sound of little feet jumping about. Armoni, a six-year-old biracial boy, and his two-year-old brother Jordan are just behind the cracked door, smiling eagerly to see who the visitors are. Louise, Armoni's 59-year-old grandmother, invites us in as Armoni and his brother run across the room and watch with curious faces as we settle onto seats at the small but functional dining room table. Hung up on the apartment walls are framed family photographs that include images of the boys with their 27-year-old White mother, Kiesha, although their 29-year-old Black father, Javonte, is nowhere to be seen in the pictures. This may be because, as we later find out after talking to Louise, that Javonte has not been involved in his sons' lives since Jordan was born. She tells us that Armoni's mom has played a more active, albeit sporadic, role over the last six years, though she has been a bit more distanced lately, even before the last three months that she has spent in jail.

During our visit, Armoni fluctuates between shyness and bursts of energy and excitement. As we sit down with him at the round marble-top dining table in the kitchen area, we cannot help but notice how the kitchen counters are covered with various belongings and countless piles of miscellaneous papers that are almost toppling over. The kitchen sink is overflowing with dishes, and the nearby garbage can is overflowing with fast food cups and other discarded items. Yet directly in front of us, Armoni leans his entire torso onto the table, placing his elbows toward the center while dipping his fingers in a jar of peanut butter, avoiding the spoon that rests gently at the rim. As his stomach pushes up against the edge of the table, his bare feet climb up the back of his chair as he licks his fingers. He is wearing a bright neon shirt full of action figures, and a pair of denim jeans that look as if he still has some growing in to do. Armoni's hair is not quite shoulder length and pulled back in tight braids to reveal his dark eyes and light brown, rosy cheeks. His front teeth, with big gaps between them, slightly poke out between his lips when he smiles. When he is not eating out of the jar of peanut butter, he shyly looks around; with the palm of his hand covering his mouth to hide a growing smirk, his eyes intently watching our every move.

Louise sits in the other room on an oversized couch with dark green fabric and faux wood trim. She wears a chunky striped turtleneck, and a pair of large, navy-rimmed eyeglasses rest crookedly on her nose. She has short, gradually greying hair. Louise is Armoni's maternal grandmother—Kiesha's mother. Louise was once married, but she is now divorced and running the household as the sole caregiver to her grandchildren. With two children in the apartment, she says that it is seldom quiet and often chaotic—but she loves the boys with her whole heart and she would not trade taking care of them for the world. Right now, Louise is not employed; she has been receiving public assistance for two years and describes her financial situation as "barely skating by" with a meager income of only $13,000 per year. She has served as the primary caregiver for Armoni and Jordan off and on throughout their lives, but this time is because Kiesha is currently incarcerated at the jail which is only a few minutes from Louise's duplex.

About a half hour into our interview, we began to ask Louise more specific questions about Kiesha's crime, arrest, and subsequent sentencing. Louise pauses for a moment, takes a deep breath seemingly to gather her thoughts, and begins to open up to us about Kiesha's substance use issues and how Armoni and Jordan actually witnessed her being arrested. She walks us through that devastating night just a few months ago, when the boys were asleep on a pair of couches in the living room at Kiesha's friend's house, across town from the duplex we are sitting in now. Louise is adamant that she was not there; she heard from the boys and her daughter that just as the sun was starting to come up, Armoni and his brother were suddenly woken up to a crash of the window breaking followed by alarmingly bright lights coming from the floor of the living room. The children were disoriented and afraid, screaming loudly but staying frozen on their makeshift couch beds, calling at the top of their lungs for their mom to come save them. Having more complete information now, Louise describes how law enforcement officers had thrown tactical devices through the living room window as part of a drug raid and then used a battering ram to destroy the front door, which was across the room from where the boys had been sleeping.

According to Louise, police officers entered the house and abruptly picked up Armoni and Jordan and set them side by side on the couch. The officers went upstairs to conduct the arrest and marched Kiesha, her friend, and three men—all handcuffed—past the children and out the door. Armoni and his brother had only one brief moment to hear from Kiesha just before she left. She quickly, though confusingly, explained that she was going to jail but was able to emphasize that it was "nobody's fault but mom's." The agents also searched the house and took out the stuffing of the several teddy bears while the boys watched, still sitting on the couch. Watching from the curb as their mom was driven away in the back of a police car to the jail for processing, the boys sat silently with a police officer until Louise could come pick them up about 20 minutes later. When she arrived, Louise described how Armoni and Jordan were visibly and audibly distressed and afraid, and they cried the entire way to Louise's apartment. Louise rated Armoni's distress after witnessing his mom's arrest on a scale from 1 (no distress) to 5 (extreme distress) as a solid 5, saying he barely slept or ate in the days that followed.

Louise also told us that "of course Armoni knows" that his mother is in jail because of her involvement in using and dealing illegal drugs. According to Louise, Armoni witnessed Kiesha's criminal activity—both the using and the dealing—countless times prior to her arrest. We asked Louise to report on that same scale how distressed she thought Armoni was after witnessing his mom's criminal activity. She told us that it was confusing and challenging for him at first but he eventually got used to it (almost numb to it, she described), so she ultimately decided to rate it as a 3. She said that the drug use was so frequent that it almost felt normal to the boys as time went on, though they hated seeing their mom in that state.

As we spoke with Louise, she began to open up about how she felt that Kiesha has done very little to rebuild her relationship with Armoni and Jordan after they witnessed such a traumatic event. She rolled her eyes seemingly out of frustration as she vented about how Kiesha seemed to be mostly concerned about staying in touch with her new boyfriend rather than staying connected to her children. Louise said this was a pattern with her, since Armoni has been in and out of his mom's care throughout his life. Their first separation occurred before he even turned one year old. With the boys playing with our researchers in the nearby room, Louise quietly retold the story of how Armoni's older half sister was abused by a live-in relative, which caught the attention of the child welfare agency in town, and, as a result, all of the children were removed from Keisha's home. She described the reason for this forced separation as being because her daughter failed to protect her child from the abuse, but also recognized the secondary trauma the boys felt from being around their sister and her abuser and from being separated from their mother. That was the first time Louise took on the primary caregiving role for her grandchildren.

Finally, at the age of three, Armoni returned to Kiesha's care for a year; but about a year ago things became more unstable again. In the eight months leading up to his mom's recent arrest, Armoni was separated from her again and moved back in with his grandma for what would turn out to be a fairly cyclical trend. For example, separations occurred when Kiesha was incarcerated for a couple of weeks last winter, when she disappeared to live with her boyfriend, and multiple times when her substance use issues resulted in eviction or left her without money for rent or hotels, resulting in bouts of homelessness with and without the boys in tow. In many ways Louise seemed to be more at peace with the boys under her watch, even saying that Armoni and his brother love living with her. She thinks that despite the stress of repeated separations from their mother and the severe trauma from witnessing her arrest, the boys are starting to feel safe—for the first time in a long time, she says.

We wondered about Armoni's adjustment to his mother's arrest and incarceration while in the care of Louise, especially given how traumatic it must have been to see his mom arrested in such an abrupt and scary way. She told us that at first, Armoni's behavior was good—suspiciously good, in fact. Louise speculated that Armoni was behaving that way because he was frightened and thought he needed to be on his best behavior so no more bad things happened. Now, just three months later, Armoni regularly exhibits defiance with his grandmother, often having angry outbursts. Louise said he has this kind of "I can do whatever I want to do" sassy attitude, and that he often lashes out at her. She thinks that sometimes he does this to gain attention but more often thinks that his refusal to abide by her directives is because he does not know how to cope with the trauma of his mom's absence, saying he often cries and relentlessly asks about her. Louise told us that on top of this anger and sadness, Armoni has also expressed fear, anxiety, depression, and loneliness in relation to his mother's incarceration. But she is glad that he is able to talk about it with her. She says that she does not keep any secrets from him and she is quick to tell him that it is not his fault that the police officers broke through the door, took away his mom, and put her in jail. She reassures him that he is a good boy and that she is there for him and his brother no matter what. They even sometimes talk about that night he saw his mom handcuffed and marched out of the broken-down front door. His grandma validates how scary it was to be around such loud noises, bright lights, and heavily armed strangers who then took his mom from him. She promises to be there for him, keep him safe, and to do her best to not have something as frightening as that happen ever again.

Louise thinks that she has really thrived as the caregiver for Armoni and his brother, and that she is doing the best she can given the circumstances.

She loves taking care of them and describes how they all have developed close bonds. Despite the outbursts, Armoni seeks comfort from his grandmother when he is upset and is learning to explore his new house and neighborhood with her encouragement. He is starting to do better in school, too, after a rough period that immediately followed his mom's arrest. It is clear that Armoni's relationship with his grandma is growing. Having the ability to live with her while working through his trauma and navigating a once-again distanced relationship with his mom has allowed him the opportunity to make sense of some of his lingering emotions from repeated separations, witnessing Kiesha's arrest, and experiencing her incarceration with a supportive adult nearby.

At Armoni's request, Louise recently took him to the jail to visit his mom. In total, he has visited her three times in the last two months. We asked Louise how the visits have been going for him, and she informed us that they were relatively normal. She told us that he looks forward to the visits and seems to take it all in stride. Typically, during the visits, he says hi to his mother but then begins to wander and becomes inattentive. At times he has a difficult time talking, but he has communicated to his mother "I love you" and "I miss you." He also repeatedly asks her, "When are you coming home?" Louise has told Kiesha that it is inappropriate to make promises to Armoni in response to his questions, especially when so much is uncertain. So Kiesha often keeps it short and simple by saying "I don't know" in response to Armoni's questions, but she reassures him that she loves and misses him, too.

### STRESSORS FOR YOUNG CHILDREN WITH INCARCERATED PARENTS

When thinking of parental incarceration as a series of events or a continuum of legal involvement instead of one singular event, we begin to understand just how much some kids have gone through. In just six short years of life, Armoni has experienced a significant amount of adversity that undoubtedly has been stressful. Of particular interest in his story (and unfortunately the stories of a significant number of children in his shoes) is the lasting toll of witnessing his parent being arrested and taken away, yet another repeated experience of separation from his mother. As alluded to, playing witness to these distressing events is not necessarily uncommon for kids whose parents are incarcerated. The ones in our study were no different, as a sizable proportion were present for their parent's arrest. As we discuss these stressful phenomena and consider them in the context of Armoni and Kiesha, we include a call for children to be protected during arrest procedures and be actively supported during and after their parent's time in jail.

*Parental Arrests*

In 2019, law enforcement personnel made more than 10 million arrests across the United States, with people of color disproportionately affected (Federal Bureau of Investigation, 2020; Mitchell & Caudy, 2015). Pointedly, these statistics cannot adequately account for how many of these arrests were of parents or the number that occurred with children present (Eddy & Poehlmann-Tynan, 2019). That said, based on what we know about parental incarceration, it is likely that most of the arrestees who then became incarcerated were parents of minor children, with a higher proportion of Black and Latinx families affected than White families (Glaze & Maruschak, 2008; Sawyer & Wagner, 2020; Shanahan & Agudelo, 2012; Shlafer et al., 2019). We roughly estimate that since about half of all those incarcerated are parents (with rates higher for mothers), it may be generally safe to assume that approximately half of those 10 million arrests were of adults with minor children back home (Glaze & Maruschak, 2008).

A recent analysis (E. I. Johnson et al., 2022) was conducted using data from the Adolescent Brain and Cognitive Development (ABCD) study, on ongoing longitudinal study that has enrolled 9–10-year-olds and their families from sites around the country in a way that approximates a nationally representative sample. At the first wave of data collection, 12.5 percent of the youth had a parent who had been arrested for issues related to drugs or alcohol, with most (75.2 percent) experiencing the arrest of their father, 16.2 percent experiencing the arrest of their mother, and 11.4 percent experiencing the arrest of both parents. Youth who experienced parental arrest exhibited higher levels of both internalizing and externalizing behaviors, especially when their mother had been arrested, compared to their peers and controlling for a number of other risk factors—which tended to co-occur with parental arrest (E. I. Johnson et al., 2022). It is unknown how many of the youth in the ABCD study witnessed their parent's arrest, however, as those data were not collected in the first wave.

Smaller regional studies have suggested that between 20 and 50 percent of children with incarcerated parents have witnessed their parent's arrest (Dallaire & Wilson, 2010; Kampfner, 1995). Given these findings, it is likely that a sizable portion of young ones whose parents are involved in the criminal legal system are not only dealing with stressful separations but also potentially traumatic (not to mention confusing) exposure to the arrest and detainment of their parents. They may also witness the parent's crime, like Armoni did.

In a 2017 publication from our research team, we reported on the children in our study who witnessed their father's crime and arrest (Poehlmann-Tynan et al., 2017). For Armoni, this included witnessing Kiesha both using and selling of drugs in and out of their various homes. We found that Armoni was not alone in this; in fact, in our subsample of 77 children between the ages of two and six with incarcerated fathers, 27 percent witnessed their parents' crime and 22 percent witnessed their arrest (Poehlmann-Tynan et al., 2017). Because of their young age and still developing cognitions, many caregivers and parents reported that children were not always all that aware or even stressed by being around the criminal activity. In this way, young children's developmental limitations might act as a sort of protective factor. But perhaps where limited developmental capacities may be more harmful are in the quarter of cases in which, like Armoni, the kids actually witnessed their parents' arrest (Poehlmann-Tynan et al., 2017). In our surveys with the adults, we found that whereas 59 percent of children who witnessed the arrest exhibited "extreme distress," only 18 percent exhibited little or no distress. This means that over half of kids responded similarly to Armoni, potentially experiencing the event as traumatic.

Because these arrests do not occur in isolation, they tend to look different on a case-by-case basis. Law enforcement officers may strategically attempt to arrest individuals, and these times may occur when children are present, as with Armoni's experience. Some arrests occurred at the child's home during the predawn period when family members were still asleep; but in some instances these efforts suddenly woke the kids up, leaving them significantly disoriented and frightened. Perhaps this was an approach that went all too wrong for Armoni's household, though it is most likely that a child-sensitive protocol was not used at all in this instance. Armoni's experience is not an anomaly—the majority of accounts we heard about when children witnessed their parents' arrest were similarly traumatizing. In another home, a law enforcement officer shot the family's dog in front of the children and it died on the coffee table during the arrest. In another instance, a father was simply stopped for a minor traffic violation but was ultimately arrested while his son was in the car after officers found out he had a significant number of unpaid citations. In this case, the child remained restrained in his car seat but was kicking his legs and flailing his arms while "crying, screaming, wanting his dad, asking why they had to take his dad." These reactions of crying, screaming, and acting confused were pervasive across the many accounts that we heard. As one caregiver stated about the child, "She started scream-crying. She said to me, 'What's going on? What's going on? Is Daddy getting taken away? Why are they not letting him go? Why can't he come with us?'" This same child then started screaming to the law enforcement officer, "Why are you taking him? Where is he going? Why isn't he coming with us?"

We found out that a sizable proportion of children were in Armoni's shoes—experiencing trauma because of witnessing their parent's arrest and exhibiting stress symptoms that have the potential to stick with them for years to come, evidenced by those who can clearly recall details of the arrest, even years later (Kampfner, 1995). Research has found that children who witness the arrest of a household member, and in particular a parent, are likely to show elevated symptoms of posttraumatic stress, elevated behavior problems, health problems, and subsequent developmental delays and missed developmental milestones (Dallaire & Wilson, 2010; Philipps & Zhao, 2010; Poehlmann-Tynan et al., 2021). To begin to examine mechanisms that may link the traumatic exposure to these adverse outcomes, our study looked at how these experiences can actually "get under the skin" of young children.

### Children's Reactions to Stress

To better understand how Armoni and many other kids in our study had experienced their parent's arrest and to learn about their distress, we used several methods to document their stress. First, we interviewed the incarcerated parent and children's caregiver about the child's experiences of the parent's arrest by asking them whether the child witnessed the arrest, how they would rate their emotional reactions, and for any details they would be willing to share about the arrest. From there, we took an innovative approach to understanding experiences of stress for kids in the study by assessing their physiological stress response as it accumulated in their bodies and was excreted in their hair follicles. By looking at the hormones stored in their hair, we were able to determine how stressed they were on a physiological level. Because the stress hormones cortisol and cortisone are excreted in hair follicles and then the hair grows outward, scientists are able to accurately capture how exposure to stress gets under their skin and into their bodies. This was the first time a study had measured the stress hormones cortisol and cortisone in a sample of children with incarcerated parents.

Cortisol, specifically, is a glucocorticoid hormone that plays an important role in health for children and adults. This hormone is released by the neuroendocrine system when the body experiences stress, and it is an indicator of hypothalamic-pituitary-adrenal (HPA) axis activity. It is normal for cortisol to increase during a stressful event. This process reflects the body's expected adaptation to stressors. Think about this in your life—when you get scared, nervous, or feel stressed, maybe your heart rate raises, your palms get sweaty, or your legs or jaw shake. These are normal physiological responses to stress—adaptations the kids in our study exhibited, too. However, longer-term changes in cortisol that occur when stressors are chronic or cumulative can affect children's developing brains and hormone systems in ways that lead to abnormal stress responses (Shonkoff et al., 2012). In other words, if these same stressful events that make one's heart rate raise or palms sweaty keep on occurring, or there is a prolonged intense or traumatic stressor, it can detrimentally impact their bodies. Abnormal stress responses are usually shown in one of two ways: (1) stress systems that express too much cortisol regularly over time (called "hypercortisolemia") or (2) stress systems that are so overwhelmed that they do not even express cortisol in reaction to normal stressors (called "hypocortisolemia" or "blunted" stress reactions). This means that one's body can produce a lot of cortisol as hormones level spike or this response system can effectively shut down and emit little to no cortisol at all. The latter response, that of blunted stress reactions, is often seen in people with posttraumatic stress disorder—their physiological stress system stops acting in the way that it normally should.'

When this stress system is working properly, elevations in cortisol get the body ready to react to potentially dangerous situations. When cortisol kicks in, often people are described as having "fight or flight" responses or "fight, flight, or freeze" reactions. This is, again, when a person's heart rate goes up, their mouth becomes dry and breathing is shallow, their pupils dilate, digestion slows, and they may become hypervigilant. This is normal—the body is preparing for action. When the stressor goes away or decreases, the body goes back to normal and we begin to see the heart rate decrease, breathing slow and deepen, and the pupils, digestive system, and cognition return to normal. This routine is not what happens in the context of high and repeated stress, however. When chronic or toxic stressors like repeated trauma, witnessing violence, or unsafe conditions are present for children—especially those who are young—the body cannot return to normal. The body *keeps* reacting, sending either too much or not enough cortisol to the brain. In this way, brain structures and functions become affected as they are developing, creating havoc in a child's body. This affects their health, learning, behavior, and ability to respond to stress in the future (Shonkoff et al., 2012).

This sort of physiological stress response can be measured by assessing cortisol in several ways, for example in samples of blood, saliva, urine, or scalp hair (Bevans et al., 2008, 2009; Xie et al., 2011). One drawback of more traditional measures of cortisol, such as those involving collection of blood or urine, is that it reflects only hours of stress response (it can also be difficult to collect such samples from young children, the focus of this study). This would not have allowed us to date physiological stress responses back to traumatic events associated with the incarceration over the last few months, like examining it for those who witnessed their parent's arrest. In contrast, and more advantageous for this study, is a relatively new measure of cortisol—scalp hair—which reflects months rather than hours of stress responses since the hormones are captured in hair follicles through which the hair, itself, holds onto and grows outward with. As such, sampling scalp hair can aid in understanding the role of cortisol as it accumulates across months because it is a reliable estimate of longer-term cortisol, and it corresponds to cortisol in the blood (Kapoor et al., 2018). Assessing stress in this way allowed us to measure cumulative cortisol exposure in a fashion that was less invasive than drawing blood or collecting urine (Raul et al., 2004; Russell et al., 2012; Staufenbiel et al., 2013). Although human scalp hair grows at different rates across individuals, about one centimeter of scalp hair growth is often used to represent about one month's growth, on average (Stalder & Kirschbaum, 2012). Therefore, by taking a hair sample and measuring cortisol, children's stress reactivity could be determined for the last couple of months, including the time period in which their parents were initially arrested before this current time in jail. It should be noted, however, that it is not possible to directly pinpoint specific sources of stress or their causal role when analyzing scalp hair—yet one can make inferences about the accumulation of stress responses over time.

### Children's Stress Hormones

Although a relatively new methodology for assessing stress processes, a growing literature has examined hair cortisol concentrations in children and adults, and we refer you to our published studies on the topic for a more comprehensive review (Muentner et al., 2021; Poehlmann-Tynan et al., 2020). Indeed, we recently published findings from our research focusing on children in this study with an incarcerated father (Muentner et al., 2021). Our analyses focused on the hair samples of 41 children along with reports from each of their incarcerated fathers and at-home caregivers. The adults reported on whether or not the children witnessed their parent's arrest and/or crime and rated the children's distress. Reports of these experiences were triangulated and combined. Children's caregivers then also reported on the child's behavioral stress symptoms in the past six months using a validated measure, the Child Behavior Checklist (Achenbach & Ruffle, 2000; see appendix B)—even before witnessing the parent's arrest (see figure 2.1). And because we collected children's scalp hair during our home visit (which occurred a few months after the parent's incarceration), we were able to assess physiological experiences of stress during that time.

When we analyzed the study data, we found that children had higher cumulative stress hormones when they had witnessed their father's arrest, on average, compared to those who were not present for such potentially traumatic events. Thus, the children who witnessed their father's arrest had more cortisol accumulated in their scalp hair, suggesting that the event was, indeed, stressful and associated with a rise in cortisol over time. In some

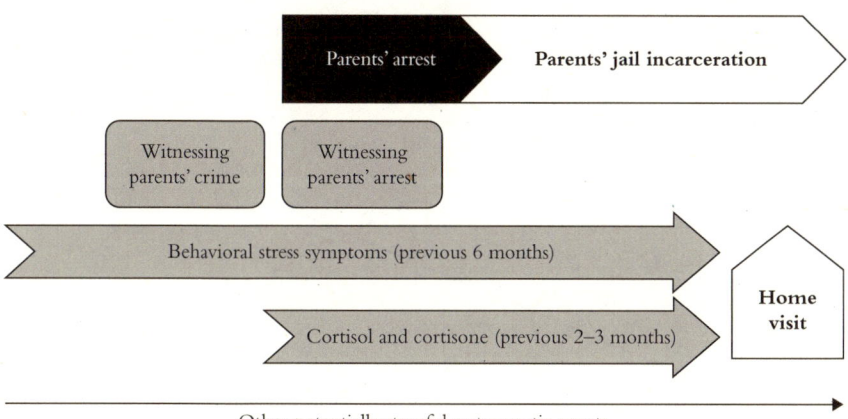

Figure 2.1. Linking witnessing a parent's arrest with children's stress responses.

ways, this may be reflective of the body's normative response to stressful events. The heightened cortisol may show how the children's bodies were doing what they were designed to—switching into "fight or flight" mode in response to being present for such a stressful event or series of events. Take, for instance, Armoni—Louise described his distress reactions, but our measures show that not only was the stress captured in his overt behavioral responses (like in his initial distress and defiance of his grandma or by his declines in behavior at school) but also in a more covert way that actually got under his skin and altered his body's physiological responses.

However, beyond just a normative response to a potentially traumatic event, we found that children who had the highest levels of behavioral stress symptoms and witnessed the arrest showed blunted stress reactions. In other words, kids in our study who were already stressed out—meaning they had been exposed to chronic stressors in their environments that even predated the arrest—experienced reactions whereby their stress systems had effectively shut down. As mentioned earlier, such reactions are often seen in people with posttraumatic stress disorder. In other words, children who were already stressed beyond what their little bodies could handle (perhaps from witnessing past negative events, experiencing repeated separations from their parents, living in poverty, experiencing discrimination and stigma, experiencing residential instability or homelessness) did not show a normal stress reaction. Their stress systems were overwhelmed and the stressor of witnessing their parent's arrest—however traumatic—did not cause the body's stress hormones to be protective in a normal way (figure 2.2). These are the children who are most at risk for showing long-term problems in their health, behavior, and learning (Poehlmann-Tynan & Turney, 2021; Poehlmann-Tynan et al., 2021).

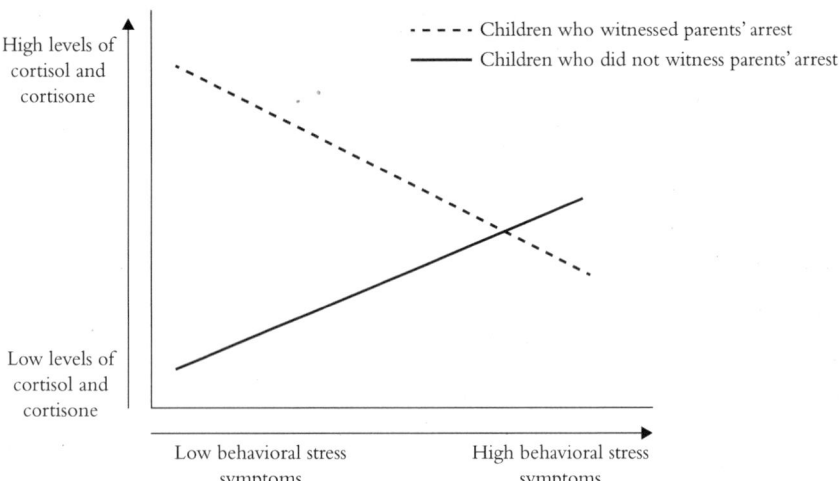

Figure 2.2. Children's stress hormones after witnessing a parent's arrest as it differs by preexisting stress symptom levels.

Importantly, these findings still held true when we controlled for other potentially traumatic events that children may have been exposed to, such as witnessing the parent's crime or domestic violence in their homes. In addition, for this book, we repeated these analyses with children who had jailed mothers. The findings in children of jailed mothers were in the same direction and about the same magnitude as the findings with the subsample of children with incarcerated fathers, suggesting similar processes as those findings from children with jailed fathers. This demonstrates that there may be something especially triggering in witnessing parental arrest (perhaps the use of force, exposure to armed strangers, or its resulting separation) that pushes young children's already stressed bodies beyond their breaking point in ways that exposure to other stressors does not. What this means, in short, is that holding constant potentially other traumatic and stressful events in children's lives, witnessing the arrest of a parent spikes stress hormones in kids who were previously experiencing normal levels of behavioral stress and blunts it in those who were already significantly stressed. As outlined above, such reactions have been shown to result in negative long-term health outcomes.

*Separation from Incarcerated Parents and Prior Trauma*

Even before the parent's judicial or carceral involvement, many of the families in our study navigated oppressive systems in which racial, social, and structural disadvantages manifested in sustained and repeated negative and even traumatic experiences, such as racism, poverty, witnessing domestic or neighborhood violence, residential instability, and diminished social mobility (e.g., Eddy & Poehlmann-Tynan, 2019). Thus, even before their parent's incarceration, many of the children faced elevated risk for stress, trauma, and social marginalization. The children may have also experienced multiple adverse childhood experiences (Turney, 2018). You began to see this in Armoni's life—his repeated separations from his mother, not having his father in his life, frequent moves, homelessness, poverty, and child welfare involvement had already amassed a significant amount of adversity in just six years of life.

The incarceration of a parent has the potential to amplify these stress and trauma symptoms, leaving a child more at risk for negative reactions to changes in caregivers, being removed from their homes, exposure to stressful corrections environments, social stigma, diminished economic well-being, and feelings of guilt or abandonment. Children with incarcerated parents may experience the presence of secondary trauma as a result of their parent's incarceration (e.g., neglect, poverty, homelessness, poor treatment by corrections staff during visits) (Arditti & Savla, 2015). To examine additional aspects of trauma, our study called on our interviews with the jailed parent and caregiver to uncover the ways in which challenging life events played out for the children, specifically noting preexisting structural disadvantages, adverse experiences, and instability in caregiving, finances, or housing.

An extensive body of research indicates that separation of children from their parents is harmful to children's short- and long-term well-being. In fact, having a parent become suddenly (or forcibly) removed from a child's life is among the most powerful traumatic stressors that young children can experience, and the effects are magnified when separation occurs under stressful circumstances, such as sudden, frightening, or prolonged circumstances (Bowlby, 1973; Pesonen et al., 2008; Pesonen et al., 2010; Teicher, 2018; Ullmann et al., 2019), like that stressful night for Armoni and his brother three months ago. Especially when they are as young as Armoni, children often react to separations by developing anxiety, depression, developmental regressions, posttraumatic stress symptoms, and other trauma reactions (Kobak et al., 2016; Murray et al., 2012; Poehlmann, 2005c). Importantly, when children are separated from parents as the result of incarceration, the younger ones can exhibit even more intense reactions over time (e.g., Poehlmann-Tynan & Dallaire, 2021; Poehlmann-Tynan & Turney, 2021).

Unfortunately, for most of the children in our study, it was not the first time they witnessed their parents walk out (or be walked out in handcuffs) during their lives. In our sample of 86 families, 66 percent of the children had experienced a prior separation from the jailed parent. These prior separations occurred for children any time from birth to the age of six for the oldest in our sample, though the most common age for this to occur was during infancy, around the same time Javonte removed himself from Armoni's life. In terms of the length of time children were separated from their parents, separations ranged from overnight (which is not generally thought of as a significant separation) to three years, with the most common length of time being 3–6 months (which is considered a significant separation). About half of the children who experienced prior separation experienced multiple separations like Armoni and Jordan. Reasons for prior separations included parental incarceration, arrest, house arrest with a monitoring device, a stay in a halfway house or treatment facility, domestic violence, alcoholism, drug use, parental relationship dissolution, or a family move. As you can see, there really was no one source of separation, but the most common reason parents were removed from their kids' lives was related to parental legal involvement. Our team has referred to this "in and out" pattern as parental "churning" in the criminal legal system. Overall, about one in three children in our study experienced this type of parental churning, with three or more separations from the parent because of the parent being jailed or imprisoned. Importantly, churning in and out of the home (or the jail) was not every child's experience. For about one in three children, the current parental incarceration was the first time that children had been separated from that parent. While this may result in complications for children so used to parents being present in their lives, it also suggests that chronic instability was not previously the norm for at least a third of our sample.

What also became clear was that children react to the separation from parents due to incarceration in many different ways. We asked children's caregivers to complete a checklist about children's initial emotional reactions to the parent's current incarceration. According to caregivers, most children expressed sadness following the parent's current incarceration, and a little more than half of children expressed anger or frustration. Loneliness, worry, fear, depression, and confusion were also common reactions. Indifference, even if temporary, was reported in 35 percent of cases. The least common negative emotional reactions that children experienced, as reported by caregivers, were embarrassment and guilt. It is likely that complex emotions, such as embarrassment and guilt, would be uncommon in young children, as implications of social stigma may not entirely hit them yet. These findings are depicted in figure 2.3.

Beyond these negative emotions, only a small number of children expressed relief and one child expressed happiness that their parent was arrested and detained. Caregivers described the relief or happiness as coming after a preincarceration period of negative emotions including fear, anger, sadness, and confusion. In these few cases, there was oftentimes a history of stress and disadvantage that intertwined with parents' negative behaviors predating the

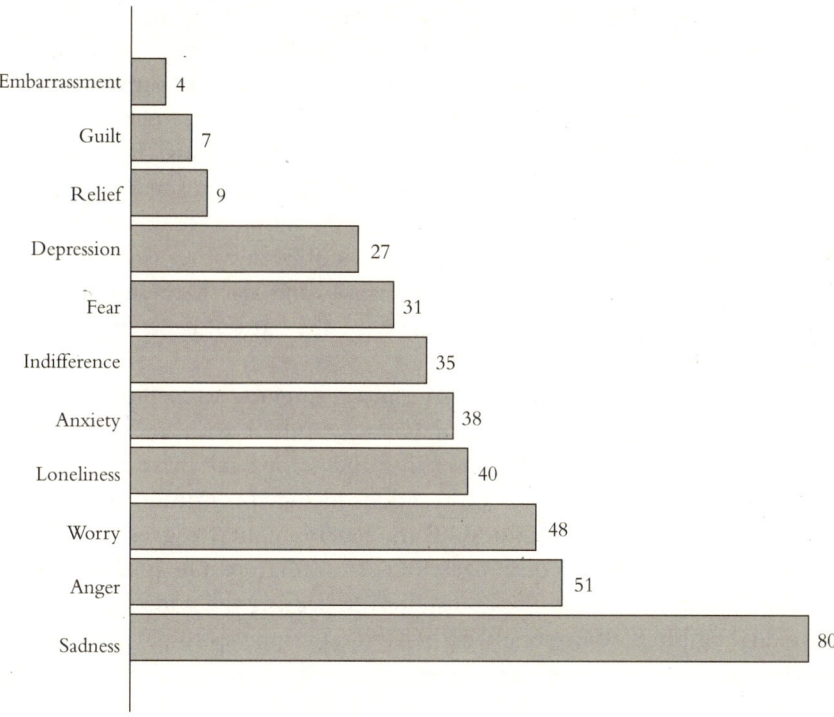

Figure 2.3. Percentage of children who exhibited various emotional reactions to parents' incarceration.

incarceration to influence children's perceptions of and reactions to their parents going to jail. This adds strength to the argument that most children feel hurt when their parents go to jail and very few express relief. The findings mirror previous work with young children who have imprisoned mothers, which found that, according to caregiver report on an emotions checklist, sadness, worry and confusion, loneliness, and anger were the most reported feelings, with relief, embarrassment, and guilt being the least reported (Poehlmann, 2005c). In other words, just because parents go to jail does not necessarily mean that their kids miss them any less than other children who are separated from their parents. Parental legal system involvement does not void the emotion, love, and care present in so many of these dyads, in fact, it may exacerbate these raw emotions and translate them into new manifestations, such as sadness and loneliness.

In a publication focusing on data from another study, we found that 3–8-year-old children with jailed parents commonly expressed sadness, anger, worry, and loneliness when the parent they lived with or were closely engaged with left for jail (Poehlmann-Tynan et al., 2021). Our study also found that when the child had existing emotional symptoms, such as anxiety, withdrawal, or depression, and the child witnessed the parent's arrest, the child showed more intense negative emotions when the parent left for jail compared to children with lower emotional symptoms (Poehlmann-Tynan et al., 2021). Again, this reiterates the point that separation from parents is challenging for kids, but it may be the most challenging for those who are already struggling. Similar to those with preexisting stressors demonstrating blunted cortisol responses to witnessing arrest, these same kids who are most stressed emotionally may have the hardest time adjusting to separation from their parents.

Content analysis of interview data in the previously mentioned 2005 study revealed that the majority of young children with an imprisoned mother expressed their sadness by crying and calling for their mother following separation. Other common reactions included confusion and worry, anger and acting out, loneliness, fear, developmental regression, sleep problems, and indifference or detachment. Similar to the present study, most children exhibited multiple reactions, reflecting the wide variation in individual children's emotional and behavioral responses to parental incarceration, which can sometimes be confusing to caregivers and other adults. Recognizing that there is no "one-size-fits-all" way for children to cope when their parents go to jail is important for recognizing stressors and designing intervention plans. Taking these findings in tandem with the physiological findings demonstrates that children respond outwardly while their bodies also process stress internally, meaning that how a child is reacting on the outside may or may not tell the entire story of what is happening on the inside.

To summarize, the findings in the present study demonstrate that the majority of children expressed sadness after the parent left for jail. Even children who previously experienced multiple separations or who were exposed to abuse in the home—like Armoni—felt sad about being away from a parent. They longed for the parent while at the same time feeling angry or hurt by feelings of abandonment. They asked when their parent was coming home and some discussed ways they might visit or talk with the parent. These are normal reactions for young children, especially when the child is in a place where they can talk about and process their feelings in a safe way like Armoni can do with Louise.

### HOW CAN WE HELP?

The findings presented in this chapter suggest at least two ways that we can help young children affected by parental incarceration. The first is safeguarding children from witnessing the arrest of their parents and the second is providing children with support to allow them to process all of their feelings about separation from a parent—even if these feelings do not make sense to adults.

### Safeguarding Children during Parental Arrest

Given what Louise disclosed about how traumatic this exposure was for Armoni and his brother Jordan, the statistics presented in our study highlight the importance of trauma-informed practices that can be put in place to safeguard children who may find themselves in the wrong place at the wrong time while their parents are arrested. Although protocols exist for safeguarding children during parental arrest, such as *First, Do No Harm* (Thurau, 2015) and *Safeguarding Children of Arrested Parents* (International Association of Chiefs of Police [IACP], 2014), these protocols were not used in Armoni's case, and we do not know how many law enforcement systems use them across the United States. Indeed, the positive aspect of allowing Kiesha to talk to her sons briefly before being taken away seemed to be far outweighed by the trauma induced by not adhering to most other aspects of these protocols, such as assessing whether any minors may be present, refraining from use of force in the presence of children to the extent possible, trying to conduct the arrest out of view and earshot of the children, and having officers talk with children, at their level (IACP, 2014).

We strongly recommend that all law enforcement personnel employ what we know are best practices for safeguarding children during a parent's arrest (IACP, 2014; Lang et al., 2013; Thurau, 2015). Training and support are essential to help officers implement best practices. National models provide guidelines and offer training resources regarding how to assess a child's presence at the scene of a potential arrest and modifying timing and methods with respect to a child's presence, including delaying the timing of the arrest to allow for the child to be moved to a different location. The guidelines also cover removing the parent from the child's sight during the arrest (including not handcuffing the parent when children are watching), not using force during the arrest if at all possible, allowing the parent to speak with the child to calm and reassure the child, having law enforcement officers speak directly to the child in a developmentally appropriate way to help explain what is happening, having the child picked up by a person known to them, and including the parent in the child's immediate and permanent placement decisions (IACP, 2014).

Law enforcement agencies—whether federal, statewide, or local—are essential in limiting the trauma that can occur to children, as discussed in *First, Do No Harm* (Thurau, 2015) or the REACT intervention (Lang et al., 2013). By changing how arrests are conducted and having protocols in place to assure the appropriate care of children during and after the arrest, including involvement of professionals to provide follow-up or wraparound services, implementation of such frameworks can help protect children (Thurau, 2015). It is important for law enforcement agencies to engage in training and collaborate with child welfare systems with goals of decreasing children's stress exposure and distress and providing services to vulnerable children. County sheriff's departments and city police forces are especially important in safeguarding children, as most arrests and incarcerations occur locally (Sawyer & Wagner, 2019). The national models are meant to be adapted locally, with special consideration for child well-being as well as the safety of law enforcement personnel. Without such protocols in place, as occurred in the locations when we collected our study data, arresting parents can lead to children witnessing the arrest, which may be traumatic, like it was for Armoni and Jordan and many other children.

*Supporting Children Following Separation from a Parent*

When children witness parental arrest or experience separation from a parent, the adults in their lives must acknowledge the pain and trauma of the events. Additional care must be provided to children to help them regulate their stress responses. At first it can be helpful to offer a comforting item to the child, such as a stuffed animal or blanket—or even a parent's item of clothing or photo—and speak to the child in a calm way using words that they can understand. Adults can help explain why the police are or were there, and reassure children that it is not their fault, like Louise did for Armoni. The adults can also explain why the child cannot be with the parent and reassure the child that the parent still loves them. Over time, children need to know that they are loved and that they are not alone. They need to hear those messages repeatedly.

It is also important that adults refrain from making promises that are impossible to keep or from providing information that may not be true, such as saying that the parent will be right back. Children's caregivers can learn about how to help children regulate their emotions, including use of breathing and other mindfulness techniques, as well as talking about feelings in a way that young children understand. There are community resources that can help with this process as well as free resources on the internet. For example, Sesame Workshop has resources designed for children in challenging situations, such as having an incarcerated parent, experiencing homelessness or trauma, and other forms of parental loss, as well as parental substance abuse. The national organization ZERO TO THREE (https://www.zeroto three.org/resources/2384-supporting-young-children-experiencing -separation-and-trauma) also has materials for caregivers of very young children experiencing trauma or separation from parents. There are several excellent children's picture books that deal with a child's experience of parent-child separation, such as *The Kissing Hand* by Audrey Penn. Such tools can help children learn ways of recognizing and coping with stressful situations, even at a young age. Other professional support, such as linking to a family therapist or looping in school social workers or counselors, may also prove advantageous if the family so chooses. Our findings emphasize how witnessing a parent's arrest can be highly stressful or even overwhelming for young children who are already stressed out and who are separated from a parent. If safeguarding approaches are absent and if support services are not in place, alteration of the child's stress system and HPA axis can have long-term consequences for their health and well-being (Muentner et al., 2021; Poehlmann-Tynan et al., 2021). In contrast, safeguarding children during parental arrest and offering supports to children of arrested parents and their families may go a long way in preventing trauma and facilitating resilience processes.

# CHAPTER 3

# "Look, It's My Family Together!"

## FAMILY RELATIONSHIPS DURING PARENTAL INCARCERATION

ELLA STANDS LEANING CAUTIOUSLY into her dad's lap, who is seated on the couch, as she watches us unpack our bag of toys. The three-year-old White girl has straight dark-brown hair decorated with glittery animal-shaped barrettes that pull back her bangs from her eyes. She is wearing bright pink shorts with a matching pink, yellow, and blue polka-dot tank top. Her nails are covered in chipped pink polish, and blue and green marker streaks span her legs from an art activity she was engaged in just before we arrived. Her dad, Mike, a strongly-built 26-year-old White man, sits back on the green, blue, and pink floral pleated couch as his daughter stands in the space between his legs, her small bare feet appearing especially tiny in comparison to his bulky black skateboard shoes. He wears a white polo shirt atop baggy white-and-green plaid shorts, an unlit cigarette tucked behind his studded ear, and a black flat-brimmed hat covering his shortly cropped hair.

Looking timidly over her shoulder at her dad for approval, Ella releases her grip from his knees and points cautiously at the set of colorful plastic blocks that are attracting her to the open space in front of the couch. She briefly makes eye contact with a member of our research team sitting near the toys and twists backward into her dad's lap, giggling at the situation and shyly burying her face into his chest. Mike gently lifts her onto the couch next to him and reaches to the floor to pick up the container of blocks that caught her eye just seconds prior. Excited to get her hands on the new toys, she scoots over so the two can play with the blocks on the open cushion between them. Outwardly, the father-daughter pair are presenting as a tight-knit duo. In fact, it may come as a surprise, given this close initial bond, but Ella only moved in with her dad a week ago. He became her primary guardian for the first time in her life, after her mom, Crystal, a 26-year-old White woman, left for the county jail, the result of a revocation caused by a technical probation violation. Ella has visited him sporadically in the past, even occasionally staying for long weekends, although this is the first time she has stayed with him at his parents' home.

Crystal was Ella's primary caregiver before she became reincarcerated. Crystal does not have a current romantic relationship—or much of any relationship, at that—with Mike. He has not provided full-time or even consistent part-time care for Ella before, but the court system decided that she should live with her father much to the chagrin of Crystal, who is not happy with this current living arrangement for her daughter. Although she has only been away from her daughter for a week now, just three months prior to this, Crystal was incarcerated and out of Ella's life again. In that previous incarceration, as well as a few before that, Ella's aunts, uncles, and grandparents stepped in as caregivers at different times. Thinking that Ella has perhaps grown numb to all of the changes in residence and caregivers as her mom churns through the criminal legal system, Crystal says that her daughter adjusts fine to the separation and that she "just kinda deals with it." Crystal herself has grown used to the repeated separations, saying that even when she talks to Ella on the phone, she does not let the distance bother her. She is not sure how long she will be incarcerated this time, but she is dedicated to resuming a parenting role when she is released, but with no specific plans about their reunification this time around.

For now, Ella lives with her dad at her paternal grandparents' house where she sleeps in a guest room in the basement. However, she spends most of her days playing in the upstairs living room we are in now—the space is large, open, and bright and features a matching furniture set where we sit with Ella and her dad. Besides the floral couch and chairs, the room is filled with two antique wooden tables with lamps sitting on top of white knitted doily mats. Across the room is a wood-framed, enclosed glass shelving unit that holds a number of delicate trinkets. There is a small television set across the room from the couch that does not seem to get much use. Above the couch on the wall hangs a series of nature-themed pictures and matching brass decorations that extends the space into the main dining room in the household. The entire space is well lit by a large bay window on the wall next to the front door, letting in the sunshine on this especially clear-skied summer day. For it being her first time living here, and for the conflict that has ensued between Crystal and Mike about Ella's living arrangements, Ella seems comfortable in the space. Mike tells us that in past households where Ella lived there was more clutter, not enough space, lots of noise, and many adults and children coming and going. He is relieved that she is finally with him in the safety and peacefulness of his parents' home.

Ella warms up to our team quickly, perhaps even too quickly, immediately inviting us to play outside with her after she is finished playing with the blocks. We move our activities outside, where she grabs a few pieces of sidewalk chalk and starts making marks on the concrete patio slab where her grandparents have an outdoor table and set of chairs. As we sit on the ground, the wind catches hold of her hair, blowing it around her face. She lets out a playful shriek, dropping her blue piece of chalk to dramatically move those glittery animal barrettes out of her face with her chalky hands. As we spent more time playing with her, we could see some of the qualities her dad would soon tell us he was concerned about, such as the one area she did not score satisfactorily on during her preschool assessment this week—exhibiting self-regulation, including both attentional and emotional control. She seems distracted and fixated at keeping the hair out of her face, shrieking every time the wind swirls it back in front of her eyes. In fact, she never went back to that chalk drawing she started after one bout of shrieking prompted a hurried run to the other side of the backyard.

Mike tells us that he has noticed more of these attention issues since Ella has moved in with him after Crystal's incarceration, and that he never noticed them as much when she previously came to stay with him for occasional long weekends. Other than that, though, he says she seems disinterested in many of the things that she used to enjoy doing when she came to visit previously, perhaps a personification of the general indifference her mom reported Ella was expressing. Briefly, Mike opens up about how Ella has had a few instances of sadness lately, for example shedding a few tears the other night and telling him "I miss her," talking about her mom. This made us wonder if the sort of "indifference" her parents were reporting truly matched the level of pain she was feeling on the inside after being separated from her mom yet again. As the home visit continues, we begin to notice more little things that may have been indications of Ella actually longing for a stable, consistent confidant, such as when she hugs the mom doll a little more closely than the others when we begin to play with the doll figures we brought outside. In actuality, Ella may very well be employing a sort of numbness, or "indifference" as her parents refer to it, as a coping mechanism to dull the acute and confusing pain she feels over the separation from her mom on top of the abrupt changes in guardianship and residence she has repeatedly—and recently—experienced.

Because Ella is already playing with the doll figures, we decide to lead her through one of our attachment assessments that uses them, which we describe in more detail later in this chapter. As we attempt to walk her through the directions and story prompts, Ella has a hard time focusing. Her demeanor wavers with sporadic bouts of seriousness and aggression as she picks up both the child and mom dolls and marches them with big movements along the sunny patio. There is something clearly on her mind, making us wonder if she is imagining the mother-child doll pair to be her and her own mother. Without receiving clarity on our curiosity, we repeat the prompt a second time. This time, her ears catch our voice, and she stares at the dolls for a moment before recentering and allowing our team to walk her through a story about a family having dinner together, with the little girl doll getting up and accidentally spilling her juice.

RESEARCHER: Oh, the juice is spilled! Show me what happens now.

ELLA: Do we have to put these away?

RESEARCHER: No no, you can use all the dolls to show me what happens now.

ELLA: They have to have a treat. [*Giggling.*] Let's get this . . . We're gonna get that, here. [*Acts out moving the dolls to go get the imaginary "treat."*] Where's the other little girl?

RESEARCHER: I think these are all the people in our story. What happened to the spilled juice?

ELLA: It's right there. But they have to have a treat! Treat, where's a treat?

RESEARCHER: What kind of treat are they going to have?

ELLA: Chocolate!

RESEARCHER: A chocolate treat.

ELLA: A fake treat . . .

RESEARCHER: Does anything else happen in this story?

ELLA: I don't know.

RESEARCHER: Alright, I have an idea for another story.

Again Ella listens as the researcher enacts the beginning of a family story, this time pretending that a family of dolls is walking in the park, with the little girl doll climbing on a rock and hurting her knee.

RESEARCHER: Boo-hoo! Ouch! I've hurt my knee! Show me what happens now.

ELLA: This girl climbs on the rock. [*Chuckles.*] Look, Mommy! She climbed the rock and she hurt her forehead. [*Ella makes crashing sounds.*] That hurt. [*Laughs and makes more crashing sounds while banging the rock on the doll.*] Ow!

RESEARCHER: What happened?

ELLA: They all hurt theyself. They hurt they head. They hurt they foot. [*Muttered words and noises.*] Wow, a big giant rock! Where's the . . . [*Words trail off*]. Let's get these to the park. [*More crashing sounds as she continues to bang the doll against the rock.*] Ow, ow! It's okay, stand up, Daddy is here. [*Stops banging the doll against the rock and holds it close to the father figurine.*] Look, it's Mommy and Daddy! It's your turn, Mommy, you do it now. [*Grabs the mother figurine and repeats the movement of it climbing the rock, falling off, and hitting the doll against the rock.*] Ow! She hurt her back. [*Giggles while crashing sounds while again banging the rock on the doll but accidentally lets go of the doll as it goes flying across the patio.]* What the . . . !

RESEARCHER: Does anything else happen in this story?

ELLA: Nope.

At this point, Ella runs to go get the thrown doll and brings it back to the researcher. In the next story, which depicts a child doll saying that she sees a monster in her bedroom, Ella simply responds by quietly laying the child doll under the covers in the bed.

RESEARCHER: What happens with the monster?

ELLA: It slid under the bed . . . it waits and then tips people over. [*Ella flips over the toy bed sending the child doll flying into the air.*]

RESEARCHER: And it tips the people over?

ELLA: Yup! Then, when they outside, it [the monster] gonna hold the people outside. And then the monster come back and lay down [under the bed again] so when [the child] come inside and get back to bed, [the monster] come back! [*Giggles.*] There's the monster! [*Ella squeals while enacting an increasingly disjointed story and moving the doll furniture around in an agitated way as if the monster is attacking the child from under the bed.*]

ELLA: [*Soothing.*] Now they watching TV. I'm done playing this. I wanna color.

RESEARCHER: Okay, let's color! Thanks for playing with the dolls with me!

Ella grabs a red marker and draws circles on a piece of paper set out for her by one of the research team members. She settles into her drawing, adding colors and giggling. She regains a cheerful demeanor as she colors and excitedly asks, "What we doin' next?" As our research team goes in and out of activities with her throughout the afternoon, these disorganized or dysregulated tendencies continue, showing us that Ella's feelings of "indifference" may only be one part of a much larger story of her coping.

### Attachment Processes in Children with Incarcerated Parents

As we learned in the last chapter, when a parent is incarcerated, many children experience feelings of loss, sadness, and anger, while only a small minority actually experience relief or even indifference in the way that Ella's parents described. This is often because family relationships can change subtly or dramatically, depending on things like family structure, living situations of family members, and involvement of the parent prior to going to jail, which can either exacerbate or mitigate the effects of separation. When the incarcerated parent has served as the child's primary caregiver, as is more often the case for mothers than fathers (Glaze & Maruschak, 2008), that parent's arrest and incarceration can cause dramatic change and chaos in both the short and long term for some families (e.g., Siegel, 2013). Separation from this primary caregiver can also cause significant disruption in a child's attachment formation or maintenance (Poehlmann, 2005c). In the case of families where the incarcerated parent is less involved or nonresidential, the effects of their incarceration for attachment processes may differ, but feelings of loss and uncertainty remain common. Indeed, these feelings often cloud family relationships and influence each individual's feelings of hope as well as their ability to rise to meet challenges and move forward together (Arditti, 2012, 2016; Eddy & Poehlmann-Tynan, 2019).

The loss experienced because of parental incarceration is often framed as an "ambiguous" loss because there are so many unknowns and uncertainties (Arditti, 2016). To cope with the uncertainties, many families choose to not talk about the parent's incarceration, only provide minimal information, or "tell a story" (i.e., engage in compassionate deception) to protect children from the stigma associated with parental incarceration (Poehlmann-Tynan & Arditti, 2018). Such responses can actually increase distress associated with a child's feelings of ambiguous loss, meaning that such untrue explanations do not necessarily help clarify the situation. Ambiguous loss can be highly stressful and impair problem solving and decision-making, leading to strain in family relationships and elevated mental health issues (Boss, 2006, 2007). For children, secure attachments to at-home caregivers can provide a source of stability, reassurance, and love while navigating experiences of ambiguous loss such as having a parent go to jail, key processes that ease adjustment, bolster coping mechanisms, and amplify aspects of family resilience.

*Disruptions in Family Relationships and the Importance of Caregivers*

As we discussed in chapter 2, separation between incarcerated parents and their children can often be challenging and even traumatic, depending on the circumstances. Beyond the risks to social emotional and physiological well-being, it can create disruptions in children's attachment relationships due to changing care situations, residential moves, family conflict, and people coming in and out of children's lives (Poehlmann, 2005c) just as Ella has repeatedly experienced. To understand the possible impacts of parental incarceration, it is also important to consider who is watching and caring for the child after their parent goes away (E. I. Johnson & Waldfogel, 2002). Most often children live with their mothers when their fathers are incarcerated, whereas other children live with a nonparental relative, and especially grandparents when the mother is incarcerated (Glaze & Maruschak, 2008;

Maruschak, Bronson & Alper, 2021). In addition, when mothers are incarcerated, children are five times more likely to be placed in foster care than when fathers are incarcerated (Child Welfare Information Gateway, 2015; Glaze & Maruschak, 2008). While Ella has managed to avoid the child welfare system so far, her frequent shifts in caregivers and moves in and out of extended family members' homes—in addition to parental conflict—have caused significant concern regarding her attachment processes. But Ella is not the only one left feeling the strain—even her caregivers struggle with such abrupt transitions associated with Crystal's incarceration.

Subsequent to a parent's incarceration—and even before, in some cases—children's caregivers often experience increased stress, residential instability, and mental health concerns (Geller et al., 2009). The well-being of a child's caregiver has a direct and significant impact on the child's present and future well-being (Poehlmann, 2005a, 2005c; Poehlmann-Tynan et al., 2017), and we cover these issues extensively in chapter 5. Unfortunately, because of the risks and changing family circumstances, many children with incarcerated parents have experienced separation from their caregivers at times, in addition to the separate loss of the incarcerated parent. Think of all the time Ella has spent away from Mike. Sure, they tried to spend some weekends together, but the constant ins and outs in Ella's wider family context have left little opportunity to build secure and trusting relationships between the two of them, despite now finding themselves in a position where they must rely on each other. That said, this routine is quite common for kids whose parents are incarcerated and many experience shifts and changes in caregivers—especially when a mother is incarcerated (Poehlmann-Tynan & Dallaire, 2021).

In our study, many kids were separated at some point from their current caregiver. This initial separation occurred anywhere from when the child was born until they turned six years old, with the most common age at separation being between two and three years—significantly later on in their lives than the initial separation from jailed parents discussed in chapter 2. Time spent apart ranged from two days to 11 months, though the most common length of separation was between one and four months. Reasons for these separations varied but included hospitalization, child welfare involvement, incarceration of the caregiver, work schedules, custody changes, and mental health issues. Even with those separations, caregivers more often provided the primary relationship stability for children when the parent was incarcerated, though we also found shifts in caregivers for some children. In terms of primary caregivers, 14 percent of children had experienced two or more shifts, whereas with secondary caregivers, 32 percent of children experienced one or more shifts within their lifetimes. This goes to show that Ella is not alone. Instead, instability in relationships is an unfortunate reality for a significant proportion of families impacted by the criminal legal system.

Although scholars and professionals readily acknowledge the importance of family relationships for children's well-being when a parent is incarcerated (Poehlmann-Tynan & Arditti, 2018), dyadic relationships, or ongoing connections that occur between two people, can be tricky to assess and understand because each person has their own internal thoughts and feelings about the other person and a fully agreed-upon consensus can be impossible to achieve. For instance, researchers need to ask each person how they think and feel, or if the child is very young, find a way to elicit such thoughts and feelings. However, most studies in the parental incarceration literature have relied on adults to report on parent-child relationship quality—usually the child's at-home caregiver or incarcerated parent (e.g., Loper & Tuerck, 2010; McKay et al., 2019; Visher, 2013), with only a few studies capturing children's perspectives on close family relationships (e.g., Poehlmann, 2005c; Shlafer & Poehlmann, 2010). This means that if we were to limit our pursuit of understanding Ella's attachments to Mike's or Crystal's reports, their perceptions of Ella's "indifference" may ultimately miss her more nuanced reactions of distress and disorganization that we were able to see in Ella's play, storytelling, and observed emotions and behaviors.

Kids like Ella represent why it is so critical to capture what occurs internally—within a child's mind and emotions, as well as what occurs externally, in the space between people—their actual interactions or words, emotions, and behaviors directed toward each other. Observations are an important way to capture these external interactions and prove to be particularly advantageous when trying to understand attachment processes with young children. In an effort to capture both these internal and external processes, we complemented observations and hands-on assessments with young children with interviews of their incarcerated parents and caregivers to inquire about family relationships.

*Measuring Attachment*

Attachment refers to the way in which a child organizes his or her behaviors (and thoughts and feelings) around an attachment figure—usually the parent—whereas the parent's or caregiver's role in the parent-child bond is referred to as "caregiving" or the "caregiving bond" (Bowlby, 1982). Some studies assess the components of parent-child relationships that involve time spent together, activities engaged in such as play or pursuing mutual interests, and discipline issues. Although these components are important for children's social emotional, cognitive, motor, and language development, the concepts differ from the core aspects of attachment as used in most of the contemporary child development literature, although they may be consistent with a sociology/criminology theory that also uses the word "attachment" (Hirschi, 1969).

According to developmental attachment theory, attachment is a deep and enduring emotional bond that connects one person to another across time and space, although it does not necessarily need to be reciprocal (Ainsworth et al., 1978; Bowlby, 1982). Attachments involve two key types of behaviors engaged in by children: "safe haven" and "secure base" behaviors. Safe haven behaviors occur when children are afraid, anxious, threatened, ill, or distressed and they seek out or return to an attachment figure to be comforted and protected. Secure base behaviors happen when children feel safe in the presence of the attachment figure, which allows them to explore the environment and venture forward to encounter new things, people, and experiences. Both types of behaviors are important for children's attachment relationships and security. In contrast, Hirschi's (1969) social bonding theory discusses individuals' attachments to prosocial institutions and people as ways to desist from crime.

According to the child development literature, children typically develop an attachment relationship with any parent or caregiver who provides regular physical and emotional care over time, starting in infancy and continuing through childhood and adolescence. However, the quality of the attachment relationship varies based on the caregiver's sensitivity, responsiveness, and consistency, as well as other contextual factors, including quality of co-parenting and the presence of family conflict (Braungart-Reiker & Garwood, 1999; De Wolff & van IJzendoorn, 1997). Often safe haven and secure base behaviors are difficult for an adult caregiver to accurately report in their own children, and social desirability is a factor (see Cadman et al., 2018). This means that sometimes parents' reports about attachment in their children are affected by what they think researchers want to hear. That said, there are several reliable and valid measures that researchers use to assess attachment in children experiencing disrupted relationships and loss that are capable of unpacking what these attachment processes look like with such kids (Roisman & Cicchetti, 2017).

In some studies that have sought to garner this information directly, children have reported on their feelings or attitudes about their relationships with incarcerated parents (Shlafer & Poehlmann, 2010), which can be helpful when children are old enough to reflect on and verbalize how they think and feel. However, very young children cannot necessarily verbally self-report about their family relationships. Thus, researchers often rely on observations of very young children interacting with their parents and caregivers. Such observations occur rarely in the literature on children with incarcerated parents, although this methodology can be particularly revealing of dyadic relationship quality from the child's perspective.

In a series of measures employed across our study, our research team gathered information from a variety of sources to document the quality of children's close family relationships and attachments with caregivers during parental incarceration, as multiple indicators of relationship quality paint the most detailed and vivid picture of family relationships. By employing these multiple measures (as detailed in appendix B) we captured components of children's attachment relationships beyond those reported by parents and caregivers—including those observed by researchers and those enacted by children in their play and drawings.

First, we completed the Attachment Q-Sort, a tried-and-true method developed decades ago and used with families around the world; the assessment is based on hours of observations in children's home environments and it has been found to be consistently reliable and valid (e.g., Waters, 1995). Second, we coded videos of naturalistic caregiver-child interactions captured in the home, again using a valid and reliable coding scheme. Third, we used a story stem completion task using dolls and other props called the Attachment Story Completion Task (ASCT; Bretherton et al., 1990) to capture how children depict their families (a portion of Ella's assessment of this was included earlier in the chapter). Finally, we collected children's family drawings and coded them with an attachment-based system. In addition to these measures, we captured the caregiving aspect of the parent-child relationship by asking adults to indicate their feelings about children.

### Attachment Q-Sort

A child's relationship with the attachment figure (i.e., caregiver) was measured using the Attachment Q-Sort version 3.0, which provides security scores ranging from −1.0 (very insecure) to +1.0 (very secure) (Waters, 1995). In our study, security scores for young children as they interacted with their caregivers at home ranged from -0.43 to 0.69, with a mean of 0.20 (standard deviation = 0.28), similar to the mean of 0.21 reported in studies with clinical samples (i.e., studies of children whose parents had mental illness or substance use problems). In contrast, a significantly higher mean of 0.32 to 0.35 has been reported in normative samples based on a meta-analysis by van IJzendoorn and colleagues (2004) as well as in other work (e.g., Cadman et al., 2018). So, while the kids in our study had similar attachment scores to that of other vulnerable groups, their averages were still lower than that of the more general population. This indicates that although their average scores were closer to the "very secure" extreme as opposed to the "very insecure" extreme, they still faced considerable risk for attachment insecurity with their caregivers.

The Attachment Q-Sort scores can also be used to classify children into secure and insecure attachment groups, with scores of 0.35 or above considered as secure attachments in young children (Coyl et al., 2002; Teti & Ablard, 1989). Using this standard, our study found that 67 percent of the children with jailed parents had insecure attachments to their at-home caregivers. Children like Ella, who have experienced numerous moves and disruptions in care, often experience challenges forming secure relationships with adults in their lives. They often develop feelings of anxiety or insecurity when approaching their caregivers and may not easily calm if they are fearful, tired, or distressed. In coauthor Poehlmann's 2005 study of children affected by maternal incarceration, she similarly found that 65 percent of children had insecure relationships with their imprisoned mothers and at-home caregivers (Poehlmann, 2005c).

Sadly, these findings indicate that two out of every three young children with incarcerated parents have not developed a secure relationship with the adult who cares for them at home. However, on a positive point, one out of three young children with incarcerated parents has a strong protective factor in their life—that of a secure attachment to their caregiver. Although these findings are important, and attachment relationships are foundational for children's development, attachment security has not been examined as a mechanism linking parental incarceration with child well-being in large population-based studies, partly because of the challenges related to measuring attachment in such samples (see Poehlmann-Tynan & Dallaire, 2021, for a summary). In Ella's case, she is starting to form new relationships with her paternal grandparents and is newly living with her father. However, they do not yet have enough positive history for Ella's cognitive and emotional expectations—as well as behaviors—to be considered secure.

Previous studies using the Attachment Q-Sort have found that security scores increase with age (e.g., Carlson et al., 2014; Clark & Symons, 2000), in part because some items focus on social behaviors that tend to improve as children grow older. In our study, we found a link between children's age and attachment security as well. Older children appear to be more skilled at showing secure base and safe haven behaviors with their caregivers, as assessed by the Attachment Q-Sort. Very young children—like Ella—appear more vulnerable to the disruption caused by parental incarceration. We see this trend in other research, as well. For example, Turney (2018) found that younger children with incarcerated parents experienced more adverse events than older children with incarcerated parents, and Poehlmann-Tynan and colleagues (2020) found that younger children with incarcerated parents were more likely to show developmental delays in the areas of language, social, and motor skills compared to older children with incarcerated parents. In their review of the literature, Poehlmann-Tynan and Turney (2021) found such age-graded effects as well; when parental incarceration occurred during their early years, children were more likely to show problems even in adolescence and early adulthood.

In our study, we also found that when children's caregivers provided safe, stable, academically stimulating home environments for children, children were more likely to develop secure attachments to their caregivers. In addition, when caregivers engaged in more positive interactions with children in the home, children were more likely to develop a secure attachment with the caregiver, similar to studies of other young children in different family structures. Although Ella's father is starting to interact with her in sensitive and responsive ways, they need more positive and consistent time together to solidify their growing attachment relationship.

### Observations of Caregiver-Child Interactions in the Home

Attachment measures look at the overall relationship that a child has developed with a parent or caregiver. In contrast, other observational measures capture children's moment-to-moment interactions with caregivers during play and structured tasks, which can be important when trying to understand children's family relationships. To obtain this fine-grained view, we videotaped 15 minutes of caregiver-child play interactions in the children's homes and later coded the videotapes with a measure called the Early Relational Assessment (ERA; Clark, 2015). For this study, we calculated two scales reflecting (1) positive caregiver emotions and behavior when interacting with the child and (2) negative caregiver emotions and behavior when interacting with the child.

As mentioned above, caregivers who were more sensitive and responsive during interactions with children in the home had children who were more likely to have secure attachments with them (Poehlmann-Tynan et al., 2017). This was the first study to report such findings in children with incarcerated parents. Moreover, high-quality interactions with caregivers in the home buffered against the relation between the parent's violent crime and children's attachment insecurity. That is, when caregivers interacted with children in a sensitive and responsive manner, there was less association between parental violence and children's attachment security. Thus, positive caregiver-child interactions seemed to function as a protective factor for young children with jailed parents.

In addition, Cynthia Burnson, who was a graduate student in our lab at the time, used a subsample of the current study to examine whether caregiving interactions could help buffer the stress associated with negative life events for children with incarcerated parents. Her findings indicated that the interaction between stressful life events and positive caregiver emotion and behavior was significantly associated with children's internalizing behavior problems such as withdrawal, sadness, anxiety, and depression. Stressful life events were only significantly related to children's internalizing behavior problems when caregiver positive interactions with the child were low

(Burnson, 2016). In other words, when caregivers interacted positively with children, there was no association between stressful life events and children's tendency to withdraw or show sadness, anxiety, or depression. However, there was not a similar buffering effect on children's externalizing behavior problems.

Similarly, prior research has found that the negative effects of stressful life events on children's behavior problems appear to be buffered by high-quality parenting (Masten & Garmezy, 1985). The importance of parent-child interactions and caregiving quality for child outcomes is central to attachment theory. Using this theoretical lens, sensitive and responsive care-giving promotes the establishment of secure attachments, which then posi-tively influence interactions with other people as well as children's ability to regulate their emotions and behaviors (Ainsworth, 1985; Thompson, 2008). Moreover, the quality of caregiving has been shown to promote resilience in high-risk children in a wide range of studies (e.g., Wyman et al., 1999), thus earning its place on Masten's "short list" of assets, or positive factors that are consistently shown to be important for positive child outcomes and resilience in the face of adversity (Masten, 2014).

*Attachment Story Completion Task*

As mentioned earlier, one cannot directly ask very young children how they think and feel about their families and expect to get a coherent and completely accurate verbal response. We could not ask Ella, for example, to tell us how she feels about her mom and dad and expect to get a verbal-ized answer that truly unpacks the nuances in their relationships. Therefore, researchers and practitioners must be creative and turn to other ways that allow children to express their thoughts and feelings about family members, in addition to observations. Thus, we also examined children's perspectives on family relationships using the ASCT, which includes dolls and props so that children can act out some of their thoughts and feelings (i.e., engage in pretend play) (Bretherton et al., 1990). Using the doll figures and props, we acted out the beginning of several family stories—like we did with Ella—and asked children to complete the stories using words and pretend play, video recording children's responses and later transcribing and coding them. You got to see how this played out in the transcript of Ella's narratives included in her story above.

We only looked at the stories enacted by the 36 children aged three years and over, including Ella's stories. (Children younger than three years of age often do not verbalize enough to code their story stem enactments, and the measure was added later in the study, missing some children.) For 36 usable narratives, we transcribed and coded them using six codes that reflected how children represented their families (content codes) and how they approached the task (structural codes). The codes included positive attachment or caregiving behaviors, family vulnerability, violence, coherence, bizarre actions, and family chaos. For more information on the measure and our coding process, please see the appendix B.

When we looked across children, examination of the ASCT data supported what we found using the Attachment Q-Sort: many of the family interactions that children depicted were consistent with insecure attachment relationships, including lack of coherence, and expression of vulnerability, chaos, and violence—all aspects also captured in Ella's ASCT stories. Ella's stories, especially the stories that portrayed a child doll who was hurt or afraid, reflect vulnerability. Violence was also depicted and, as the stories went on, an increasing amount of chaos and lack of coherence, suggesting that she may have internalized somewhat problematic or disrupted family relationships, especially in time of need or distress. Yet again, about one-third of the children in the study depicted positive family relationships in a coherent way despite their experience of parent-child separation and parental incarceration. These children consistently enacted story completions that reflected supportive, loving, and caring family relationships, suggesting that young children can internalize highly positive family relationship dynamics even under stressful conditions. Children who represent family relationships in a more positive way address the core issue in each of the story stems in a way that resolves the story.

For example, in the "spilled juice" story stem we described earlier in the chapter, a more securely attached child pretends that a doll cleans up the juice or pours more juice for the child. In the "hurt knee" story stem we asked Ella to continue, a more securely attached child would pretend that someone helps the child or cares for the child doll's knee, or the child doll is portrayed as climbing that rock again without hurting herself (mastery). In the "monster in the bedroom" story stem, the more securely attached child doll would successfully get help and have the "monster" disappear or go away. But for Ella, the core issues in the story stems are not resolved. The problems introduced go on and the stories become more disorganized, without a resolution. This means that Ella is probably feeling much more than just a numbness or "indifference" about her attachment figures—she is likely emotionally struggling with whether or not she can rely on the adults in her life to keep her safe, secure, and loved because of the frequent separations from her mother and other caregivers. As seen through these attachment measures, the unstable family environment she has grown accustomed to appears to have complicated her ability to form secure attachments with the family members in her life, which translates into her internalizing a sense of insecurity.

We also found that chaos in the home, as observed by researchers and reported by children's caregivers (see appendix B and chapter 5), predicted children's representations of family chaos and disorganization in their story stem completions of the ASCT. That is, children represented in their play and narratives what researchers saw using other methods, suggesting that the children were internalizing aspects of the environments in which they lived, just like Ella. In addition, the ASCT codes of family chaos and vulnerability were also significantly associated with children's behavioral dysregulation as rated by researchers in the home. When children depicted their family interactions as including potential for hurt and disorganization, they were more likely to actually show difficulty regulating their behaviors and emotions when observed by researchers, again like Ella. However, not all children are dysregulated in the context of insecure attachments. Some children show an outer brightness and affability—or even indifference—while inside they are feeling anxious and fearful. We also found that older children were more likely to enact positive representations of family relationships, similar to our Attachment Q-Sort findings as well as other studies. Once again, very young children appear to be particularly vulnerable in families affected by parental incarceration—findings that hold for children with incarcerated fathers as well as mothers.

### Children's Family Drawings

In our study, coauthor Hilary Cuthrell, who was a graduate student at the time that we collected these data, used an attachment-based family drawing method to contribute to our understanding of how children think and feel about their families (Pace et al., 2021). Cuthrell analyzed 32 drawings from 16 children who participated in the family drawing task in their homes and during a visit with their incarcerated parents in the jail. She found that children's attachment security scores from previous measures were positively correlated with the elaboration and imagination of the pictures and negatively correlated with exaggeration, rigidity, and omissions. What this ultimately showed was that children with more secure attachments with caregivers produced drawings that were more imaginative, complete, and elaborative and that they were more likely to depict a sense of energy in their pieces. The secure children also produced drawings that depicted minimal fluctuations of the size among the figures and were void of exaggerated body parts and facial features (even controlling for children's age). On the other hand, children with more insecure attachments did not have these qualities. Take for instance Ella's drawing from her home visit (figure 3.1). Although her depiction of family included herself with her mom, dad, and maternal grandmother in close proximity, with the type of bodies that 3-year-olds often draw, the broad strokes of purple, pink, red, and blue are chaotic, possibly reflecting anxiety or conflict, and contribute to what we know from our other attachment measures, indicating trends toward insecure attachment.

Figure 3.1. Ella's family drawings during the home visit.

We were also interested in how children's drawings in the home compared to their drawings in the jail, especially regarding different emotions that children may express in their creations. We found that signs of happiness, positive emotion, and completeness were higher in the jail compared to the home, whereas the exaggeration of body parts and distanced proximity of figures was lower in the jail compared to the home. We see this in Armoni's drawings, the child we introduced in chapter 2 (figures 3.2a and 3.2b). During the home visit when he was prompted to draw a picture of his family, he drew a beautiful self-portrait with proportional body parts and a smiling face. However, when reminded of the prompt to draw his family, he matter-of-factly replied to the research assistant, "This is all of the parts that I want to draw of my family." This may reflect feelings of loneliness and isolation that have occurred, especially since coming to live at his grandma's house following his mother's arrest and incarceration. Throughout the drawings of children in the study, we saw similar trends—conceptualizations of family following a parent's arrest and jailing were complicated. Yet, the drawings completed in the jails included more complete depictions of the family.

There are several reasons why this somewhat unexpected finding may have occurred. First, the child's visit with the incarcerated parent may have

Figure 3.2a. Armoni's family drawings during the home visit and jail visit: Armoni's home visit drawing showing "Me" (Armoni).

prompted the child to feel a sense of family togetherness, inclusiveness, pride, and positive emotions that may not have been as salient in relation to the whole family at home. Supporting this finding, scholars and practitioners have argued that supported visits between children and their parents in jail or prison can positively build family connections during parental incarceration (Poehlmann-Tynan & Pritzl, 2019). Second, the jailed parent's absence from the home may decrease the salience of a child's sense of positive emotion regarding the whole family. Third, perhaps some of the concerns and ambiguity surrounding the parent's whereabouts and safety were ameliorated at the jail because the child had an opportunity to see where their parent was staying and personally verify their parent's presence and

Figure 3.2b. Armoni's family drawings during the home visit and jail visit: Armoni's jail visit drawing. Top: "Me" (Armoni); bottom (left to right): Uncle, Aunt, Cousin, Brother (Jordan), Grandma (Louise), Mom (Kiesha).

well-being. The latter explanation is consistent with ambiguous loss theory and prior findings regarding children's visits to their parents in corrections settings (see chapter 6). Fourth and finally, prior research has found that the vast majority of young children who visit their parents in jail engage positively with their parents for at least some of the time (Poehlmann-Tynan et al., 2015). The sense of reconnection that occurs during a visit may allow children to experience a temporary alleviation from their feelings of loss regarding the parent's incarceration, with fewer "distortions" in the figures that the child drew. For many families, positive visit experiences can function as a protective factor regarding parental incarceration, although caregivers who bring children to the visits often report that the visits can be quite emotional or stressful depending on many factors (Poehlmann-Tynan & Pritzl, 2019; Tasca, 2016).

To walk you through what this sort of family drawing process looked like in our study, please consider Armoni's drawing again, this time comparing the drawing from the jail visit to that of the drawing from the home visit (figures 3.2a and 3.2b). While his home visit drawing is positive in many ways, it may depict signs of isolation; in contrast, generally speaking his jail visit drawing is vibrant, colorful, and overall depicts a connection between family members. It is evident that Armoni has invested energy into the detail of the figures in his drawing—he uses multiple colors and great detail in the figure's feet, faces, and hair. The figures have positive expressions and they appear grounded and smiling. However, Armoni still drew himself at a distance from his family. This may again be reflective of the emotional distance and isolation he has been feeling since witnessing his mother's arrest, but at the jail he feels reassured by the support of his family, recognizing it enough to include family members in his drawing this time. In fact, this example aligns with what we found across the sample. When given the opportunity to visit incarcerated parents at the jail and accompanied by their caregiver, children produced more complete and elaborative depictions of family and were more likely to demonstrate energy with their pieces. Taken together, these drawings map on to other measures of attachment in our study.

Given what we know about Armoni's attachment styles with his grandma Louise and his mom Kiesha, the variation in these family drawings may not be all that surprising. For instance, the pain he is feeling from the traumatic separation from his mom may have made him reconceptualize his inner image of family so much so that he was the only one he felt comfortable depicting. However, after developing a more trusting relationship with his grandmother, and spending time with his mother at the jail, Armoni includes a number of his attachment figures in the picture along with other key providers of social support, like his uncle, aunt, cousin, and little brother. When he finished the drawing in the waiting room at the jail, he eagerly ran back over to hand it to us, gleefully saying, "Look, it's my family together!"

*Parent and Caregiver Reports of Family Relationships*

In addition to measures that focused on the child, we also asked adults to report on their feelings about family relationships to better understand the larger family emotional climate. Using the Inventory of Family Feelings, we asked jailed parents and caregivers to rate their relationships with the young children in their care, and we asked jailed parents and children's caregivers to report on their feelings about each other (more detail is shared in appendix B; see also Lowman, 1980). Each adult reported on their emotions of warmth, loyalty, and trust toward their child. Scores can range from 0 to 38, with higher scores indicating more feelings of trust and security, loyalty, warmth, and affection. Although a few adults felt that they had a conflicted relationship with the child, the norm was a highly positive rating.

Parents who were incarcerated, on average, reported more positive feelings about children's caregivers than caregivers reported about the incarcerated parents. One caregiver even said that he had no relationship with the child's jailed parent, so he would not complete the measure—this was Ella's father, indicating significant problems in the relationship between her caregiver and incarcerated parent (which Crystal also told us about). Despite the differences in average scores, the ratings of jailed parents and at-home caregivers toward each other were positively correlated, meaning that if a jailed parent felt positively about the child's caregiver, the child's caregiver was likely to feel relatively positively about the jailed parent and vice versa. These findings fit with previous literature indicating that some caregivers are frustrated or even angry at the incarcerated parent for leaving them to face the family's financial burdens, childcare, chores, and the other stressors of managing a household in addition to facing the stigma that often surrounds a parent's incarceration (Arditti, 2012).

## How Can We Help?

Parental incarceration can trigger cascades of uncertainty or family conflict that have implications for family relationships. These negative cascades may even resist healing when more family stability is achieved or when the parent is released from jail or prison. Expectations and pressure from family members, friends, and others; social stigma; and institutional policies and practices often make it difficult for formerly incarcerated parents to reestablish relationships with their children and reintegrate into family life (Hairston, 2007), especially when caregivers remain stressed and recidivism occurs. These findings suggest that supporting children and their families during and following parental incarceration is critical so that affected children can develop and maintain positive family relationships at home.

### Expand Services for Incarcerated Parents That Engage Caregivers

Right now, most interventions for families affected by parental incarceration in the United States occur within prisons (Eddy et al., 2019). The programs, such as Parenting Inside Out (Eddy et al., 2008), InsideOut Dad (Turner et al., 2021), or responsible fatherhood programs (Fontaine, Cramer, & Paddock, 2017), focus on parenting and are administered to incarcerated parents (usually fathers) during the incarceration period. In contrast, few programs are available for caregivers in the community when a parent is incarcerated (Wildeman et al., 2018). In addition to general poverty prevention programs as described by Berger and colleagues (see Noyes et al., 2018), programs that strengthen family relationships (e.g., Strengthening Families Program, Miller et al., 2014) and attachment relationships in particular, such as the Circle of Security intervention (Cassidy et al., 2010; Powell et al., 2013), Attachment and Biobehavioral Catch-Up (Dozier & Barnard, 2017), Mediational Intervention for Sensitizing Caregivers (MISC, Klein et al., 2017) or Triple P-Positive Parenting Program (e.g., Sanders, 2008) interventions, are needed for caregivers of young children with incarcerated parents. Because so much is happening with young children on a day-to-day basis in their homes, focusing on the child-caregiver relationship can be positive.

By engaging both incarcerated parents and children's at-home caregivers, multiple intervention goals can be supported, possibly facilitating positive co-parenting processes and decreasing family conflict in addition to fostering secure caregiver-child and parent-child attachment relationships.

### Talk to Children in Developmentally Appropriate Ways

Because children with incarcerated parents often experience ambiguous loss in their family relationships, it is also important to engage in open communication with children in a way that takes their age and capacity for understanding into account. Open communication is seen as a cornerstone of secure attachment (see, e.g., Bretherton, 1985, 1995). This includes providing available factual information presented in a developmentally appropriate way, even to young children. Although compassionate deception around a parent's incarceration is well-meaning, it may actually increase children's experience of stigma and isolation because they think the issue is so bad that their family cannot talk about it. Sesame Workshop's Emmy-nominated initiative Little Children, Big Challenges: Incarceration includes a caregiver guide that provides suggestions for how to talk to young children about a parent's incarceration. A recent study using a rigorous randomized controlled trial design evaluated these Sesame Workshop materials and found that caregivers in the intervention group were more likely to feel comfortable talking to young children (age 3 to 8 years) about the parent's incarceration; indeed, they were more likely to tell children the simple truth about their parent's incarceration using developmentally appropriate language compared to caregivers in the control group (Poehlmann-Tynan et al., 2021). Children who were told the simple truth about where the parent was also had a more positive visit with the incarcerated parent in the jail compared to children who were told nothing or a distortion. In addition, children in the intervention group indicated more positive feelings about their families (using an innovative iPad assessment technique) after watching the Sesame Workshop incarceration videos than children in the control group who watched general Sesame Street videos (Muentner et al., 2022). Thus, we recommend using these materials with young children whose parents are incarcerated to help dispel some of the ambiguity associated with the loss of a parent to incarceration and to support positive family relationships.

### Recognize and Support Caregivers

Finally, we recommend supporting children's at-home caregivers when a parent is incarcerated, including attending to their parenting and mental health in addition to making sure basic needs for shelter, food, and safety are met. Previous research (Turney, 2021; Wildeman et al., 2012) has documented mental health concerns in individuals with an incarcerated family member, including caregivers of children with incarcerated fathers. For example, using the Family History of Incarceration Survey (FamHIS), a nationally representative survey of adults in the United States, Turney (2021) found that having any family member incarcerated has negative implications for adult mental health. The findings did not depend on various demographic factors, suggesting that it was not simply an economic effect or an effect limited to one gender. Mothers who are caring for their child during paternal incarceration also show a propensity to use harsh discipline on the child (Turney, 2014a). Given these factors, as well as the findings of the present study, it is important for interventions to support the mental health and parenting of children's caregivers during and following parental incarceration. Doing so can help children like Ella, who are struggling.

Although the quality of relationships varied across families in our study, the children generally experienced more strained family relationships than children typically experience, similar to other clinical samples. About one quarter of young children in the study experienced at least one significant separation from their caregiver before age six in addition to separation from the incarcerated parent, suggesting significant disruptions in care for some children. In addition, only one in three children had developed a secure attachment to their at-home caregiver. While some of the children internalized positive family relationships and interactions, most of the children assessed internalized relationships characterized by disorganization and vulnerability, as demonstrated with Ella. Among children who visited their incarcerated parents, some had an easier time representing their families through their drawings. Although most of the adults reported feeling positively about the children in their care, suggesting strong caregiving bonds, adults rated each other lower, on average, suggesting tension in many of the co-parenting relationships. Caregivers were especially harsh in their judgments of the incarcerated parents, often reflecting frustration or resentment about being left to provide care for the child and handle responsibilities at home, often alone, during the incarceration period. All of these factors suggest a need for support for families with young children during parental incarceration.

# CHAPTER 4

# "We're Still Working on It"

## CHILDREN'S HEALTH AND DEVELOPMENT

THROUGHOUT JASMYNE'S MOM TANISHA'S young adult life, she has been passionate about helping people. While growing up, Tanisha's mother worked as a personal caregiver for several aging, disabled, and chronically ill folks around the town where she grew up. She remembers accompanying her mom on some of these visits when childcare could not be arranged, where she would sit at a distance but pay close attention to the delicate care her mom gave to her clients. After arriving home from an energizing day tagging along to these appointments, Tanisha would scurry up to their third-floor flat and quickly open up the old lunch box she had playfully repurposed as her medical bag to grab her toy stethoscope and run it over to her dolls she had left scattered around the room. Gently resting the earpieces in her ear, Tanisha remembers how she would lightly rub the circular end of the chest piece down the doll's torsos and arms until she found a make-believe pulse while uttering "You'll be okay, Dolly!", just as she saw her mom do in the hours prior.

Once she turned 16, Tanisha found it necessary to begin working since her dad had become incarcerated, thus halting child support payments, and her mom was struggling to make ends meet with her care work income alone. Still passionate about any and all things medical, she turned her search toward health care. Feeling too young to obtain her CNA (certified nursing assistant) certification and without a car of her own to make personal caregiving appointments like her mom did, she decided to settle as dining room staff at the local assisted living center to at least get her foot in the door in a health care setting. One day, after being there only a few months, she started getting stomach cramps and feeling nauseous during one of her shifts. Able to manage the discomfort and stick it out for the duration of her shift but unsure if she could continue to work through the cramps for the night, she stopped at Urgent Care on her way home to see what was causing this newfound pain, only to receive the news that she was pregnant.

Tanisha and her boyfriend, Lamonte, had been together for about three months—since around the time of her sixteenth birthday. Though they were both young and had only recently gotten together, they were dedicated to raising their child together as a family. Lamonte's love and support became necessary throughout Tanisha's pregnancy, which proved to be more complicated than the two expected. Though she was receiving regular prenatal care, Tanisha's stomach pains only heightened over the next few months, constantly causing her to feel nauseous and lightheaded. These pregnancy-related medical issues forced her to cut back her hours at the assisted living center, even further tightening their budgets and cutting into their savings. One day during Tanisha's sixth-month of pregnancy, while staying home to nurse a particularly rough flare-up of stomach pains and lightheadedness, her water broke. Unsure what to do, she called her mom, who immediately rushed home from running errands to take her to the hospital.

Because of a number of medical concerns, the doctors decided to rush her into an emergency delivery. In only a few hours, Tanisha and Lamonte were introduced to Jasmyne, their two-pound, five-ounce, baby daughter. Jasmyne was immediately taken by the delivery nurses to the neonatal intensive care unit (NICU) where she stayed over the next two months. After a week-long recovery herself, Tanisha made daily visits to the NICU to watch her baby grow and develop. Over time, Jasmyne became stronger—her little body grew and put on weight, her bald head started growing small patches of peach fuzz, and eventually she was set free from the tubes connecting her body to air, fluids, and nutrients.

Now fast-forward a few years later to the day we meet Jasmyne. The two-("and a half!" as she would assert)-year-old Black girl sits cross-legged on her living room floor as we unpack our bag that is filled with never-before-seen toys. Her short braids swing through the air as she excitedly rocks back and forth awaiting the last block, car, and stuffed animal to leave the bag; her green, pink, and orange hair beads clicking together in the air. Her stature is petite and takes up little space on the print rug where we sit together—a likely reflection of her premature birth—though her charm and vibrant personality fill the room from wall to wall. She immediately reaches for the white fuzzy bunny rabbit and holds it tightly to her body, almost losing sight of the stuffed animal's fur against her white T-shirt; its colored ears resting against her brightly colored, patterned shorts. Her mom, now 19 years old, sits closely nearby and smiles softly at Jasmyne's warm response. Besides the fashionable black-and-pink glasses and matching headscarf, her outfit mirrors Jasmyne's and makes it look as if she is an older, more mature version of her daughter. The two clearly have a strong bond, to which Tanisha says is, in part, due to the medical complications that she experienced throughout pregnancy and immediately postpartum. She loves her little girl with her whole heart and cannot fathom seeing anything bad happen to her.

That said, Jasmyne's health complications and their associated family stressors have not necessarily stopped over the years. She recently received an asthma diagnosis and is also experiencing some fairly significant speech and motor skills delays. She has been taking advantage of occupational therapy services, made available to her through her Early Head Start program (a federally funded initiative that helps provide family-centered services for low-income families with very young children) seeing the specialist monthly for more than a year to work on some of these developmental issues. While Tanisha tells us she has seen some improvements in Jasmyne's motor functioning—such as Jasmyne being able to eat her favorite food (cereal) from a bowl—she was hoping to notice a bit more progress by now. On top of that, Tanisha expresses concern to us over how Jasmyne seems to get sick more than others her age, has difficulty sleeping, has always eaten irregularly, and is not all that sure how to make sense of her newfound breathing and asthma issues. She tells us, too, that Jasmyne's language acquisition is only in the 50th percentile of those her age, based on an assessment done through Early Head Start. Tanisha often thinks back to the patience and care she witnessed her mom give to her patients; and though she remains quite worried about her daughter's ongoing health and development, she strives to mirror her caregiving to that of her mom's—which she has so adamantly admired for years.

However, on top of all of the stress surrounding Jasmyne's health and developmental well-being, support from her dad, Lamonte, has recently (and suddenly) changed. After the financial stress of having a new baby and the high cost of the associated medical bills, 17-year-old Lamonte began selling marijuana to bring in extra money for his new family. He continued doing so up until about six months ago, when he was arrested and charged with possession with intent to sell. Jasmyne's now 19-year-old father is incarcerated in the county jail only a few miles from her home, but the physical and emotional separation have been difficult for her. Tanisha explains to us how this stressor has seemed to further exacerbate some of Jasmyne's developmental issues. She gives us an example that has been causing significant frustration around their home lately. Even though Jasmyne has been potty-trained, she has started wetting her bed. Tanisha says that multiple times a week Jasmyne wakes up in the morning having wet the bed in her sleep. On top of that, Jasmyne has not been listening as well to her mom since her dad's arrest, and whenever she sees someone in public talking on their cell phone, she asks her mom, "Is that Dadda?"

Tanisha has been struggling with this, too. She has since decided to not really talk to Jasmyne about her dad's incarceration, saying that it's Lamonte's responsibility to tell her, because when Tanisha was younger, her dad's time in prison was especially hard on her. Lamonte speaks with Jasmyne on the phone most days. He tells Jasmyne that he is in trouble and just has to go away for a while to a place that he cannot leave, a place called jail. Jasmyne has questions about this, like when is he able to come home, is there cereal, and where does he sleep? Lamonte answers her questions the best that he can, although he does not know when he will be home. For Lamonte, the hardest part about being separated from Jasmyne is not being able to be with her, not seeing her every day like he used to, and knowing she is still struggling with her health. He tells us that he is heartbroken to see his daughter's developmental situations potentially worsening while he is away, but he feels trapped and like there is little he can do from the jail while he is away from her, especially given that he does not feel comfortable telling her full information about where he is and exactly how long he will be gone.

## Parental Incarceration and Other Adverse Childhood Experiences

The sorts of health and developmental concerns that Jasmyne's parents shared with us are not all that uncommon in the larger population of those with incarcerated parents. In fact, many other kids whose parents are in jail struggle with similar health-related risks and developmental needs. One common correlate of some of these health issues in youth with incarcerated parents is the amount of hardship the young one faces across their childhood, commonly referred to as adverse childhood experiences or ACEs. Parental incarceration is often included in lists of ACEs that are used to measure the cumulative amount of children's exposure to challenging or traumatic events. Other examples of ACEs that typically show up on these screening tools include experiencing abuse or neglect, death of a parent, parental substance abuse, parental mental illness or suicide, domestic violence, or parental relationship dissolution (i.e., divorce) in addition to experiencing racism and exposure to other trauma. Importantly, each of these instances of adversity is not meant to be directly comparable, but rather reflects the variety of ways in which children's exposure to hardship and trauma can influence their health and well-being in critical ways.

The first ACE study was conducted through a health maintenance organization from 1995 to 1997 and involved collecting data at two points in time on more than 17,000 adults receiving physical exams (Felitti et al., 1998). The original study, and many later studies conducted through the Centers for Disease Control and Prevention in various states, have found that multiple adverse experiences in childhood strongly relate to the development of risk factors for physical and mental health problems as well as overall well-being throughout the life course. Recent research has also found that parental incarceration is associated with other ACEs (Turney, 2018), as has been the case for Jasmyne since Lamonte has gone away as well as for Tanisha when her dad was incarcerated.

Specifically, individuals who experience the incarceration of a household member during their childhood (typically a parent) are more likely to experience four or more other ACEs (see, e.g., Gjelsvik et al., 2014), about the same number of hardships that Tanisha and Jasmyne have both experienced. Not only have Tanisha and Jasmyne navigated complications associated with parental incarceration, they both have lived in poverty. In addition, Lamonte occasionally used substances in the home prior to his incarceration, and their neighborhood is not the safest, so Jasmyne and Tanisha have witnessed community violence—all stacked on top of experiences of racial discrimination. These experiences amount to a significant accumulation of adversity in Jasmyne's life. This is especially relevant given the host of studies that have found that experiencing four or more ACEs is related to a higher occurrence of health and mental health problems and poorer quality of life, implications of which have been found to extend well into adolescence and adulthood, as depicted in figure 4.1. Particularly when these ACEs are cumulative, they have the potential to elevate risk for additional trauma, toxic stress, physiological dysfunction, disease, and mortality (Anda et al., 2006).

Across the field, numerous studies have asked parents to report on their children's ACEs. As alluded to, the vast majority of these findings indicate that when children experience the incarceration of a parent, they are also likely to be exposed to other ACEs. For example, Murphey and Cooper (2015) analyzed data from the 2011–2012 National Survey of Children's Health (NSCH), a representative sample of children under 18 in the United States. Controlling for demographic variables such as race and income, incarceration of a resident parent was a significant predictor for children to experience more traumatic life events. This means that kids like Jasmyne are more likely to live through significant adversity than their peers throughout their life course. This study also found that for children under the age of six years old—like those sampled in our study—the number of additional ACEs a child experienced was directly linked to developmental delays and potentially lasting health-related challenges for children. Turney (2018) more recently analyzed 2016 NSCH data to examine children's exposure to ACEs and the salience of having an incarcerated parent. Findings indicated that children with incarcerated parents experienced five times the number of ACEs as their peers who never experienced parental incarceration, even controlling for background characteristics of study participants. Yet again, the link between parental incarceration and exposure to other ACEs was stronger for children aged 0–6 years than for older children, suggesting that young

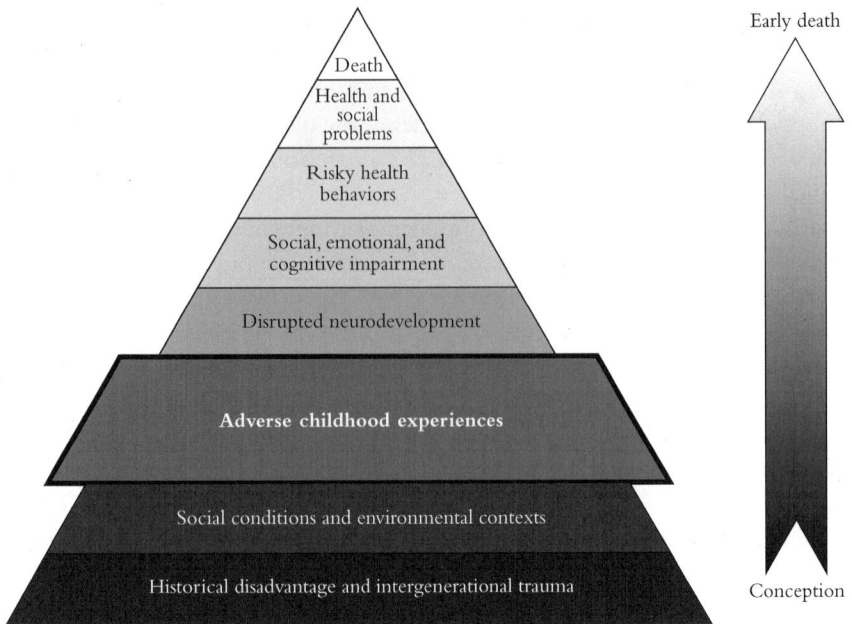

Figure 4.1. Proposed mechanisms by which adverse childhood experiences may influence children's health and well-being across the life course.

children with incarcerated parents are particularly vulnerable to experiencing additional hardship and trauma, contributing to significant risk for their health and development.

In our study, we asked caregivers to report on potentially challenging or even traumatic life experiences that the children had experienced using the Life Experiences Questionnaire (see appendix B). While a handful of items on the questionnaire asked about traditional ACE questions (i.e., asking about homelessness, parental divorce, exposure to violence) it also included indicators for experiences such as death of a close friend, funds being cut off by a government agency, and questions specific to stressful situations with siblings, resulting in a total of 32 questions asked in regard to the previous 12 months. Children experienced an average of 6.6 significant life events in the last year, ranging from 1 to 14 events per child, reflecting a significant number of transitions and stressors for these young ones. Because some items on the questionnaire depicted situations that called for household adaptation but were not inherently negative for the child (e.g., another adult moved into the home, mom started working), we also extracted exclusively the negative events that map more closely onto traditional ACE measures. Within a range of 0 to 12, children in our study experienced an average of 5.1 of these negative life events (in addition to parental incarceration), with more than two-thirds experiencing four or more of these events (the threshold found to be a tipping point for health and developmental consequences in other studies). The most frequently reported stressful life experiences were having difficult household financial situations (71 percent), residential instability (51.4 percent), and parents struggling with substance use (42 percent). Indeed, for just under half of our sample (44 percent), caregivers reported that the past year had included an above-average amount of stress for their young children, with only one out of five caregivers stating the last year was not all that stressful for the kids.

Though interesting descriptively and helpful in identifying risk for health and well-being, the additive count of ACEs (or stressful life events more generally in our study) does not paint the entire picture of the consequences that parental incarceration has in the everyday lives of children and families and its links to health and development. Items such as exposure to violence can vary from one to many, and the type of violence exposure can differ as well. For instance, children who experience parental divorce can be exposed to different levels of conflict and disruption depending on parental communication and how the separation or divorce unfolds. Of note for this work, parental incarceration is more than just an "ever" or "never" experience as most typical ACE measures account for. Many factors vary, such as (1) the nature of the parent's crime, (2) the frequency of arrests and jail or prison incarcerations, (3) the duration of time that the parent has spent in corrections settings, (4) what the child knows about the incarceration, (5) whether the child lived with or has contact with the incarcerated parent, and (6) whether the child witnessed the parent's crime or arrest, among others. These factors also intersect with children's caregiving environments and wider contexts to create unique experiences for families touched by the criminal legal system.

Take for instance Jasmyne and her family. Jasmyne was routinely exposed to the sort of behaviors that ultimately sent her dad to jail and, though this is his first time away, she is already experiencing significant risks in her health and development (such as her uptick in bedwetting). When these specific factors stack onto her other lived experiences of adversity, they may very well launch Jasmyne on her own path of troublesome health and development. Certainly, one can imagine how these details contribute to children's feelings, relationships, and experiences day to day, as the above factors may vary widely across families, communities, and cultures. So too do they contribute to variation in children's physical, physiological, and mental, physical, and behavioral health outcomes, as well as aspects of their development, including potential developmental regressions.

## Children's Health while Parents Are in Jail

Despite parental incarceration being considered an ongoing public health crisis, we are still making sense of its consequences for children's health and development—particularly for young children. Jasmyne's poor baseline health was already front and center in Tanisha's mind, but she worries that since Lamonte has been away, her daughter may be further slipping behind her peers. She is not alone in her worries about this. In our study, about 40 percent of parents in jail expressed fairly serious concerns about their young children's development, with most concerns focusing on children's ongoing (and in many cases worsening) behavioral and emotional issues. Though important, these indicators of how children are adjusting tell only part of the story. Indeed, when we more holistically examine how negative health-related consequences of parental incarceration intersect with preexisting conditions and physiological measures of health functioning, we are able to further examine just how layered this public health crisis may be for young children.

### Physical Health

When considering children's overall health, behavior problems and emotional well-being often rise to the top of the most-studied outcomes for those with incarcerated parents. Indeed, despite parents generally perceiving their incarceration as negatively impactful for their children's health (Correa et al., 2021), limited work has examined aspects of children's physical well-being or even preexisting conditions. Even still, the scarce research that does examine this finds ultimately detrimental consequences of parental incarceration. Indeed, younger children have been found to be at increased odds of poor sleeping and eating behaviors (Jackson & Vaughn, 2017), physiological distress (Muentner et al., 2021), and elevated risk for psychopathology—in other words, significant psychological disorders and maladaptive behaviors (Murray & Murray, 2010). This concern is particularly troublesome given the long-term health consequences seen for children with incarcerated parents across the life course, such as poor health-related quality of life (Gjelsvik et al., 2014), generally problematic health behaviors (e.g., poor diets, smoking cigarettes, drinking and drug use, risky sexual practices; see Heard-Garris et al., 2018), diabetes (White et al., 2020), and foregone health care (Heard-Garris et al., 2018). Qualitative work describes the physical toll that parental incarceration takes on a person as they grow into adolescence and adulthood, with reports of it contributing to hypertension, anxiety, and depression. As one adult reflected, "The stress [of having a previously incarcerated parent] . . . is gonna kill me" (Greib et al.

2014, p. 1189). Physical health remains largely unexplored in samples of younger children with incarcerated or recently released parents, a gap our study sought to fill.

Despite the children in our study being six years old and younger, many were already dealing with preexisting health conditions that complicated their current well-being and contributed to issues exacerbated by their parents' incarceration. Nearly 15 percent of children (Jasmyne included) were born preterm, and nearly half of the mothers had complications of some sort during their pregnancy, while a handful received no prenatal care at all. As a result, almost one in five children in our study spent some time in a special care nursery or the NICU, as did Jasmyne. This ranged from a couple of hours to nearly four months for some children. About this same proportion (20 percent) had been exposed to substances in utero (the most common of which were alcohol and marijuana, but a smaller percentage included cocaine or crack cocaine, and opioids).

Since birth, about one out of six children in our study had been diagnosed with a developmental, mental health, or genetic condition. That said, an additional handful of caregivers expressed concern over children having some sort of condition despite their young ones receiving no formal diagnosis yet. The range of these concerns varied, though many caregivers thought that children struggled with attention-related conditions such as attention-deficit/hyperactivity disorder (ADHD) (e.g., "He has too much energy and is always hyper, he was prescribed ADHD medicine but his mom doesn't give it to him"), speech and other language issues (e.g., "She has a fairly serious speech impediment, in fact her daycare teachers thought she may have been deaf for a while during her first year, but she's been in speech therapy for about a year and a half now"), and other mental (e.g., anxiety, posttraumatic stress disorder) and physical health (e.g., heart problems, brittle hair/nails, inhibited perception of pain) conditions. That said, less than 10 percent of the children in our study were receiving mental health services, such as counseling. Despite the number of those experiencing health problems, 15 percent were taking medication for a health condition, which included both chronic conditions like Jasmyne's asthma but also more temporary illnesses like an ear infection. This shows that, even with a significant proportion of children in the study experiencing health-related issues (both preexisting and ongoing), uptake in service utilization and treatment regimens remained limited.

These findings complement recent results from our lab (and our collaborator at the University of Minnesota-Twin Cities, Rebecca Shlafer) based on a different study of children with incarcerated parents between the ages of three and eight years (Poehlmann-Tynan et al., 2020, 2021). In that work, we asked caregivers to rate children's health on a scale that ranged from poor to excellent at two different time points (Poehlmann-Tynan et al., 2021). We found that despite children's general health being rated relatively well overall, the young ones who were highly anxious or depressed after witnessing their parent's arrest had less optimal health. In other words, child health can be exacerbated by their own emotional reactions to the jailed parent's arrest and departure for a corrections facility.

This evidence is concerning given what we found in the current study around preexisting health conditions and limited service availability. When combined with stressors related to parental incarceration, lower service utilization and availability can further worsen children's health. In many ways, adverse reactions to events surrounding a parent's incarceration as well as lack of access to treatment may be part of what contributes to health risks in adolescents and young adults experiencing parental incarceration (Heard-Garries et al., 2018; Hiolski et al., 2019). In addition to such health risks, some scholars have hypothesized that toxic stress may play a significant role in linking parental incarceration with subsequent negative outcomes in health and well-being (e.g., Haskins & McCauley, 2019).

*Physiological Stress*

In a novel contribution to the field, Lindsay Weymouth, a graduate student in our lab during the study, documented children's hair cortisol and cortisone concentrations as neurobiological markers of children's ongoing development and adjustment to stress, as we discussed in chapter 2 in the context of witnessing a parent's arrest. Prior to the current study, no previous research had documented stress hormones in children with incarcerated parents despite the burgeoning literature suggesting trauma symptomatology as a pathway to poor outcomes (e.g., Arditti & Savla, 2015; Bocknek et al., 2009). We know from more general community samples of children (i.e., those without incarcerated parents) that trauma exposure is linked to alterations in basal cortisol levels and lower cortisol reactivity (Bevans et al., 2008, 2009; Jaffee et al., 2015). In other words, children's exposure to traumatic events—including parental arrest and incarceration—can influence the body's hormones that respond to stress and affect a wide range of the body's everyday processes (like metabolism and immune response) in a negative way.

Our study used scalp hair samples from 62 children (some are excluded because of a delay in getting study protocols approved by the institutional review board and others because they either did not assent to hair collection or had shaved heads and thus no hair could be collected). At the home visit, we cut hair about the size of a pencil eraser from four areas at the back of a child's head and toward the top of the scalp (called the posterior vortex; more comprehensive information about data collection is included in appendix B). This method is used as a biological marker of cortisol and cortisone secretion accumulation over approximately three months, and is correlated with other methods of physiological stress measurement, such as the analysis of hormones in saliva and urine (Stalder et al., 2012). Descriptively, the concentrations of cortisol and cortisone in children's hair in our study were significantly higher than those of children from community samples and even clinical samples of children experiencing significant distress and even toxic stress (Weymouth, 2016; Pritzl, 2022). Toxic stress—which occurs when stress is overwhelming or chronic—can have adverse impacts on young children's developing brain architecture, especially when extreme events occur during early childhood, like parental incarceration in this study. Such exposures can have a dysregulating effect on brain circuits and stress response systems that are crucial for children's behavior, health, and development moving forward (Blair & Raver, 2016; McEwen, 2012).

A recent publication of ours (which was covered in more depth in chapter 2) discusses children's physiological stress reactions in the context of witnessing a parent's arrest (Muentner et al., 2021). As mentioned, we found that prolonged exposure to stressful events (e.g., being exposed to a father's arrest on top of already high behavioral stress symptoms) results in stress mediators that are no longer protective and may make children more sensitive to future stressors. Chronic stress in children with jailed parents, as documented in both Weymouth's (2016) dissertation and Muentner and colleagues' (2021) publication, can affect the morphology and chemistry of brain regions such as the hippocampus, prefrontal cortex, and amygdala. These changes are largely reversible if the chronic stress only lasts for weeks. However, it is unclear whether prolonged stress for many months, as reflected by these hair cortisol data, may have long-lasting effects on the brain (McEwan, 2009), compounded by the vulnerability of the developing brain in young children and combined with vulnerable caregiving contexts. Such factors may ultimately increase children's risk of experiencing health issues, from heart disease and obesity to anxiety and depression (see, e.g., Ranabir & Reetu, 2011). This is particularly salient and concerning evidence, given the general worry of caregivers and parents over the poor health and development demonstrated in children in our study.

### Behavioral Health

Exacerbated behavioral health problems, common indicators of social-emotional strife, are among the most consistently documented examples of challenges that children with incarcerated parents face (Poehlmann-Tynan & Turney, 2021). For instance, we know from analyses of the Fragile Families and Child Wellbeing Study that children with incarcerated fathers are more likely to manifest externalizing behavior problems compared to their similarly

disadvantaged peers without incarcerated parents (Geller et al., 2009; Wakefield & Wildeman, 2013; Wildeman 2010). These adverse outcomes may
be even more stark for boys than girls (Gellar et al., 2009; Wildeman, 2010)
and for children who lived with their fathers prior to incarceration (Gellar
et al., 2012). That said, possible effects of maternal incarceration on behavioral health have been mixed and heterogeneous (Turney & Wildeman,
2015; Wildeman & Turney, 2014). Results from the Pittsburgh Youth Study
are similar, indicating that boys with incarcerated parents had heightened
behavior problems compared to counterparts with never-incarcerated parents (Murray et al., 2012).

   A child's behavioral health can be reflected in a handful of ways, depending on the developmental stage. For instance, older children may exercise
more delinquent tendencies, substance use dependence, or risky sexual behaviors. While these are all warranted extensions of the concept (and ultimately
prove applicable in samples of those with incarcerated parents across adolescence), they are largely irrelevant for the young children in our study. Instead,
focusing on internalizing behaviors as a measure of emotional health, as well
as externalizing behaviors like aggression and impulsivity to capture
children's overt responses, is a more advantageous approach for this group.
For instance, elevations in internalizing behaviors, or behaviors and emotions
directed inward at oneself such as withdrawal, anxiety, depression, or thought
problems, have been linked to parental incarceration (Murray & Farrington,
2008), with high-quality parent-child relationships acting as a potential protective factor (Davis & Shlafer, 2017). Other work has found that children
with incarcerated parents are also at risk for trajectories of high externalizing
behaviors, which are directed outward and can include bouts of physical
aggression, disobedience, or destruction of property (Kjellstrand et al., 2018),
with instances of family instability further worsening these symptoms (Muentner et al., 2019).

   To measure behavioral health in our study, we used either the Preschool
Child Behavior Checklist (CBCL) for children between the ages of two and
five years or the School-Age CBCL for children who were six years of age
(more measurement information is included in appendix B; see also Achenbach & Rescorla, 2014). High scores on the internalizing and externalizing
subscales indicate more problematic behaviors; indeed, T scores (calculated
based on age and gender using data from the standardization sample) can
indicate "clinically significant," "borderline clinical," or normal levels of
behavior problems. In our study, means were relatively high, with an average score of 51.60 and 50.28 for internalizing and externalizing problems,
respectively. According to caregivers' reports on the CBCLs, 41 percent
of the children in our study exhibited clinically significant or borderline

externalizing behavior problems and 26 percent exhibited clinically significant or borderline internalizing behavior problems. Additionally, 80 percent of the children scored below the Social Competence Scale community sample mean (2.68) for preschoolers (Gouley et al., 2008). Thus, a significant proportion of young children of jailed parents were not doing well in regard to their behavioral health. Despite these concerns, however, there is good news, too: the majority of children in our study did not display clinically significant behavior problems, and the proportion of children rated as having above-average social competence should not be understated.

Like previous studies, though, our study documents the development of behavior problems in children with incarcerated parents—especially fathers—across both internalizing and externalizing spectra. Recognizing that common ways that young children can cope with having a parent go to jail include withdrawal, depression, and anxiety or also through acting out, disobeying, and increasing aggression, these measures of behavioral health shed light into how children are adjusting. For a smaller, yet significant and sizable, portion of our sample, adjustment processes were so adverse that they hit clinical cutoffs of problem behaviors. When young children are nearing such high levels of problem behaviors, intervention-related support may be necessary. Indeed, mental health services offered by trained professionals, increased support and involvement with caregivers who support children's secure attachments, and developmentally appropriate conversation with young ones around where their incarcerated parent is may all jointly support children in processing their emotions and mitigate against risk to their behavioral health.

### Children's Skills across Developmental Domains

There are multiple approaches to measuring children's developmental outcomes. For instance, one could observe children's fine motor skills in how they spoon cereal into their mouth or one could examine a child's gross movements as they jump off playground equipment. Another area of potential observation is language acquisition and vocabulary skills. Regardless of how development is conceptualized, children with incarcerated parents face significant risk across a number of domains of development, with young children being particularly vulnerable. Because young children have less developed cognitive capacities and language skills to understand and discuss what is happening when a parent is arrested and then incarcerated (Eddy & Poehlmann-Tynan, 2019; Poehlmann, 2005a), they may be at an increased likelihood for associated stress and experiencing feelings of ambiguous loss. This calls for more attention to be paid to young children as they grow and develop while parents are incarcerated.

*Physical/Motor Skill Development*

For a subset of children and families for whom we observed jail visits, we asked caregivers to complete the Parents' Evaluation of Developmental Status: Developmental Milestones (PEDS:DM) form (Glascoe et al., 2006). With this tool, caregivers reported on four significant motor skills (both gross and fine) that children are expected to complete by their chronological age. For example, caregivers of the five-year-olds reported about whether the child could take off loose clothes such as pull-down pants or a coat as well as if the child could scribble with a crayon or marker without going off the page much. Overall, we found that 40 percent of children met three or four of these motor skill milestones that were appropriate for their age, with 33 percent meeting two and 27 percent meeting zero or only one milestone. (It would generally be expected that children could complete these milestones, so meeting zero or one milestone is considered an affirmative screening for possible developmental delay.) In the aforementioned study with a larger sample of children aged 3–8, about 45 percent of children displayed a motor delay, which is relatively comparable to that in the present study (Poehlmann-Tynan et al., 2021). Pointedly, the developmental screeners conducted at the jail in this study significantly correlated with assessments of developmental skills conducted at home, an important contribution for prevention and intervention work discussed later on in the chapter.

*Language and Learning*

On top of risk for motor delays, studies have found that parental incarceration is associated with less optimal child, adolescent, and young adult cognitive and educational outcomes, including developmental delays, learning disabilities, special education placement, grade retention, suspension, and expulsion (Haskins, 2014, 2016; Jacobsen, 2019; Murphey & Cooper, 2015; Turney & Haskins, 2014; for a review, see Poehlmann-Tynan & Turney, 2021). Even for young children, parental incarceration has been associated with lower preschool readiness (Testa & Jackson, 2021).

In our study, we assessed the same subset of children for developmental milestones around language skills (both receptive and expressive language) and learning (preacademic skills of early literacy and numeracy), again using the PEDS:DM. For language skills, no children were in the top range that met most or all of the language milestones appropriate for their age. Approximately 57 percent of the children met two milestones, but the remaining 43 percent did not hit any or only one of the language skills, such as if they could point to various parts of their body and label them as "head," "legs," "teeth," "toes," etc. That said, learning skills were a bit higher, with an even 33 percent split across groups who met 3–4, 2, or 0–1 milestones (e.g., being able to draw a triangle or recognize objects when asked). In the other study of children aged 3–8 that we mentioned, 43 percent of children showed an academic or learning delay, 42 percent a language delay, and 30 percent a social/adaptive delay (Poehlmann-Tynan et al., 2021).

The learning and language delays in the present study are considerable given that more than 60 percent of children involved were in some sort of formal schooling or Head Start or Early Head Start program like Jasmyne. On top of that, only one in eight children were receiving special education or learning-related services (the majority of whom were receiving speech therapy services). When we asked caregivers how the child was doing in their program or school, responses varied considerably. For instance, some shared sentiments that reflected concerns, such as "He's doing very bad and is very naughty—he acts out all the time and is at the very, very bottom of his class for learning." Oher caregivers were more positive about the child's development: "She's doing above average in most things and is a gifted kid." More common were sentiments that described children's learning as a work in process, for example: "It's going fine but we're still working on it; her academic skills are delayed, and it's taken her a while to catch up." In some instances, having a parent go to jail seemed to get in the way of paths to success, for example: "In comparison to last year [before the parent's incarceration], he seems to wander off more and is having issues with attention and focus."

Beyond interviews with caregivers, we also completed cognitive assessment with children in their homes. We used the abbreviated version of the Stanford-Binet Test, which gauges children's cognitive skills, including both nonverbal and verbal skills (see Roid & Barram, 2004; Roid & Pomplun, 2012). Children's cognitive skills and vocabulary skills assessed in the home ranged from delayed to accelerated, with average scores of 88 (compared to a standardized average score of 100) resulting in about 18 percent of children scoring in the "significantly delayed" range. We also used the Peabody Picture Vocabulary Test (PPVT) to measure children's one-word receptive vocabulary (Dunn et al., 2003). In comparison to the standardization samples where average PPVT scores are 100, children in our study scored an average of 95.6 (ranging from 54 to 128), with 21 percent of children scoring below age-appropriate vocabulary levels. Although these findings are concerning, they also indicate that 79 percent of children were at or above age-appropriate vocabulary levels.

Although language and cognition for children in our study were closer in line with the standardization samples than for their behavioral health, there were still children who showed significant delays, reaching levels of clinical concern. These sorts of learning delays (and lack of services and intervention supports as previously discussed) may have dire implications

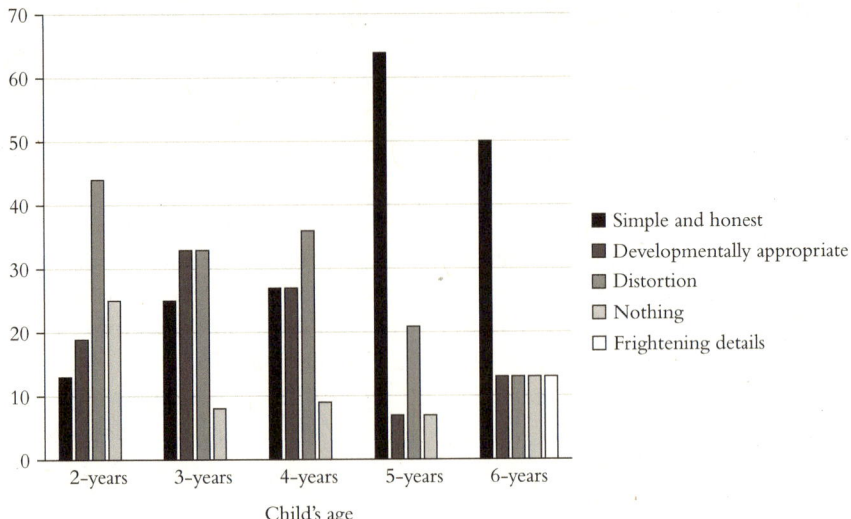

Figure 4.2. Percentage of children who were told different explanations about their parent's incarceration, by child's age.

for children's school success. However, learning delays have more immediate consequences for the ways in which young children can communicate and understand specifics related to their parents' incarceration.

For instance, when children are young, caregivers often have questions about what children understand about the parent's time in jail. We asked children's caregivers about what they told children about where the absent parent was (figure 4.2). About 14 percent of caregivers said that they did not say anything about the parent's incarceration, the same approach Tanisha used with Jasmyne. These parents preferred to ignore children's questions about it and did not bring up the topic. About 17 percent of caregivers indicated that they told children a "story" about where the parent was, such as "Your daddy is at work" or "Your mommy is in school." We sometimes refer to this as "compassionate deception" because of the well-meaning intent to protect children from distress or stigma. A total of 69 percent told children either a simple, honest explanation like "Your daddy is in jail, a place where people have to go if someone says that they broke a grown-up rule called a law" or a developmental explanation like "Your mommy is in a really big timeout because she did something wrong." This is similar to the route that Lamonte chose in his conversations with Jasmyne. Although she had follow-up questions that he struggled to answer, he felt that this approach at least opened the door to conversation with Jasmyne and made him feel like he was still an active part of her life rather than a mysterious figure who had suddenly disappeared. Previous research has found that young children who are told simple, honest, developmentally appropriate explanations are more likely to have a secure attachment to their caregivers (Poehlmann, 2005c), to express more positive emotions during visits with their incarcerated fathers (Poehlmann et al., 2021), and to have more regulated behaviors following the parent's release (Muentner, 2021).

Thus, materials developed for caregivers of young children who have a parent in jail or prison have emphasized the importance of open communication and simple honesty for children (e.g., Sesame Workshop's materials for children with incarcerated parents)—but not oversharing details about the parent's crime, arrest, associated violence, or alleged criminal activities. As children grow older, they are more likely to overhear the truth from relatives or once they become computer savvy, they can even look up the information themselves on the internet. Some details are unknown, even to the adults, like how long a parent may be gone, so it is important to be honest about where uncertainty lies as well. What the child has been told does not equate with what the child understands, especially if children show any language or cognitive delays. However, keeping the lines of communication open so children feel free to ask questions is often helpful.

Caregivers are also sensitive to children's age. In our study, they tended to share more honest explanations about the parent's incarceration with older children. The most common explanation of where the parent went was a "distortion" for two-year-olds, while the most common explanation for children ages five and six was the simple truth (figure 4.2). Potentially frightening details about the parent's crime were only shared with six-year-old children, not with younger children. In a recent study that considered the implications of what children were told about their parent's incarceration as it pertained to how they coped when that parent returned home found a similar age gradient in outcomes, highlighting more positive outcomes for younger children (Muentner, 2021). Indeed, older boys exhibited more behavior problems than younger boys postrelease (including learning-related outcomes like thought and attention problems) when they were given more detailed information about the parent's incarceration, suggesting potential concerns about oversharing. That said, refraining from sharing information is not necessarily the solution; rather, it again stresses the need for supportive and trusted parents or other adults to have honest, developmentally appropriate conversations with children across age groups given the benefit of this dialogue seen in each of these previous studies for young children (Muentner, 2021; Poehlmann, 2005c; Poehlmann-Tynan et al., 2021).

*Developmental Regressions*

Though beyond the scope of the current study, another project conducted in our lab in 2005 with young children with imprisoned mothers found developmental regressions following the incarceration as a serious concern for children (Poehlmann, 2005c). Remember back to Tanisha's frustrations over Jasmyne's return to bedwetting since Lamonte has been incarcerated? Unfortunately for many young children like Jasmyne, such loss of key developmental milestones previously acquired is a reality. In the previous study of children with incarcerated mothers between the ages of 2.5 and 7.5, 22 percent of children experienced developmental regressions like this, most often related to toileting, as was the case for Jasmyne (Poehlmann, 2005c). Other caregivers in that study talked about relapsing into acting like a baby again, both in terms of language use and clingy behaviors (Poehlmann, 2005c). A smaller proportion even talked about how some reverted back into frequent significant emotional distress of that of an infant or young toddler, describing children who would be crying so much at the separation that they could not even eat (Poehlmann, 2005c). These examples holistically depict significant developmental concerns for one out of five young children when parents go to jail as they regress even further behind from where they started, which is already often lagging behind their peers.

Taken together, the findings from the present study spark significant concern for the growth and development of many young children who experience parental incarceration, although many of the children were doing well and developing normally. Children who witnessed more incarceration-related events seemed to be at particular risk for poor outcomes. For instance, other work has found that witnessing a parent's arrest and exhibiting distress about it is linked to missing developmental milestones, particularly in the area of early learning and academic skills (Poehlmann-Tynan et al., 2021). What this suggests is that the magnitude of the effect of parental incarceration on children's overall development may be influenced by a culmination of multiple vulnerabilities, including those related to the parent's incarceration. As these young children grow older and receive regular schooling and even additional support services, they may "catch up" in some of their skills. However, the gravity of the issue as detailed in this study puts an added emphasis on supporting children now so that they do not fall even further behind.

## How Can We Help?

*Expanded Services in Educational Programming*

Findings from our study presented in this chapter point to the critical need for educational and learning-related services that better support children's developmental and intellectual outcomes in the context of parental incarceration. First and foremost, more efforts need to be made to mitigate missed language, motor, adaptive, and cognitive developmental milestones and ultimately improve school readiness. To begin, steps can be taken to support caregivers in the home to improve children's likelihood of success. This includes providing a language-rich environment where children engage in daily communication, book reading, and other literacy and numeracy activities. In addition to books and other written materials, exposing the children to educational toys and games helps them to encounter more words per day, thus improving their vocabulary and also preparing them for socialized aspects of storytelling, listening, and imaginative play. Children can be provided with support to complete their daily routines like dressing, toileting, eating, and getting ready to leave the house, in an increasingly independent way. These efforts can help to improve children's self-regulation, executive functioning, planning and sequencing, self-care, and even motor functioning.

On top of this, expanded access to free high-quality early childhood care and education is important. Whether this be school or home based, developmentally appropriate educational opportunities have been found to improve young children's academic trajectories, and increasing access to programs such as Head Start and Early Head Start (both federal initiatives that support young children's growth and development through early learning, health, and family services) allows more children from low-income households to receive services similar to those enjoyed by their more affluent peers. Along with this, working with the children's childcare educators to identify developmental delays, regressions, and signs of missed milestones allows for appropriate referrals and supportive collaborative care that usually improves children's developmental outcomes. Starting on this early and continually monitoring progress will help to keep children on track with their peers and prepare them for future opportunities in an equitable way.

*Developmental and Health Surveillance in Pediatric or Public Health Sites*

Beyond missed learning-related developmental milestones, children in our study exhibited significant health-related concerns, some of which were even associated with disadvantages that predate their parents' incarceration. For all children, regardless of parental involvement in the legal system, expanded screening for developmental concerns is necessary. Importantly, it would be helpful to incorporate developmental screenings within the context of families' "touches" with primary care, urgent or emergency care, and public health settings. This would allow for children to be identified early and monitored often regarding their overall developmental functioning, helping to identify problem areas and outline intervention goals. Hand in hand with this should be efforts that make access to health-care services affordable or free. This includes expanding the breadth and capacity of basic services, such as Medicaid, and efforts to eliminate waitlists for community-based health access programs. Even for those with private insurance, efforts can be made that give families a broader set of service options and less stringent timelines and requirements for service uptake and utilization. Improved access to health-care services and ongoing developmental surveillance within the health-care system would not only help to reduce challenges associated with preexisting conditions (like complications from being born preterm or with mental health and attention diagnoses) but also better situate children within community-based services that improve their growth and development, such as linkages to occupational and speech/language therapies.

More efforts also can be made within the criminal legal system to support the health and well-being of children whose parents are incarcerated. Our study found that developmental screenings, conducted within the jail when children come to the facility to visit their parents, were significantly correlated with screenings administered at the child's home. This means that correctional facilities might be able to collaborate with public health and child welfare agencies to better provide screening and triage services for children whose parents are incarcerated, integrated into ongoing activities such as visiting. If social workers or child development specialists can be present within institutions to monitor the health and development of children who come through the door of a jail, they can also support children's caregivers in getting community-based services needed to intervene on identified challenges and concerns. Indeed, partnering with local public health programs and other nonprofit services could allow jails to connect children with incarcerated parents to health-related resources. Including jailed parents in these conversations is equally important, given their documented concern for children's well-being and potential to assist caregivers in decision-making about parenting issues while incarcerated and assist hands-on upon release.

Having an incarcerated parent is increasingly being seen as a growing epidemic with significant public health consequences. Recognizing this, children with incarcerated parents are a particularly vulnerable group who face adversity across an array of health outcomes with both immediate and long-term physical, behavioral, and learning concerns for children. Though risk for health concerns and developmental delays warrant attention and support in their own right, they by no means make up all that each of these children are. Take, for instance, Jasmyne, who we continue playing with in her mom's bright, blue-carpeted, white-walled apartment. As she brushes the fur on the toy rabbit she just grabbed, her mom tells us all about how despite her preexisting health conditions with being born preterm, recent asthma development, and ongoing speech delays, she displays significant resilience. Every morning, she wakes up early to eat breakfast with her mom before spending most of her days playing with her cousins and grandma. Even with all of her health concerns, she is perceptive and learns quickly, already able to sort her blocks by colors and turn on cartoons by herself, and she is learning more words every day. She is outgoing, readily saying "Hi!" to anyone walking past her on the sidewalk. And she is kind, always willing to share her toys and cereal (which she insists on trying to make herself). Her innumerable strengths undoubtedly shine through despite the developmental and behavioral challenges she has been experiencing. Certainly, her undeniable love for candy and all things sweet is in line with other kids her age, regardless of their parents' incarceration history. The measures suggested here may help Jasmyne's positive characteristics continue to flourish, despite the adversities she has experienced.

# CHAPTER 5

## *"Just Temporary"*

CAREGIVING AND CHILDREN'S
HOME ENVIRONMENTS

AS WE MAKE OUR WAY to the house where Carlos resides,
we walk up a gravel driveway covered in deep snow, being sure to maneu-
ver through the recent tire tracks so as not to let snow fill our shoes. The
two-story farm home where Carlos lives is located in a rural area, in the
middle of snow-covered cornfields, with no other houses visible on the hori-
zon. We step up to the front door, knock loudly, and are soon welcomed by
Martina, a 24-year-old Latina woman, and her four-year-old Latino son Carlos. As we say our greetings and get introduced to Carlos for the first time,
we are left standing in a foyer-type space that feels more like an exterior
than an interior space because it is constructed of plywood and thick plastic
wrap. The space feels nearly as cold as outside. We remove our shoes in this
front entry space and enter the house. We look around briefly to what seems
to be a cramped space storage or "mud room" space before being directed
around the corner to the basement steps, escorted by Martina and followed
by Carlos.

When we enter the basement living space, we sit with Carlos and his
mom on top of the mattress that is on the floor of the bedroom that they
share. The basement seems to be half renovated and half-unfinished—
shaggy carpet remnants line portions of the floor as beams remain exposed
in the ceiling. The full-sized mattress we sit on is where Martina sleeps, its
lilac-colored comforter with mauve flowers complementing the cream shag
carpet well. The bed is made up neatly, with multiple soft blankets covering
the underlying sheets and pillows. Placed orderly around us is nearly everything the small family owns—clothes stored in green plastic totes as substitutes
for dressers, canned food on plastic shelving units, a large box-set TV across
from Martina's mattress, toys neatly piled in the corner, and a stack of
children's books in both Spanish and English. Less than five feet away from
the side of the mattress is a set of metal-framed bunk beds where Carlos
sleeps along with his two-year-old brother Vicente (whom Carlos lovingly

calls "Vinny"). The space feels cramped, but manageable for the three of them. As we get settled in, the sort of reconstruction phase that the basement is undergoing becomes even more evident. Many of the walls are missing insulation, the concrete floors are exposed beyond the sleeping space, and interior doors have been replaced with fabric blankets hanging in their place. The downstairs room is somewhat chilly, relying on a floor heater at the base of Martina's bed and a rolled-up rug placed delicately against the base of an exterior door as the only combatants to the cold Midwestern winter. Seemingly embarrassed by the state of their living situation, Martina tells us early on in our interview with her that this (as she motions around to the state of the room) is "just temporary." In fact, she says that before this, they had been in and out of short-term leases, spending nights on friends' couches, and even had a bout where she and the boys stayed in a family shelter in a neighboring town. After that time, she told us that "enough was enough," and she moved in with her children's father's family to give her some time to get back on her feet.

Seemingly used to battling the frigid indoor temperatures, Martina wears a thick white winter coat with a furry hood zipped up the entire time we are together. Along with that, she has on dark gray sweatpants and black fuzzy slippers, her hair tossed into a messy bun. Carlos, on the other hand, contrasts his dark brown hair and black-rimmed eyeglasses with light-washed denim jeans, a semi-stained short-sleeved white shirt, and well-worn sneakers. Carlos sucks on a lime green popsicle for the first portion of our visit, appearing rather unbothered by (or perhaps accustomed to) the crisp air throughout the house. Since we have been with them in their home, he has been energetic and active, scooting around on the floor and leaping from one activity to another. Even more so, though, he has been kind in how he has actively welcomed us into his space, engaging in conversation with us while peering through his long eyelashes that hit the lens of his glasses when he blinks in between licks of his popsicle.

Carlos is a charming kid whose silliness and creativity shine through in most interactions. For example, as we work with him on a number of vocabulary and language tasks, he takes a quick peek at the set of pictures we are asking him to identify and then covers his eyes and "guesses" correct answers, as if magically responding without sight. He giggles as he says, "I'm going to close my eyes now and guess the answer, but I'm not looking!" Like most kids his age, he has quirks. His mom tells us that he has a fear of birds, and his dad, whom we interviewed at the county jail, told us that Carlos fears the grass snakes that they occasionally find behind their house. Recently, his mom has given Carlos household responsibilities by assigning a set of chores, specifically to keep his corner of the room clean. His parents applaud him by saying he is smart, happy, and remembers things well. However, Carlos has

begun having noticeable behavior shifts as he goes through streaks of having "really good days at school and then suddenly having bad days," and
these are becoming more apparent since his dad has gone to jail. Carlos and
his dad, Rodrigo, a 28-year-old man who emigrated from Mexico during
his own childhood, have been separated for about a month and a half
because of an operating while intoxicated charge that sent Rodrigo to the
county jail.

Initially after being arrested, Rodrigo was concerned about Carlos, and
he felt guilty for not being there to parent him. At first, Carlos did not pay
much attention to his dad's incarceration, but now Carlos says he misses
him and is starting to ask more questions. Soon after these questions arose,
he began misbehaving because of frustration at not being able to see his dad
whenever he wanted. Rodrigo notes that he is the one to enforce the rules
around the house. At the beginning of his incarceration, when they could
only talk over the phone, he did not discipline Carlos because he "didn't
want him to get angry." It was not until after Rodrigo told his son, "Even
though I'm in jail, I still know what you're doing," that Carlos began to
start behaving a bit better again. Since then, Carlos has come to the jail to
visit twice, despite the 45-mile drive. Before the visits, Carlos is happy at
the prospect of seeing his dad, his cheerful attitude continuing throughout
the visits, which makes for quite a positive visit experience. However, when
it is time to go home, Carlos begins acting sad and depressed again. Recognizing this, Rodrigo is still worried about his son but is thankful that he and
his brother are able to stay living with their mom, specifically because
Rodrigo was separated from his own mother and father when migrating
to the United States at a young age, and that was and still is really difficult
for him.

The home where Carlos lives with his mom and little brother actually
belongs to Rodrigo's sister and her husband, and the upper level is also the
residence of Carlos's grandparents. Rodrigo's family has been living together
on this farm since they arrived in the United States nearly two decades
ago, although now they rent out the adjacent cornfields instead of farming
them. Despite the interior that is in the process of being remodeled, the
environment is safe and quite supportive for Carlos to learn and grow, and
he and his brother have ample space to run and play outside. Family members talk with Carlos and Vinny, and they play together and read books.
Since his dad's incarceration, the five adults in the household have stepped
up to support him, and his mom works part time at the motel in town to
contribute to the family income. She qualifies for food assistance and is
happy about the additional support, although in this rural area there are not
as many parenting support services as she would like. When she gets headaches or feels tired, Carlos's grandparents step in to take care of the kids,

talking to them in Spanish and telling them stories. Carlos loves spending time with his grandparents and other family members and he has developed close relationships with them. The positive effects of this support are clear, as Carlos continues to do well socially and is surpassing his expected reading level in school. His teacher consistently remarks how impressed she is by this, applauding Carlos's abilities as a dual Spanish- and English-language learner. He has a wild imagination, commonly making up silly stories to tell his friends at school and family. On top of this, he loves doing crafts, singing, and playing on the computer. Martina tells us that Carlos already has big plans for doing activities with his dad once he's released, including swimming, biking, and fishing—the pair's favorite hobbies before being separated.

## CHILDREN WITH INCARCERATED PARENTS' HOME AND FAMILY ENVIRONMENT

In chapter 3, we focused on the importance of children's family relationships for child well-being, honing-in on children's attachments to their caregivers. Such relationships occur in the context of the home and family environment, the focus of this chapter. This includes potential changes in family structure and income, residential stability or instability, caregiver mental health and co-parenting, family chaos, and academic and social stimulation in homes and neighborhoods. Each of the 86 homes that we were welcomed into was unique—they varied in size, style, and location. The one thing that rang true about every door we walked through and each floor we sat on was that love filled the spaces, and each family was trying their best to support their young ones navigating parental incarceration.

### Changes in Family Structure

Parental incarceration can cause significant daily changes in family structure, as it did for Carlos's family, including who lives in the home, where the family lives, and how the environment and family interactions are organized. The removal of a parent from a family unit, even if the parent did not live with the child prior to incarceration, typically alters norms and expectations about how a family functions. As a response, the at-home caregiver often assumes additional roles and responsibilities. In Carlos's family, his father's incarceration means that the family now lives doubled up with his aunt, uncle, and grandparents, and his mom is taking on extra parenting responsibilities. However, she is not doing it alone. Rodrigo's family members have repeatedly stepped up to provide not only shared housing for his family while he is incarcerated but also day-to-day instrumental and emotional support for Carlos and his mother.

Who cares for minor children after parental incarceration depends on whether it is a mother or father who becomes incarcerated. When fathers are incarcerated, mothers assume the caregiver role for 80–90 percent of children (Glaze & Maruschak, 2008; Maruchack et al., 2021). In most cases, grandparents or other nonparental relatives assume the primary caregiver role during maternal incarceration, and foster care is also more common than during paternal incarceration (Glaze & Maruschak, 2008; Maruschak et al., 2021). Although most of the families in our study consisted of incarcerated fathers, with mothers acting as the children's caregivers during paternal incarceration, we also had incarcerated mothers and their families in our study. We spoke with a range of other family members (e.g., fathers, grandparents, and aunts) who were caring for children during maternal incarceration—a population trend that has steadily increased and significantly affects changes in family structure and processes for children and families. Across families experiencing an incarcerated family member, many women—including mothers, sisters, or aunts—step up to provide significant support both during and after incarceration, if not as primary caregivers to children, often as secondary caregivers, or at a minimum providing some sort of economic, instrumental, or relational support (Western, 2018).

Throughout the last several decades, the rising number of women experiencing incarceration has been of great concern to researchers, practitioners, and advocates. Recent reports indicate that local jail population rates for women have increased significantly over the last several years. As reported by Zeng (2020), the Bureau of Justice Statistics found that the U.S. jail population of women rose 10 percent between the years 2005 and 2018. At the same time, incarceration rates for men in local jails decreased by 14 percent. The rates are not limited to jails. Within the last four decades (between the years 1980 and 2019), the incarceration rate for women has increased by more than 700 percent (Lane, 2020). Further, most incarcerated women are mothers of minor children. It is estimated that more than 60 percent of women confined in state prison facilities are mothers of minor children (Glaze & Maruschak, 2008) and 80 percent of jailed women are mothers to minor children (Swavola et al., 2016). Taken together, the drastic increase in incarcerated women has contributed to an increase in mothers behind bars, which translates to a growing number of children affected by maternal incarceration.

When their mothers were in jail, some of the children in our study stayed with their grandparents, similar to other children across the United States. These informal placements are often preferred by families because then the child does not have to go into foster care (Hanlon et al., 2007). Grandparents rarely seek legal custody of their grandchildren, even when mothers have longer sentences, as this can symbolize a parent's inability to care for the child or represent permanent changes in family structure (e.g., Ruiz & Kopak, 2014). Instead, grandparents and other kin often care for children with incarcerated parents unofficially or informally (i.e., without legal guardianship) (Hanlon et al., 2007), which can be positive but also have negative implications for a family's economic well-being. Many non-parental family caregivers view their caregiving role as temporary because they hope that children and parents can reunite quickly following the incarceration period. However, informal caregiving may mean that grandparents do not qualify for financial support or other supportive services, such as food assistance, publicly funded health insurance for the child, or family respite care that would otherwise be offered in more formal out-of-home care placements. Additionally, without the legal authority to make decisions for their grandchildren, grandparents may experience financial strain, have problems enrolling children in school, or even navigating the health-care system.

*Poverty and Material Hardship after Incarceration*

Economic hardship is not foreign to many families impacted by parental incarceration. In fact, children experiencing poverty are three times more likely to experience the incarceration of a resident parent (Murphey & Cooper, 2015). Many families with jailed parents struggle with material hardship and food insecurity as a result of the incarceration. The incarcerated parent usually can no longer work and help provide for the family financially through provision of income or payment of child support. Indeed, both of these streams of income are typically immediately halted when parents go to jail. At the same time, at-home caregivers take on more childcare and financial responsibilities, although they may not be able to work as many hours at their places of employment because of increased childcare responsibilities. These factors often result in more dependence on public assistance, but with less access to other services, following parental incarceration (Geller & Curtis, 2011). Indeed, the sudden shock of parental incarceration can push families already living within the realm of poverty or financial insecurity to the point of homelessness and hunger while disqualifying them from the exact federal programs supposedly designed to pull people in those positions out of poverty. Like Carlos's family, many caregivers of children with incarcerated parents may have to live doubled up or even in a shelter for a time (Muentner et al., 2019).

Beyond the loss of income, a number of additional financial burdens are imposed on the family because of a parent's incarceration, including the costs of maintaining contact with the incarcerated parent through visits, phone calls, or letters (see chapter 6), paying for legal expenses, and assisting the incarcerated individual with material needs during incarceration (Christian et al., 2006). Even after the parent's release, affected families often struggle with poverty or underemployment because of restrictions or stigma from the government or employers (e.g., being unable to get a driver's license in some states or being prohibited from working in some professions), making it difficult for formerly incarcerated individuals to obtain and keep a job (Brown & Bloom, 2009; Celinska & Seigel, 2010). This often results in a vicious cycle, wherein those with criminal convictions are left with little credit to meet requirements to apply for housing; even if they are approved for housing, they may struggle to pull together enough funds for security deposits and the first month's rent, let alone purchasing necessary items to fill the apartment or home. Without stable and safe housing, adhering to regular work schedules or conditions of parole or probation can be challenging, not to mention the significant challenges caused by limited financial resources in accessing transportation services to even make it to work. For those simultaneously navigating the child welfare system following incarceration, securing stable housing can be a prerequisite to regaining access to their children. All in all, these examples illustrate how much incarceration can exacerbate cycles of poverty, with direct implications for children's well-being and overall family functioning.

In our study, we used several methods to learn more about the families, including issues related to poverty and housing but also basic demographics, caregivers' stress levels and mental health, home environments, and co-parenting during parental incarceration. We found that the caregivers in our study ranged in age from 18 to 62 years, with an average age of 31 years. In addition to the focal child in our study, caregivers reported having between 0 and 14 dependents in their care, with an average of 2–3 additional dependents. Most caregivers reported being single—most had never married, but some had been separated, divorced, or widowed. Only 12 caregivers were currently married, although about half reported being in a romantic relationship with someone (many of whom were still partnered with the jailed parent in some fashion, just like Martina).

In terms of employment, of the 86 caregivers in our study, 50 reported having either full- or part-time jobs. In fact, the employed caregivers worked anywhere from 8 to 75 hours per week, averaging out at about full-time hours (nearly 40 per week). While these caregivers were at work, some children were either in school or attended day care centers, although 36 children were cared for by some sort of secondary caregiver or regular care placement offered by family, friends, neighbors, or in-home babysitters—most often grandparents. This mirrors Martina's arrangements, with Rodrigo's parents and other relatives often providing care for Carlos and Vinny when Martina puts in her hours at the motel. Family incomes in our study ranged widely, from $0 to $140,000 per year (not counting public assistance), but averaged only $15,300 per year, with many falling even below that. In fact, 74 of the 86 families reported receiving some kind of public assistance, primarily in the form of food assistance, housing assistance, or income supplements like kinship care funds. Caregivers reported receiving between 0 and 204 months of assistance, with an average of 48 months of public assistance. For most families, use of public assistance predated the parent's incarceration, although the actual use of such assistance increased, on average, because of the parent's incarceration. Given family incomes relative to family size, 79 percent of the families were living below the federal poverty line, rates that were similar across race.

### Family Chaos

When a family is challenged by poverty, the household is more likely to lack routines, have more people coming in and out of the residence, move more often, and have louder noise levels, interruptions, and conflict (Evans et al., 2010). Individually, these experiences are a normal part of life and can occur temporarily in families with young children. But taken together— and when they occur frequently—such factors can be referred to as "family chaos." Take, for instance, Carlos's family. They are part of the 79 percent who fell under the federal poverty line in our study, which they feel all too intimately given that Martina's part-time employment is not nearly enough to support her and her two boys. When Rodrigo went away, they had little to no choice but to move into his family's home, after having moved around quite a bit before the incarceration, as well. Without anywhere else to turn, Martina moved in, with Carlos and Vinny in tow. However, in the already cramped space, the only room for them was in the unfinished basement, and the adjustment has been difficult. Rodrigo's brother-in-law works the night shift at a local factory so is up opposite hours as the boys and frequently wakes them up with his walking around upstairs. Additionally, Martina says she has little to no privacy without doors and says she can overhear conversations going on in the other rooms. She uses the word "chaotic" to describe their day-to-day environment, but she is also adamant that she is incredibly appreciative that Rodrigo's family welcomed them in and offers as much support as they do.

When we met with Martina and the other caregivers in the study, we asked them to complete a form that reflected the number of changes that the child experienced in caregivers, in addition to the routines or rituals that they engaged in (e.g., "child goes to bed at a regular time"), and environmental confusion or noise (e.g., "You can't hear yourself think in our home"). Table 5.1 shows responses from 63 of the caregivers, as we did not have the form ready for the first set of caregivers. Caregivers reported that some experiences were common, like rushing or having commotion in the household. However, many of the experiences reported were positive and probably helped foster resilience processes in the children. Some common

TABLE 5.1

*Percentage of children whose caregivers reported different elements relating to household chaos*

| Item | Percentage |
|---|---|
| There is very little commotion in our home. | 55.7 |
| We can usually find things when we need them. | 88.5 |
| We almost always seem to be rushed. | 29.5 |
| We are usually able to "stay on top of things." | 83.6 |
| No matter how hard we try, we always seem to be running late. | 31.1 |
| At home we can talk to each other without being interrupted. | 72.1 |
| There is often a fuss going on at our home. | 24.6 |
| No matter what our family plans, it usually doesn't seem to work out. | 16.4 |
| You can't hear yourself think in our home. | 19.7 |
| I often get drawn into other people's arguments at home. | 16.4 |
| Our home is a good place to relax. | 83.6 |
| The telephone takes up a lot of our time at home. | 13.1 |
| The atmosphere in our home is calm. | 80.3 |
| First thing in the day, we have a regular routine at home. | 95.1 |
| We eat together as a family once a day. | 90.2 |
| We have an evening bed time routine with [focal child]. | 86.9 |
| [Focal child] has a regular after school routine. | 75.4 |
| [Focal child] goes to bed at a regular time. | 78.3 |
| We set aside time for talking with our children each day. | 93.4 |
| [Focal child] does his/her homework at the same time every day. | 42.3 |
| Our children do regular household chores. | 62.3 |

positive experiences included children engaging in regular morning routines, talking with others in the home, eating together, and doing regular household chores.

Using these items, Lindsay Weymouth created a family chaos index as part of her doctoral dissertation using data from this study (Weymouth, 2016). The negatively worded items were summed whereas the positively worded items were first "reverse coded" (i.e., scored in the opposite manner) and then summed, so that higher scores on the index meant fewer routines, less calm, more moves, more interruptions, and more changes in caregivers. Findings indicated that young children experiencing higher levels of family chaos showed more problematic behaviors at home, including more externalizing behaviors (acting out, aggression, impulsivity), internalizing behaviors (withdrawal, depression, worry), and symptoms of stress. However, children in more chaotic households were not more likely to have higher stress-hormone levels show up in measurements of their hair.

In addition, as we saw in chapter 3, more family chaos was associated with representations of less secure attachment relationships in children aged three years and up. These data show how many children begin to act out in ways that mirror their environment. When the space around them is hectic and unpredictable, then so too are children's behaviors (and even the ways they make sense of relationships with their families). Even if a more chaotic home environment does not negatively influence their physiological stress markers, it certainly complicates the way they cope behaviorally while parents are incarcerated. The flip side of the coin is that many of the children's households had low chaos scores—and low chaos related to fewer behavior problems and more secure attachments in the children.

While we were in the children's homes, we also observed positive aspects of each household using the Home Observation for Measurement of the Environment (HOME) scale (see appendix B). The items observed included the presence of items and interactions such as cognitively stimulating toys, books, and games, positive language interactions between children and adults, organization of the environment, adequate space, use of nonpunitive discipline, having a pet, and taking trips outside of the home. We found that children in homes with more academic and social stimulation had higher cognitive test scores, even controlling for family income. In addition, children in homes with more academic and social stimulation were more likely to show secure attachment to their caregivers. Examining the positive aspects of children's home environments is one way to understand how some children thrive despite the experience of parental incarceration, whereas other children struggle. These findings are important given the discussion in chapter 4 around gaps in children's learning and cognitive development. Given that so many children in our sample were experiencing developmental delays, these findings point to positive home environments as being consequential in mitigating developmental risk and setting children up for future success.

### Residential Transitions and Instability

Carlos, his brother Vinny, and his mother Martina rely heavily on Rodrigo's family for shelter, food, money, transportation, and childcare while Rodrigo is incarcerated. These factors contribute to Carlos's well-being. Without the support offered by Rodrigo's family, Martina and the kids may have had to continue couch surfing or wind up more regularly in a shelter; instead, they are doubling up with a loving extended family. It is easy to see how important social and familial ties can be during parental incarceration. Across many of the families we met, family relationships and support systems could be incredibly beneficial for families during the time of parental incarceration. On a national level, when compared to their peers, children with incarcerated parents are more likely to experience residential instability or frequent moves (Geller et al., 2009). Some families may experience eviction or other forms of housing instability as a result of parental incarceration, while others may have experienced housing instability even prior to the incarceration. As noted by Tasca and colleagues (2011), experiencing housing instability prior to parental incarceration may further expose families to unsafe neighborhoods or offer a lack of employment options, both of which can contribute to additional involvement with the criminal legal system.

To better understand how often children, their caregivers, and their incarcerated parents experienced transitions, we examined their living situations within the year leading up to the current incarceration. When we assessed frequency of changes in children's residential environments, we found that a majority of children had moved residences three or more times within their lifetime. This is noteworthy given that children in the study were all six years old or younger. In fact, nearly 30 percent of the young children in our study had moved residences five or more times in their lifetime, which is significantly higher than the national average (Murphey et al., 2012). In an analysis of data from this study, coauthor Luke Muentner and colleagues (2019) also found that children often experienced multiple housing transitions along with their parents. Importantly, more housing transitions for children were also associated with elevated behavior problems. In other words, not only were adverse behavioral responses common when home environments were more chaotic, they were also elevated by each and every move.

We asked each incarcerated parent, including Rodrigo, to think about where they had been staying on a weekly basis in the year leading up to their incarceration. Together, we mapped out a depiction of their recent residential history on a calendar. We then asked the incarcerated parent to describe their dwelling—such as whether they lived in an apartment, house, correctional facility, treatment center, or shelter, with whom they were living, and if they were contributing to the mortgage, rent, or cost of the shelter. Lastly, we asked them to tell us about any transitions they made between one living establishment and another throughout the past 12 months, and why the transition from one living situation to another was initiated, such as a move for a job, eviction, or completion of a program. When we sat down with Rodrigo, he corroborated the residential mobility that Martina had recounted. On the housing calendar that we created together, he reported living in two different apartments with his small family during the year. Additionally, he recounted the month they spent couch surfing with friends and family on top of the week he spent separated from his family because he had to stay in the men's homeless facility (because it did not allow for women or children), as Martina took the small boys with her to the family shelter.

From our interviews, we found that Rodrigo and his family were not alone. Indeed, most incarcerated parents—more than 70 percent—reported one or more housing transitions in the year prior to their recent confinement in jail. In fact, just under half of the incarcerated parents told us they experienced at least two residential moves within the year leading up to their incarceration. Overall, the incarcerated parents reported moving anywhere from zero to nine times in the last 12 months prior to their confinement (Muentner et al., 2019). Nearly all of those in our study indicated they had experienced at least one previous spell of incarceration in their lives, and one-third had been incarcerated at least one other time within the last year (Muentner et al., 2019), illustrating how chronic such churning in and out of jail can be. Although incarceration length varied, nearly a quarter of jailed parents indicated they had been incarcerated for six months or more within the last year.

### Homelessness

Closely tied to residential instability are spells where children and families have no place to go, similar to some of the experiences that Carlos's family had had the previous year. Descriptively, it was more common for jailed parents to experience homelessness than it was for their children (Muentner et al., 2019); in other words when parents faced potential homelessness, most of it did not include their children. In our study, only seven children experienced homelessness since their parents had been incarcerated, although they were homeless in different ways and for variable lengths of time. Two children experienced living with their family temporarily in a shelter or their car; one child lived in a motel; two couch surfed; and six families lived doubled up with another family at some point. This does not necessarily account for the number of children who had ever experienced homelessness (like the nights Carlos spent with his family sleeping on a friend's floor or the time spent at a women's shelter with his mom before his dad's current incarceration).

Qualitative analysis of data from these young children and their families was conducted by Kerrie Fanning, who was a doctoral student and member of our research team at the time, for her master's thesis. She found that the children in the families who experienced couch surfing and motel living appeared to be struggling the most developmentally and behaviorally, as these experiences were associated with increased uncertainty, lack of routines, and financial strain for the families, even more so than other types of homelessness (Fanning, 2018). Research with homeless unaccompanied youth has found that couch surfing frequently creates daily changes in a person's residence (Hail-Jares et al., 2021); it can also involve searching for someone—a family member, friend, or acquaintance—with whom they can stay for the night, which can be particularly stressful. In addition, hotel or motel living can be extremely costly and provides only a small temporary space (K. A. Thomas & So, 2016). Even though living doubled up, sleeping in a car, and staying in a shelter (especially in the case of long-term shelters) may provide families with some certainty in their residence, these are also highly stressful living arrangements for children.

For example, Carlos, his mom Martina, and his brother Vinny are living doubled up with his paternal aunt, uncle and grandparents while his dad is in jail, and the house is in the process of being renovated to accommodate them. Remember that many of the walls are missing insulation, floors are exposed, and fabric blankets are hanging in place of interior doors. Carlos shares a crowded bedroom with his mom and younger brother, sleeping on the lower half of a bunk bed next to a mattress on the floor, where his mom sleeps. Although crowded and unfinished, the area is safe and Carlos seems comforted by the constant presence of his mom as she sleeps nearby. Martina expresses a sense of sincere relief for being in this space, too. Just knowing that they have a roof over their head (even if it is exposed to pipes and ongoing drywall repairs), with family living upstairs, is enough to make them rest easier at night.

### Caregiving Stress and Mental Health

Shifts resulting from parental incarceration can increase stress levels for adults and children in the family (Turney, 2014b). Regardless of the continuity or abruptness in this caregiving role, caregivers take on full responsibility for maintaining day-to-day family functioning and many also assume the role of facilitating communication between children and their incarcerated parents. This multifaceted role can be taxing and even overwhelming for many caregivers. For example, caregiving women are at additional risk for experiencing distress, loneliness, depression, anxiety, and increased parenting-related stress, which may be linked to less optimal parenting (e.g., Turney, 2014a).

We asked children's caregivers to report about their depressive symptoms using the Center for Epidemiological Studies Depression (CESD) measure, which includes items that refer to fatigue, sadness, hopelessness, and general psychological distress. More information on this measure can be found in appendix B. On the CESD, 21 percent of caregivers in our study scored in the clinical range, with the mean score at the clinical cutoff, suggesting significantly elevated depressive symptoms.

We also asked caregivers to complete a longer, more comprehensive form about their mental health called the Adult Self-Report (ASR; see appendix B), which is scored based on the adult's age and gender. The most common set of mental health concerns reported were somatic problems, with 22 percent of caregivers scoring in the subclinical or clinical range—three times the average of the standardization sample. Somatic concerns involve symptoms that often appear in the body, such as headaches, bodily aches and pains, and fatigue. Items on the ASR that are seen as potentially needing clinical attention (called "critical items") were endorsed at the subclinical or clinical level by 21 percent of caregivers. In addition, 15 percent of caregivers reported attention-deficit/hyperactivity disorder (ADHD) symptoms and 13 percent reported anxiety problems. ADHD includes symptoms of restlessness, impulsivity, and difficulty paying attention, while anxiety includes symptoms such as worrying and overthinking. Only 6 percent of caregivers reported problems related to substance use, which is about the same as the standardization sample. What is evident then is that caregivers' mental health is significantly depleted, resulting in chronic somatic-, attention-, and anxiety-related symptoms. We did not have access to the kind of longitudinal data that would help us understand whether or not these symptoms predated or were exacerbated by their co-parent's incarceration, as some caregivers thought that was the case. Pointedly, Martina and many caregivers opened up to us about how their mental health had worsened significantly while their partners had been incarcerated, including how they hoped the co-parent's eventual release would offer them some much needed relief.

To further examine these issues, we considered how indicators of mental health concerns in caregivers may be connected to parenting stress. When we looked at the association between mental health and parenting stress scales, we found high correlations across the board. That is, for caregivers in our study, higher parenting stress was associated with significant elevations on all of the mental health measures. Stated differently, when caregivers were more stressed by taking care of children, they also reported more mental health symptoms. This further emphasizes the need to support caregivers of children whose parents are incarcerated. Not only are many struggling financially, a significant proportion report seriously concerning mental health symptoms. Because parenting stress and caregiver mental health are strongly intertwined, efforts to reduce parenting stress—including stressors related to housing, finances, and childcare could help caregivers' psychological well-being and have spillover effects that improve child-level outcomes.

### Co-Parenting

While Rodrigo is incarcerated, Carlos and Vinny have experienced a change in their parents' disciplinary roles and expectations, similar to many

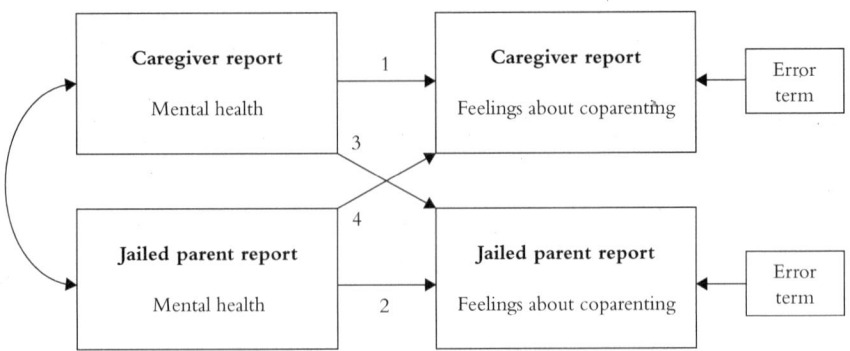

Figure 5.1. Actor and partner effects for jailed parents and at-home caregivers.

families affected by parental incarceration. Rodrigo struggles to maintain a parenting role (albeit from a distance) with Carlos during the incarceration, although he wants to continue to parent his children. Establishing new ways of parenting, such as communicating and engaging in discipline remotely, is one area of co-parenting that can be challenging during a parent's incarceration. In speaking with the parents in our study, we heard various approaches to co-parenting.

A positive co-parenting alliance occurs when adults who are parenting a child coordinate their care in a way that supports the child (McHale et al., 2004). Incarcerated co-parenting is when a parent or caregiver is engaged in parenting discussions, decisions, or remote interactions with a parent who is in jail or prison (Tadros et al., 2021). In our study, we asked both the caregivers and jailed parents to complete the Parenting Alliance Measure—which assesses co-parenting quality—along with the ASR, and the Inventory of Family Feelings (see appendix B) to assess adult mental health symptoms and feelings about children in their care, respectively. Given that co-parenting is a process that occurs between two people who influence each other, members of the co-parenting dyad (i.e., caregivers and jailed parents) are not independent from one another, and so we used methodologies that allowed us to account for the interdependence within the dyads (figure 5.1). Eman Tadros, a professor at Governor's State University in Chicago, collaborated with us on these analyses, as she is an expert in the area of incarcerated co-parenting.

In our analyses, we found a "partner effect" that went from caregivers' externalizing symptoms to incarcerated parents' co-parenting alliance perceptions, but not the other way around. That is, higher internalizing and externalizing mental health symptoms as reported by caregivers related to jailed parents' view of the co-parenting alliance as less optimal. This finding means that when caregivers reported more mental health symptoms, jailed parents reported that the co-parenting alliance was weaker or in some way problematic.

In addition, a significant "actor effect" also emerged, but only for incarcerated parents, regarding how they felt about their children. This means that better co-parenting, as reported by the jailed parent, related to more positive feelings about children. For Rodrigo, this means that Martina's positive co-parenting alliance with him during his jail stay helps him feel closer to Carlos and Vinny. Caregivers' perceptions of their relationships with children were less dependent on the co-parenting alliance. This makes sense because caregivers have daily access to children, whereas incarcerated parents usually depend on their co-parents (i.e., children's caregivers) to connect with their young children (see chapter 6). Overall, these findings suggest that caregivers have more power in the co-parenting alliance, whereas incarcerated parents are the more vulnerable member of the co-parenting dyad. In short, caregiver mental health affects how incarcerated parents experience co-parenting; and how incarcerated parents experience co-parenting, in turn, affects how they feel about their children.

## How Can We Help?

When a parent is incarcerated, children's well-being is often a barometer for how well the family is doing, including how stable their living situation is, how the household is organized, and family stressors related to poverty, mental health, and parenting. Improving caregiver well-being and family functioning is likely to have positive effects on children too.

### Poverty Prevention and Residential Stability

While some families, such as Carlos's, garner enough support from extended family or friends to meet the changes and challenges presented by parental incarceration, others do not have access to such resources. Most families affected by parental incarceration live in poverty, as was true in our study. Some families even become homeless for a time, while others struggle with provision of basic items such as food and clothing. Meeting basic needs of families is essential before, during, and following incarceration. Connecting families to poverty prevention programs and facilitating their access to resources that combat food and housing insecurity are important goals that can have positive effects on children's development (Noyes et al., 2018).

Programs that focus on parents inside corrections facilities should include information—and even support through family specialists who connect with co-parents and other caregiving family members—so that families on the outside are able to access housing and food assistance and other economic and supportive resources during the parent's incarceration. Community programs should be sensitive to the issues that accompany a parent's incarceration, including problems with housing instability and homelessness, and make efforts to reach out to families involved in the criminal legal system in a timely manner. Similarly, when a child comes to the attention of a state child welfare system, it is important to assess whether or not the child has an incarcerated parent and ensure referrals to necessary supports (de Haan et al., 2019).

Because grandparents and other relatives often provide primary care for children with incarcerated mothers, we also recommend that parents be informed about options for assigning temporary guardianship that may allow caregivers to enroll children in economic assistance, health, and academic programs. It is important to eliminate barriers so that, at the time of a parent's incarceration, such guardians can become eligible for temporary food and housing assistance and insurance programs, if needed, to ensure that children's basic needs are being met. Sustained ties to community programs could help provide stability to many families, as sometimes jail stays are brief, and many challenges are also present prior to and following the incarceration. Such assistance may be particularly important in rural communities, where children are more likely to experience parental incarceration in the United States (Murphey & Cooper, 2015).

### Support Children's Stimulating Home Environments

In addition to experiencing poverty, some families experience strain in the day-to-day organization of the household and some caregivers feel overwhelmed. Young children are often sensitive to these issues, and stress and disorganization in the home can be reflected in children's behavior problems, health issues, and cognitive or language development. On the positive side, caregivers who create at least moderately organized, academically and socially stimulating households with routines often have children who respond positively, even if they have experienced life stressors or previous changes in their lives. In Martina and Rodrigo's family, Carlos and Vinny have the benefit of bilingualism as well as having multiple adults speaking directly to them, playing with them, and reading to them. The results from our study are similar to the findings of developmental researchers across disciplines and methodologies who have identified processes consistently associated with positive outcomes for children and families experiencing risk factors. In her book on resilience, Ann Masten has summarized the research to create a "short list" of factors that can promote resilience processes in children (Masten, 2018). The short list consists of individual, family, relational, and contextual variables such as self-regulation, secure child-caregiver attachment, supportive family relationships, positive parenting, and community social support. Chapter 8 will discuss resilience in more detail.

In families affected by parental incarceration, household chaos—and efforts to ameliorate it—may be one underexplored route regarding how poverty affects children's well-being. Poverty among children with incarcerated parents is ubiquitous. However, their environments differ enormously depending on supports and contexts within the household that can stimulate children's development. The physical world in which children live is an important consideration, especially when viewed along with their social world consisting of attachment relationships, extended family connections, neighbors, friends, and teachers—the latter of which become more important as children grow older. Findings from this study suggest that young children with incarcerated parents may be less likely to struggle with their development and behavior when both the proximal physical environment of the home and the larger social contexts are more organized, safe, and supportive.

### Support Caregivers' Mental Health and Relationships

Findings from our study demonstrate that many caregivers of children with incarcerated parents, like Martina, are stressed and may need additional supports. As we noted in chapter 3, parenting programs can be helpful, but they cannot focus solely on the incarcerated parent. Family mental health support services could be implemented as part of family programs that are offered during parental incarceration in coordination with local jails and county or state departments that focus on child welfare or public health. It is important that services for incarcerated parents extend into the community (including following release), as that is where children are, and that is where the vast majority of incarcerated parents will return. Support groups for grandparents (or other extended family members) raising grandchildren, respite care, and drop-in childcare are all options that caregivers mentioned as particularly important community resources.

Prior research has found that strengthening the parenting alliance between co-parents is associated with positive interactions among family members (e.g., Loper et al., 2014). Supportive co-parenting may also help decrease feelings of parenting stress (Durtschi et al., 2017). In studies of families experiencing divorce, positive co-parenting relationships are associated with better emotional and behavioral health in children (Ferraro et al., 2016). Previous studies have found that incarcerated parent-caregiver co-parenting may influence a parent's relationships with their children through parent-child contact during and after incarceration—contact which is often regulated by caregivers when children are young (Arditti, 2012; Tasca, 2016). Thus, parenting programs that are offered in jails and other correctional settings may also want to garner support from children's caregivers, especially when parent-child contact is part of the program. At minimum, recognition of the importance of co-parenting during parental incarceration may help support young children.

Caregivers of young children with a jailed parent appear to struggle with parenting stress as well as mental health issues. Because many report somatic symptoms and depressive symptoms, caregivers may benefit from approaches that address those issues, such as integrated health and behavioral health interventions. Community mental health services that reach both parents and children are particularly important and can be one route to increasing resilience in families affected by parental incarceration.

# CHAPTER 6

## *"It Is So Good to Hug You!"*

VISITING AND OTHER FORMS OF
PARENT-CHILD CONTACT

ON A COOL, fall Saturday morning, we enter the waiting room of the visiting area of a county jail after passing through a security screening. Across the room on a bench, we see Meekah sitting in between her mom, Jade, and her older brother, Tristan. Meekah is an adorable five-year-old Black girl with a serious look on her face. Her hair is pulled back tightly by a silver, glittery bow into a bun that sits on the top of her head, complementing the red cable-knit sweater and black leggings she is wearing, as well as the silver necklace with a heart charm that is dangling over her sweater. Sitting on the bench directly across from the kids is their mom's friend Carla, who drove Meekah, Tristan, and Jade to the jail this morning because they did not have other transportation.

As Meekah sits patiently, waiting for the time to come when she can go into the visiting space to see her dad, she looks quite somber, having a furrowed brow and pursed mouth. However, her emotions quickly turn to smiling and laughing when Tristan jumps off the bench and runs over to playfully tug on the heart at the end of Meekah's necklace. After settling down, we slowly approach Meekah and ask her if she would like to draw us a picture of her family, giving her paper and a standard set of markers. She does some warm-up doodling and then quickly gets to drawing each one of the people she considers to be in her close-knit family (figure 6.1). Switching between the pink and purple markers, she soon finishes the drawing of herself before grabbing the blue marker to draw her brother Tristan, the two connected by holding hands. Extending off of Tristan's other hand, she draws a figure she tells us is "Mommy"—a tall, colorful, and smiling character with hair that mimics the depictions of Meekah and Tristan. After finishing her mom's purple facial features, Meekah grabs the red marker and begins on a fourth figure. Situated a bit at a distance and not connected to the other three figures by holding hands, she draws a smiling character. We ask her who that is, and she shyly says, "Da-a-a-ddy," smiling broadly,

Figure 6.1. Meekah's family drawing during the jail visit. Top: Daddy (Cedric); bottom (left to right): Mommy (Jade), Brother (Tristan), and "Me" (Meekah).

before covering up the red marker and sliding the sheet of paper back to us. Looking at it, the drawing may be indicative of how close Meekah feels to her family, the figures' smiling faces illustrative of how happy she is to be able to see her dad that day.

After the drawing task, the five- and six-year-old siblings go back to playing quietly with the heart necklace for a few seconds before their mom checks her phone and notices that it is time for them to head to the visiting space. Carla waits where she is, as just the family is allowed into the visiting space. Jade puts their belongings in a locker and, along with her children, heads toward the security line where Meekah experiences a neutral interaction with staff and stays in close proximity to her mom as she goes through the security checkpoint. This time, Meekah's mom shows her identification and they get through without any extra safety procedures being performed. In the past, Meekah has seen her mom patted down, told to remove her shoes or outerwear, and had her purse searched with a metal detector wand.

The family is escorted to the visiting room where they will be having an in-person contact visit with Meekah's dad, Cedric, this morning—a contrast to their usual visits that occur behind a clear plastic partition. While she's waiting for her dad, Meekah's eyes ferociously scan the room, stopping on other groups of people visiting at that time. Now, she seems a bit hesitant, regaining the serious look on her face and hiding behind her mom, clinging to her, and playing with her hair. The noise level in the room is modest—you can hear murmuring voices but still clearly understand the person next to you speaking in a normal voice. The space is clean, with surfaces looking as though they have been recently wiped down. The visiting room has a number of materials for children like Meekah and her brother to play with, including some books, coloring supplies, and a few toys. Meekah eyes the dolls while Tristan grabs a book.

Meekah's dad Cedric, in his worn teal jail uniform, appears—escorted into the room by the jail security personnel—and the kids soon spot him. He is tall with a slender, yet strong, build and has buzzed hair, just like Tristan. Cedric walks in with a type of charm and energy that feels contagious. Meekah sees him coming near and immediately runs toward him. She jumps in his arms and hugs him, seeming very excited to see her dad. Jade stays seated at the table with Tristan as Cedric carries Meekah the rest of the way back to the table to meet the others. Meekah's dad sits her down in a chair back at the table, but Meekah pleads to get picked back up again; her dad responds with a big smile, lifting Meekah high into the air, bringing her down and hugging her tightly. As he squeezes her, he says, "It is so good to hug you!" Meekah smiles and laughs loudly, filling the room with love and excitement. The two sit down on the one remaining vacant chair and Cedric eagerly greets the others at the table. The visit officially begins, and Meekah's previously somber look has transformed into happiness. She switches her clinginess from her mom now to her dad, whom she has not seen for a few weeks. The adults begin talking, and Tristan is immersed in a picture book, but Meekah stays close to her dad—sitting, standing, and jumping around his space, often touching him.

After a few minutes, Meekah goes to the other side of her dad to look at the book in which Tristan is seemingly engrossed. Cedric reaches for her hand to hold in the meantime, bending down to face level with his children to tell them the exciting news that he is getting released on community supervision next week and that the two of them can come stay with him again in just a few short days. Meekah first appears slightly confused, not sure what that information means for her, but then looks up from the book with a big smile on her face.

For the next block of time, the adults continue talking—sharing updates on friends in the neighborhood, funny stories illustrating some of the things the kids have done in the past few weeks, and checking in on how Cedric has been doing at the jail. During this time, Meekah seems to zone out a bit, looking at the pictures in a new book while seated beside her family but separated from the conversations at hand. After seeming a bit more distant than at the beginning of the visit, her dad grabs her hand again and asks, "What's going on, Meekah, why are you so quiet? Are you doing okay?" Meekah looks up with a big toothy smile and exclaims, "Yeah, Daddy!" Her dad mirrors her smile and reaches for her belly to give her a big tickle. Meekah roars in laughter, dropping her book on the floor beside her chair. The two giggle back and forth like this for a few moments before they settle back in, Meekah to her book and Cedric to the adult conversation happening within the group.

The room gets loud temporarily, and Meekah puts her fingers in her ears to soften the voices. To get some distance from the commotion around her, she walks toward the other side of the room and reads a sign issued by the sheriff's department, exclaiming "Look, Dad, I can read!" as one final shot to gain back her dad's attention. Cedric looks over and nods, but continues listening to Jade's story, this time about one of her friends who is going through a rough situation with her boyfriend. Appearing saddened, Meekah moves back over to the table and starts leaning on her mother, tapping her with a piece of paper she has grabbed off the table. She whines to her, "Is it almost time to leave yet?"—this remark comes about 40 minutes into their 45-minute visit. Nobody answers her, and she resumes playing alone with her necklace for the rest of the visit, just as she had been doing in the waiting room.

Once Meekah senses that the visit is coming to an end, because people begin standing up and hugging good-bye, she perks up again. She goes and stands behind her mom's chair, pulling at her hair and making silly faces behind her shoulders and ears to her dad across the table. Her dad makes silly faces back, which makes Meekah buckle over in laughter. The adults begin to stand up, hugging each other good-bye. Meekah is the last to bid farewell, taking two slow steps closer to her dad who lifts her high into the air again, brings her back down, and embraces her in a tight hug.

They wave and begin walking away when Meekah starts looking concerned, exclaiming "Mom, where are Dad's clothes!?" Jade had brought a new pair of jeans along, on the slight chance she would be able to give them to him to wear when he is released—but they had to leave them in a locker. Her mom shushes Meekah to be quiet, holding her hand and escorting her out of the room. After going back through security, they collect their belongings, meet back up with Carla, and leave the facility. Once outside, Meekah skips down the sidewalk with her arms wide open and spinning around, a contrast to her closed-off demeanor at the start of the visit and indicative of how liberating the opportunity to hug and laugh with her dad this morning was for her.

## Parent-Child Contact during Parental Incarceration

Although most prolonged separations between children and parents, including parental military deployment, divorce, or deportation, share some common elements of loss and anxiety, separation because of parental incarceration is unique because it is enforced by the carceral system and carries a high level of stigma for the child and family (Glick et al., 2022). After a parent is arrested, which can occur abruptly without warning, some await conviction in jail while others are released on bail or bond; if they are convicted, many also may have to wait in jail for a sentencing determination. Because a variable amount of time may pass before sentencing occurs, many incarcerated parents may not know how long they will be incarcerated until they have served several weeks or months in jail—and thus it can be a time of uncertainty and confusion. Although jail stays tend to be much shorter than prison stays, the average stay in jails across the United States is 26 days, although for larger jails the average stay is 36 days (Zeng & Minton, 2021). From a young child's perspective, even a 26-day stay can feel long and have a disruptive effect on day-to-day routines, especially when the incarcerated parent lived with or cared for the child (Eddy & Poehlmann-Tynan, 2019). From an incarcerated parent's perspective, separation from children is often described as the most difficult part of confinement (see, e.g., Poehlmann, 2005b). One way that families mitigate the negative effects of enforced separation for parents and children during parental incarceration is to stay in contact during the incarceration period (Poehlmann-Tynan & Pritzl, 2019).

Most incarcerated parents have some form of contact with their children while confined. A report from the Bureau of Justice Statistics found that more than three-quarters of parents in prison had some type of contact with their minor children at some point during their incarceration (Glaze & Maruschak, 2010). Types of contact include phone calls, in-person or video visits, and letters, with some facilities starting to offer email or instant messaging as options. The most common method of communication for parents in state prison is via telephone, followed by letter writing and visiting (Glaze & Maruschak, 2008; Shlafer et al., 2020). Similar statistics regarding parents in jail are limited. However, visiting in jails seems more common than in prisons, given that jails are typically located in communities where families live, in contrast to prisons, which are often located further away from families (Shanahan & Agudelo, 2012). Like many family members, Jade tells us she thinks it is important to help facilitate any and all contact between Cedric and their kids. She says that Meekah especially loves visits because it allows her to see her dad and verify for herself that he is doing okay, and she much prefers the in person contact visits involving hugs than the visits behind glass, which can be confusing. Jade goes on to say that sometimes phone calls are challenging for Meekah because she gets distracted easily and is occasionally frustrated that her dad cannot see the things that she tries to show him on her end of the phone, similar to other young children. That said, she loves sending her dad drawings that she creates at school, often running into the house after a school day with a piece of art in hand exclaiming, "I made this for Daddy!"

Often families take advantage of as many opportunities as possible to stay in contact with their incarcerated loved ones, although forms of communication have changed over time with the advent of smart devices and the COVID-19 pandemic. We collected the data in our study before the pandemic and during a time when remote video visits, emails, and instant messaging services were not offered to most incarcerated people. In a recent article using our study's data (Pritzl et al., 2022), we reported what each jailed parent told us about their weekly contact with their child, be it through visits, calls, or letters. The parents told us that the most common form of communication they had with their child each week while they were in jail was through phone calls. About one in five told us they had daily calls with their children, with nearly half saying they talked on the phone at least once per week. However, just over 42 percent said they did not exchange any calls with their children on a weekly basis. Visits were the second most common form of parent-child contact, with one out of three parents saying their children visited them at least once a week (with under 10 percent reporting multiple weekly visits); meanwhile, nearly 60 percent had no regular visits at all. Similarly, 66 percent reported no letter writing with children throughout their time in jail. For those who did, about a quarter wrote roughly once a week while less than 10 percent reported multiple letters each week.

### Types of Contact and What They Mean for Children

Each facility or corrections system, whether a local jail or a state or federal prison, has rules about different forms of communication and contact between incarcerated individuals and their families, including modality, frequency, and length, and each form of contact comes with different costs and benefits. For example, contract agreements with communication providers that carry a service surcharge (Wagner & Jones, 2019) are most often paid for by the families of incarcerated individuals (Christian, 2005; Christian et al., 2006; Grindstead et al., 2001). Recognizing this, staying in contact with an incarcerated loved one can be expensive for families (Lewis & Lockwood, 2019b). Based on interviews with family members visiting their imprisoned loved one, Christian and colleagues (2006, p. 449) indicate that "one can estimate that it would not be unrealistic for a mother, wife, or girlfriend intent on maintaining a strong relationship with her loved one in prison to spend anywhere from \$200 to \$600 a month." Such costs can be prohibitive for many families (Comfort et al., 2016). Indeed, children whose families have lower incomes visit with their incarcerated parents less often (Rubenstein et al., 2021). Like many families, Jade says that the cost of staying in contact with Cedric has been a bit of a challenge for her and her household. In fact, she told us that because the local county jail is located only about a 20-minute drive from her house, and she is able to get rides from her friend, she would rather come to the facility once or twice a week for free visits than spend such a significant sum of money on phone minutes. Cedric tells us he understands the barrier and while he would love to have daily phone calls with his girlfriend and children, he understands why it is not possible and tries to channel the sadness into excitement when he receives a letter, gets a chance to call, and for when they do come to visit.

### Letter Writing and Email

It is estimated that more than half (52 percent) of parents incarcerated in state prisons exchange letters with at least one of their children on a monthly basis (Glaze & Maruschak, 2008). If children are old enough, letters can be a good way for children to express their thoughts and feelings to their incarcerated parents. In addition, incarcerated parents can be thoughtful and reflective in their responses to children, as opposed to the immediacy that is demanded when responding in a phone call or visit (Poehlmann et al., 2010). Despite the incarcerated population being comprised of a significant proportion of individuals who cannot read well or have reading and learning challenges (see, e.g., Dowling, 1991), letter writing remains a primary source of communication. This may be partly due to the freedom it gives parents or children to draw, doodle, or sketch pieces of art that may be more illustrative of how they are coping. That said, this "freedom" is largely determined by restrictions each jail or prison setting puts on ingoing and outgoing mail.

For instance, the jails in our study had strict policies about items that could be accepted in the mail, limiting them to legal paperwork, cards, or letters (but no musical cards) and photographs (non-Polaroid only and without gang signs or nudity). They required that the mail be sent exclusively through the U.S. Postal Service without allowing for any mail to be dropped off at the jail. As such, there are often stringent requirements on what will get processed through the corrections mail system, including:

- Envelopes must not be more than 1″ in thickness.
- No boxes or large envelopes are allowed.
- No packages larger than 10″ × 13″ are allowed.

- Items sold through the inmate commissary will not be accepted through the mail.
- Mail sent in bubble wrap envelopes, or paper insulated envelopes will be recycled and the contents placed in a Sheriff's Office approved envelope.
- Mail and/or envelopes containing perfumed contents will be returned to the sender.
- Mail and/or envelopes containing lipstick kisses will be returned to the sender.
- No stickers or glued-on items will be allowed.
- Those sending mail to inmates must hand-write their return name and address.
- No return labels, stickers, or other affixed items will be allowed.
- Musical greeting cards or greeting cards with string, ribbon, or artwork affixed will not be allowed.
- Greeting cards must be a regular, flat paper greeting card.
- Photos cannot be glued or affixed in any way to anything else.

As alluded to, these policies can vary significantly from institution to institution. For example, another jail in the study had a policy indicating that all incarcerated individuals' incoming and outgoing mail would be subject to inspection. This included legal mail between incarcerated individuals and their attorneys, courts, elected officials, state probation and parole officials, the sheriff, a jail administrator, or the even their physician, psychiatrist, or other health-care professional. When such mail would come in, all items would be opened and inspected, and all staples or binding removed before turning it over to the incarcerated person. At that point, the original envelope would be set to be discarded and the incarcerated individual would quickly need to request a copy of the return address before it was disposed of, otherwise the sender's information would be lost. Another restriction was that general mail that exceeded five pages would not be screened and would be placed directly in the incarcerated individual's secure property (and not accessible until release). Incarcerated individuals could request this restriction be waived once per month, but not all requests were granted and were contingent upon a showing of good cause and at the sole discretion of the jail supervisor. This jail, too, had stringent requirements of what mail items would make it through, stating that the following would not be accepted:

- Mail containing any potentially harmful chemical substance.
- No commercially produced or homemade greeting cards or post cards.
- Nothing containing tape, glue or any other adhesive or binding agent.
- No mail containing envelopes or stamps within the mailer.

- No pages or cut outs from calendars, magazines, newspapers or books.
- No mail containing stickers, cosmetics, stains, glitter or any foreign substances of any kind.
- No mail exhibiting perfume or other odors.
- No food items outside of the established commissary system.
- No Polaroid photos.
- No photos or drawings containing overt sexuality, nudity, violence or gang activity.
- No photos or drawings containing exhibitions of currency, alcohol, drugs, smoking or vaping.
- Nothing marked or written with markers, colored pencils, crayons or anything other than a standard ballpoint pen or pencil.
- No oversize mail will be accepted (paper larger than 8.5″ × 11″)
- No mail containing contraband (e.g., electrical music devices, lights, stamps, newspaper articles, envelopes, calendars, etc.).

There were strict rules for outgoing mail as well, including specifics for how items being sent out must be addressed, and even limiting incarcerated individuals' access to writing paper (eight sheets) and stamped envelopes (four) every two weeks.

The ways in which correctional facilities regulate the mail that incarcerated individuals receive have direct implications for children and families. Because many facilities do not allow colored ink, crayon, glue, glitter, or other media, families often send photos of the multimedia artwork that young children use to express themselves, rather than the artwork itself. Correctional administrators fear that materials such as crayons, paint, and paste might be mixed with illicit drugs that have been liquefied and passed into the correctional facility.

In the notes app on her smartphone, Jade keeps a list of things like this that are and are not allowed when they send mail to Cedric because it is so hard for her to remember. Cedric, too, says he has a hard time keeping everything in mind, especially remembering his monthly request of the waiver for mail over five pages to come to him rather than directly into his secure property. He told us there have been times where this request has not been granted, so longer letters (or ones where Jade compiles different notes and drawings from their kids and family into one envelope) are forced to go unread. These nuances are the exact points that Jade jots down in her notes. She tells us that she really has to keep this in mind with the art projects that Meekah brings home from school. It devastates her to have to tell her daughter that she cannot send her new favorite art project to her daddy. Instead, Jade tries to redirect Meekah by saying "Let's keep this one at home with us and draw Daddy a copy of what it looks like on this paper" as she hands her a jail-approved size sheet of paper and a writing utensil that is allowed. When this alternative is not possible, she takes a photo of the art-work and prints out the photo to mail. These factors can be confusing for Meekah, who has a hard time understanding why she cannot just send the original artwork, but more often than not she takes her mom up on the offer to make a replica, excited for any opportunity to send something to her daddy.

In an attempt to get around all of these policies related to written com-munications, some correctional facilities have begun to digitize incoming mail. By doing so, incarcerated parents can receive their letters via email after they are scanned. Arguably, this strategy allows incarcerated individuals to hold on to their letters without them being lost, stolen, or damaged and have ongoing access to the digitized versions of mail. Although this approach allows children to write letters to their incarcerated parents using various types of materials, including color beyond just standard ink, digitizing all incoming and outgoing mail is often managed by a third-party vendor that charges money for this service. In addition, the incarcerated parent and children do not have the actual letter to hold on to, which may have mean-ing for them.

However, as recently detailed by Kam (2021), the decision to switch physical mail to a scanned format has prompted concerns and even outrage from family members of incarcerated individuals. Caregivers and children have privacy concerns about digitizing mail and the physical items allowed to be received by incarcerated parents, such as photos. Families feel that scanning these items minimizes the connection and bond they so eagerly try to maintain through letter writing. Correctional facilities have consid-ered this approach because it relieves the burden of delegating manpower to sifting through mail and it eliminates the possibility of contraband coming into the correctional facility through mail service, but at what cost to the children and families of the incarcerated? Personally, Jade tells us she does not feel comfortable with this process. That is another reason why she is so adamant about bringing the kids to come see Cedric. She says if they can-not send him pictures to remind him of us and show him how much the kids have grown, the best she can do is come visit as much as is possible for them.

Despite the many barriers to communicating through letter writing, there is evidence to indicate how this form of contact can be positive for families. A study conducted by Tuerk and Loper (2006) found that letter writing between imprisoned mothers and their children was associated with more positive maternal feelings and sense of parental competence. Similarly, Loper and colleagues (2009) found that letter writing from incarcerated parents to their children is associated with a more positive co-parenting alliance between the incarcerated parents and the children's caregivers (co-parenting alliances are discussed in more detail in chapter 5). Importantly, there is no research suggesting that receipt of letters from incarcerated parents is associated with problems for children's development (Poehlmann-Tynan & Pritzl, 2019).

In some corrections facilities, email and instant messaging are now allowed as ways for parents and children to communicate, as a growing number of incarcerated individuals have access to tablets or computers. Usually there is a cost associated with such forms of communication, although it is often lower than telephone charges. Because these forms of communication are relatively new, research to date focusing on children with incarcerated parents has not yet included email and instant messaging. Future work should pay attention to how these electronic forms of communication take into account children's digital literacy, developmental capacities, and equitable access.

### Telephone Contact

Within corrections facilities, telephone calls can only be placed one-way, meaning that the incarcerated individual can call out from the correctional facility (placing a collect call) but the family cannot dial into the correctional facility. For many families, telephone contact is utilized as a way to stay in touch without traveling to the correctional facility to visit. Connecting via phone can allow for children and families to arrange a time for the incarcerated parent to contact the family on their own time and without leaving the house.

Despite some advantages, telephone contact can present various challenges. One barrier to talking via phone while incarcerated is sheer access to the phone itself. As described by Buckley (2021), there are a limited number of phones available to a large population of incarcerated individuals. Some individuals may manipulate or overuse the available phones, deterring others from access to the phones. Money is also a factor in that many families of incarcerated individuals do not have the funds necessary to pay for a call to contact with their loved one (Comfort, 2008), as is the case for Cedric and Jade. Calls from correctional facilities range in price, with many correctional institutions (or the private companies offering phone service to those incarcerated) establishing high-priced rates per minute or additional surcharges and fees. However, given that jails do not have one singular entity overseeing them, such as a state Department of Corrections, the cost of calls from each jail locale varies significantly and can be upward of three times that of prisons (Wagner & Jones, 2019). In fact, the average cost for a 15-minute phone call from jail is $5.74 but can be upward of $20 or more in some parts of the country (Wagner & Jones, 2019). Many nonprofit organizations, advocates, and state and federal governments have discussed the implications of costly phone services in this context. In fact, the Federal Communications Commission (FCC) has assisted in bringing about policies aimed at capping rates of local and long-distance phone charges from prisons—although the FCC rules do not apply to locally run jails.

Another set of barriers to phone communication between incarcerated parents and children has to do with the age and developmental capacities of children, as summarized by Skora Horgan and Poehlmann-Tynan (2020). Very young children rely on visual and tactile cues when communicating and thus find it difficult to talk with someone whom they cannot see—this is what Meekah struggles with most. Children like her may point to reference objects or use other forms of nonverbal communication, such as nodding, which cannot be seen by the person on the other end of the phone. Young children also have limited attention spans for telephone calls, and they may walk away or start doing something else.

Despite the many barriers that exist in the realm of telephone contact, previous research suggests that telephone contact between incarcerated parents and their children is associated with positive family relations (Poehlmann et al., 2010). For example, an earlier study conducted by Poehlmann (2005b) consisting of incarcerated mothers and their young children found that parents who reported having frequent phone calls with children also reported more positive mother-child relationships. Jade agrees that she finds the calls more helpful than not, however she just thinks that visits may be a more meaningful form of contact for Meekah.

### Video Visits

Video visiting, or televisiting, is a relatively recent visit platform that has quickly expanded throughout correctional facilities. Video visits are essentially a timed video connection that is scheduled in advance. Incarcerated individuals usually connect from their housing unit or a designated space on the secure side of the correctional facility, and visitors connect via video either remotely from home (or a specific designated location such as a library) or on-site, from the nonsecure side of the correctional facility itself. Video visits are sometimes free, but typically are offered through a third-party contracted carrier that operates as a service provider, similar to phone calls, which means that the incarcerated individual's family often pays a significant amount per session.

This form of communication provides opportunities for incarcerated parents to stay connected to their children in ways that were previously impossible or unavailable. When the video visits are conducted remotely, such as from the home, children are able to connect with their parents without encountering the barriers of transportation, long wait times at the correctional facility, security procedures, or any interaction with correctional staff. Further, many families have children or caregivers with circumstances that may have limited their ability to physically visit a loved one at the correctional facility itself and now have an opportunity to connect via remote video visiting. Lastly, allowing children the option to connect via video visits offers the opportunity for them to open up and engage in conversation in a way that is otherwise not permitted during standard contact or barrier visitation. During remote video visits, children can show their incarcerated parents their artwork, how well they have cleaned their room, how they ride a bike, dribble a basketball, their newest dance moves, or their prowess on a musical instrument. Incarcerated parents can be virtually present for family meals, birthday parties, homework times, daily routines, or playtimes (Charles et al., 2021; Kerr et al., 2022). Young children often experience video visiting with their incarcerated parents in a similar way that they experience FaceTime, Skype, or Zoom connections with other relatives who live at a distance (Skora Horgan & Poehlmann-Tynan, 2021).

Although remote video visiting can open up opportunities for parent-child communication during parental incarceration, it can become a problem if the corrections system uses video visits to entirely replace in-person communication. To better understand the experiences of family members connecting with their loved ones through video visits, The Marshall Project conducted a study spanning 32 states and comprising 161 participants (Lewis & Lockwood, 2019a). More than one-third of the respondents indicated they had an incarcerated family member located in a facility (mostly jails) that did not offer any form of in-person visiting. Many families reported concerns about video visits replacing in-person contact visits. These televisiting options can provide barriers for some families, while other families may benefit. On the one hand, video visits can be costly; however, for some, this may be a positive option as it is convenient and may allow some family members to see their loved one's face (although remotely) when they otherwise may not been able to due to lack of visiting space or restrictive on-site policies.

### In Person Visiting

Rules and restrictions abound regarding the days and times allotted for visiting, the platforms or methods that people can use to visit, and security procedures around individuals coming into the jail (Boudin et al., 2013). For example, some correctional facilities may offer 20-minute periods of visiting multiple times per week, whereas other correctional facilities may offer two-hour periods of visiting only once per week, whereas other facilities offer daily opportunities for visiting in-person. Typically, state prisons offer in-person visits, whereas jails are more likely to offer visits that occur through video or behind glass (Shlafer et al., 2015). Across jail sites in our study, there were fairly big differences in the types of visits offered and what security procedures were used. At one site, most visits occurred through clear plastic or Plexiglas. Contact visits at tables in a visiting room, like the visit that occurred when Meekah and her dad could hug, occurred less than 4 percent of the time and were only available to those on work release. The other site used exclusively Plexiglas or on-site video visits.

Families who go to a correctional facility to visit their incarcerated loved one are subjected to the policies and procedures imposed by correctional administrators and staff (Dallaire et al., 2021), the same types of rules that Jade has also learned to include on the list on her phone. Visitors are exposed to security procedures that range from checking one's identification and children's birth certificates, going through metal detectors, physical pat downs, and numerous rules about clothing that can and cannot be worn into the correctional facility and items that can be brought in (Dallaire et al., 2021). Although specific security procedures varied from jail to jail in our study, most common was having adults show their IDs, walk through metal detectors (and needing to remove their shoes), and having bags searched and ultimately stored in lockers. In our study, children were not frisked or patted down.

Based on our observations across jail sites, we found no significant variations in the ways in which jail staff interacted with children. In fact, most exchanges were rated as neutral or even slightly positive. There were also no differences in terms of cleanliness. All that said, strict visiting rules make things complicated for families just trying to stay in contact with their loved ones. Indeed, multiple barriers exist for families—especially low-income families—who want to visit, including the distance and time required, transportation issues, cost, difficulty following facility's stringent policies (e.g., making sure each visitor is listed on the approved visiting list and has a proper form of identification), and even family conflict (e.g., Rubenstein et al., 2021). Transportation has certainly been an issue for Jade and Cedric. The one car that they previously shared has broken down and, although Jade can take the kids on public transportation across town to the jail, the 20-minute drive turns into nearly an hour-and-a-half commute with transfers—and that is just one way. That is why Jade has recently started calling on her friends for assistance. Carla has stepped up to the plate quite frequently lately, saying that she is happy to help in any way that she can because she knows how much Cedric loves his babies.

Although incarcerated parents often prefer contact visits with their children, some caregivers feel hesitant about bringing children to a correctional facility, and Jade definitely did at first. For example, in a study consisting of children aged 4–15 years, along with their imprisoned parents and the children's caregivers, Shlafer and Poehlmann (2010) found that caregivers largely reported problematic depictions of visits. Similarly, in Tasca's (2014, 2016) research on incarcerated individuals and their families, caregivers also described their visit experiences as primarily negative. Caregivers described their concerns around exposing children to the overall correctional environment as well as negative interactions that sometimes arise between correctional staff and the incarcerated parents. Sometimes there is a substantial amount of caregiver–incarcerated parent conflict as well, which can contribute to negative perceptions and fewer parent-child visits and other forms of communication during parental incarceration (A. Thomas et al., 2022). Through trial and error, Jade has found ways to make this experience positive for her, Cedric, Meekah, and Tristan.

Barrier visits, which are also an option in many jails, come in several forms. In some cases, a metal screen with perforated holes is used as a barrier, or a piece of wood separates the table, creating a barrier several inches high between incarcerated individuals and visitors. More often, clear acrylic or plastic or thick glass is the barrier and visitors can only hear and talk to the incarcerated individual through a headset or phone. Barrier visits allow incarcerated individuals and their visitors to see each other, but touching is not possible with a full barrier; in other types of barrier visits, visitors are sometimes only permitted to have a brief hug or handshake as a greeting or good-bye. Typically, there is only a small amount of space between each visiting station, creating a lack of privacy, many distractions, and sometimes long waits (Shlafer et al., 2015). The telephone receivers offered in most Plexiglas visiting stations resemble a hard plastic payphone tethered by a short metal cord. These phones are heavy and too big for young children to listen and speak into at the same time. Often, there are not enough telephone receivers offered in these small visiting spaces for a family to have a multiperson conversation. As a result, young children may become bored or disinterested in the visit (Poehlmann-Tynan et al., 2015). This happens quite a bit for Meekah when Plexiglas visits occur with Cedric. She loves to touch and hug him and gets frustrated by the clear plastic pane in their way. And although she tries her best to communicate, her head is just too small to be able to press her ear to the phone and listen and talk at the same time in a clear manner. Because of this, she loses interest quickly and often becomes more enamored with conversations going on in the booths right beside her where she can see and hear clearly.

Contact visiting allows for face-to-face interaction as well as physical touch. Typically, an incarcerated individual sits at a table in the visiting space, and their visitors join them for an allotted amount of time—for Cedric and his family, that was 45 minutes. Incarcerated individuals may be able to exchange a short physical greeting such as a hug or kiss once they enter the visiting space and just before their visitors leave. Some contact visiting policies also allow for young children to be physically close to their incarcerated parent during contact visits, permitting the child to sit on their parent's lap, hold their hand, climb on them, and so on. Contact visits arguably allow for more interaction between children and their incarcerated parents. These types of visits are often the most desired form of visiting for incarcerated individuals and families, and Jade was so happy to hear that that is what they would be having on the day that we observed Meekah's visit.

However, parents' attitudes toward visiting are not uniform, and although most incarcerated parents indicate that they want to see their children and contact visits are often preferable, some incarcerated parents voluntarily eschew visits with their children. In a qualitative analysis of data from Black fathers in our study, Alvin Thomas and colleagues (2022) examined whether or not children visited, and if not, why. Some incarcerated fathers said that they did not want their children to "see them this way," whereas others remembered not liking visiting their own father behind glass when he was in jail during their childhood. Still other fathers felt that exposing their children to the carceral environment might make it more likely that they would continue intergenerational cycles of incarceration. In some cases, fathers wanted visits but the child's caregiver was unwilling to bring them for various reasons, including cost, time, distance, or a conflicted relationship with the incarcerated father.

We were able to systematically observe those parents and children who did choose visits and were able to successfully have at least one visit. In an article published in 2015, we examined young children's behavioral and emotional reactions to Plexiglas and video visits with their parents in jail using data from observed jail visits with a subset of parents, children, and caregivers (Poehlmann-Tynan et al., 2015). These visits lasted between 20 and 90 minutes, largely dependent upon wait times at the correctional facilities and how long the visits were permitted to last. Visits included on-site video, Plexiglas barriers, or face-to-face contact visits. During the video and Plexiglas visits, only one family member could speak to and hear the jailed parent at a time, although multiple family members could see the incarcerated parent—another challenge for Meekah who wants to be part of every conversation. We then used the Jail-Prison Observation Checklist (Poehlmann, 2012; see appendix B) to rate children's attachment behaviors and emotions during the jail visits. With this tool, our research team rated the presence or absence of security procedures (metal detectors, frisking, bag searches), facility noise and cleanliness, interactions with jail staff, and also children's behaviors and affect during entry, while they waited, and during the visit, both toward caregivers and incarcerated parents.

We found that most families needed to show some form of identification, as Jade did, when they entered the jail (often a driver's license for adults and a birth certificate for the child). About half of young children were asked to walk through a metal detector and a smaller proportion were asked to remove their shoes, though none were ever frisked. Most children stayed close to their caregivers upon entry, through security, and into the visiting area. In many cases, this continued throughout the visits as children stayed sitting on the caregiver's lap, clinging to their leg, or holding their hand. Interestingly, although no children displayed aggressive behaviors toward their caregivers at the front end of visits, by the end nearly half engaged in avoidance or even hit their caregivers. All children appeared to be happy at some point during their visits, though there was also an increase in negative affect as the visits continued (due in part to fatigue, hunger, confusion, increased sadness, and even upticks in anger), though only 10 percent expressed indicators of fear. In fact, the most commonly observed emotional responses for children were happy and serious or somber facial expressions. Meekah embodied most of these responses—a predominantly calm and collected demeanor that ebbed and flowed with sincere and genuine happiness at seeing her dad. Although she did have one bout of more negative affect, seemingly spurred by the commotion in the visiting area, she was able to self-regulate and calm herself back down (with the help of her loving parents, of course).

At the visits, all children engaged in visual contact with their jailed parents and about 95 percent of the young ones talked to and listened to their parents, with about four out of five expressing a loving sentiment (e.g., blowing a kiss or saying "I love you."). Nevertheless, a similar proportion avoided engaging with the jailed parent in some way throughout the course of the visit, as many children acted restless and moved around the room, seemed disinterested, or acted distressed. Elements of the jail's visiting procedures seemed to play a role in this. For instance, many children were not familiar with the hand-held device that allowed them to listen to their parents in the context of Plexiglas or on-site video visits. While this device looks like an old-fashioned telephone receiver, most families had cellular phones and touch screen devices, limiting children's exposure to such outdated technology, and, again, the size of the device caused challenges for children's ability to speak and hear efficiently. On top of that, having other people's visits in close proximity to children was challenging not only for Meekah; many young ones found this to be distracting as they constantly overheard neighboring conversations that in some instances could be inappropriate for children. In some facilities, children could even see behind their incarcerated parents and into the cell block or housing unit where the incarcerated individuals were taking the visit. In the case of video visits, the visit can seem to end abruptly from a child's perspective, with the screen turning off with little to no warning, to which some children react with sentiments like "Where did Daddy go?" while becoming teary.

In a 2017 article using the observational data collected for this study, our team sought to examine young children's attachment behaviors toward incarcerated fathers in the context of visiting (among other predictors like witnessing the father's arrest and the child's home environment) (Poehlmann-Tynan et al., 2017). We found that of the subset of children who were observed visiting their fathers in jail, the vast majority (nearly 90 percent) were brought by their mothers, with a few cases of grandmothers facilitating the contact, while siblings or other children were present in about one-third of the cases. Wait times leading up to the visits averaged about 15 minutes, though they ranged from no wait at all to more than an hour of waiting. Visits themselves tended to be about a half-hour long, but ranged from 12 minutes to nearly an hour. In the jails where our study was completed, nearly half of the observed visits were barrier visits through Plexiglas, about 40 percent occurred through video monitors, and less than 10 percent were face-to-face with opportunities for contact.

At these visits, children's behaviors toward jailed parents were classified, in the order of frequency in which the constellation of behaviors occurred, as (a) listening, responding, happy, excited, and loving; (b) avoiding, paying attention to other visits, angry, and whining; or (c) fearful, sad, and confused. Toward the caregivers at these visits, children's behaviors and emotions were characterized as (a) avoiding, whining, being angry or sad; (b) seeking close proximity, sitting on lap, not being confused; or (c) hitting or pushing or acting fearful (Poehlmann-Tynan et al., 2017). Younger children tended to respond in more avoidant and angry ways toward their caregivers, but attachment processes played a significant role in these behaviors. In other words, even when controlling for children's age, children rated as having more secure attachments at home were likely to respond positively toward the caregiver during the jail visit. We could clearly see this for Meekah and Jade. Their strong bond and secure attachment built at home transferred seamlessly to the jail, where Meekah often relied on her mom as a secure base to help facilitate her coping, such as when they went through security and when the visit was ending. We saw this illustrated in the drawing that Meekah did while waiting for the visit to begin—a chain of holding hands connected her to her mother, smiles on each of the figure's faces. In our analyses, children's expressions of aggression, avoidance, and fear with the caregiver were significantly correlated with fear and sadness directed toward the jailed parent, as well. However, this is not always the case. Simply stated, when children felt more distanced from the caregiver and dysregulated in the home, they were also less likely to have positive reactions toward the jailed parent. The inverse is true as well, such as we positively saw with Meekah's family: children's security and affection with their caregivers also correlated with positive emotions and behaviors exhibited toward the jailed parent.

Interestingly, wait time played a significant role in children's behaviors, such that the longer they waited the more avoidant, distracted, or upset the child became. Beyond that, children were more likely to be avoidant and angry with the caregiver as well as fearful, sad, and confused toward the jailed parent during Plexiglas visits as compared with any other type of visit. Because young children can see their parents through the glass but are unable to touch them, these visits in particular may activate a child's attachment system and trigger anxiety that cannot be easily relieved since the parent–child separation continues following the visit.

For Meekah, the overall tone of the contact visit with her father was positive, with opportunities for engaging with her dad in a number of ways, including talking, listening, and laughing with him. She expressed a number of emotions toward him, and her initial confusion and somberness were more than outweighed by happiness, excitement, and love, even though she did experience periods of disengagement, avoidance, or distraction during the visit.

### Child-Friendly Visiting

Although we did not observe any explicitly child-friendly visits occurring in the jails as part of this study, we have conducted observations of such visits in the time period since, both at prisons and at jails. Child-friendly visiting is a type of contact visit that facilitates supported, structured interactions between incarcerated parents and their children. Elements of the space are specifically tailored to young children, designed to welcome and encourage children to communicate and interact with their parents. Children and their incarcerated parents can utilize materials such as games, puzzles, books, and arts and crafts to engage with their incarcerated parents in a developmentally appropriate way and they have snacks or a meal together. Typically children's caregivers are not present at these visits, allowing incarcerated parents and children to focus solely on each other. Incarcerated parents and their children are allowed to have physical contact such as hand holding, hugs, and sitting on laps. Parents and children engage in preparation for the visits and have contact with each other in between the visits. Although child-friendly visits appear to be the best way for children to have contact with their incarcerated parents, opportunities for such visits are limited across the United States at the present time.

Child-friendly visits have been associated with improved outcomes for children (Poehlmann et al., 2010; Poehlmann-Tynan & Pritzl, 2019). In a recent white paper from the Urban Institute, Cramer and colleagues (2017) reviewed research and conducted interviews with eight experts regarding parent-child visits during parental incarceration, concluding that child-friendly visits appeared the most helpful for children when they are embedded in family-support programs that also include elements like identifying and working through underlying issues to promote healthy parent-child and family relationships. Family-friendly visiting policies include more relaxed, child-sensitive security procedures, longer visit periods, opportunities for families to engage in positive activities together (such as playing games and eating together), and conducting visits in a less stressful setting (i.e., a designated family visiting room) as opposed to the stark surroundings of most adult visiting environments (Arditti, 2016).

Enhanced visits are also important ways for helping children to connect with their incarcerated parents. Enhanced visits are usually conducted using the principles of child-friendly visiting but typically involve visit-specific events hosted for incarcerated parents and their children. Each correctional facility is different, but some offer enhanced visit events monthly, quarterly, or annually. Examples include pizza parties, dances, holiday gift exchanges, talent shows, game nights, and family picnics. Enhanced visit events are opportunities for families to connect in a way that is partially similar to a common event outside of the correctional institution. Like other types of child-friendly visits, these events allow opportunities for children to have unstructured play and physical contact with their incarcerated parents.

Correctional administrators tend to focus on rewarding, or incentivizing, positive behavior by way of enhanced visit events for incarcerated parents. For example, enhanced visits are often planned by correctional administrators near the completion of a parenting program as a reward. This way, parents who have participated in and completed a program successfully can celebrate with their families during an enhanced visit. Similarly, correctional administrators often provide enhanced visiting as reward for positive behavior within the correctional institution.

*Frequency of Contact and Children's Well-Being*

Previous studies have investigated the link between frequency of parent-child contact during parental incarceration and child well-being, with nuanced findings. A literature review published in 2010 found that in the presence of interventions (such as offering child-friendly visits or parenting programs), parent-child contact was positively related to child well-being (Poehlmann et al., 2010). Conversely, in cases when interventions were not present or when visits occurred behind a barrier, findings were generally less positive. For example, a study conducted by Dallaire and colleagues (2012) found that more frequent visiting between jailed parents and their children—which occurred behind glass at a jail—was associated with difficulties in monitoring, supervision, and obedience. A study conducted by McClure and colleagues (2015) also reported mixed findings regarding the association between frequency of contact and child well-being.

In our study, we worked with team member Kaitlyn Pritzl, who analyzed data for her honors thesis, to examine the association between different types of contact and child behavior problems, as measured by the Child Behavior Checklist (Pritzl et al., 2022). We found that jail policies played a significant role in the association between frequency of parent-child contact and children's behaviors. At the site that relied almost exclusively on Plexiglas visits, more in-person parent-child visits related to more externalizing behavior problems in children. In contrast, more frequent visits with parents incarcerated at the jail that offered families a choice between Plexiglas and video visits related to fewer child externalizing behavior problems. This relation existed even though the jail site that relied solely on Plexiglas visits had fewer security procedures and was less crowded than the jail using both Plexiglas and video visits. These findings are similar to research emphasizing the negative impact that "glass walls and locked doors" can have on families during noncontact barrier visits in jails (Arditti, 2003) and highlight the role of family choice. Some families prefer face-to-face visits whereas some prefer video visits.

### COVID-19 and Visits

During the COVID-19 pandemic, corrections facilities worldwide suspended in-person visits to limit transmission of the virus. Visits moved to video only for facilities that had video capabilities, whereas other corrections facilities moved to telephone and mail communication only. A survey of state prisons in the United States conducted during the pandemic found that only 25 state Departments of Corrections had video visits before the start of the pandemic lockdown in March 2020, with 16 of those offering free video visits with family members during the pandemic (Dallaire et al., 2021). In addition, 15 states offered free email access to residents of state prisons during the pandemic, whereas 10 states offered free postage. Such offerings occurred so that incarcerated individuals with limited means—and especially those who relied on in-person visits for contact with family members prior to the pandemic lockdown— could still have some contact with their loved ones.

Video visits have been met with mixed emotions, as sometimes the internet connections are poor, the visuals are pixelated, the audio difficult to hear, or the visits just drop or end abruptly because of technology issues (Lewis & Lockwood, 2019a). Since the height of the pandemic, some facilities have begun to reopen for in-person visits but with visits occurring behind plastic barriers only, whereas others are still prohibiting face-to-face visits. Some facilities had reopened for contact visits as of summer 2022, especially visits behind glass.

During the pandemic, a study in a mid-sized county jail surveyed 33 adults, the majority of whom were Black men and half of whom were parents, to assess their experiences around COVID (Charles et al., 2021). Respondents indicated that COVID-19 significantly disrupted day-to-day activities in the jail, negatively affected their health, and strained family relationships. Suspended in person visits, with limited opportunities for alternate forms of family contact, contributed to challenges with feelings of isolation and diminished mental health in addition to increased worry about the well-being of children and other family members.

## How Can We Help?
### Implementing Child-Friendly Visits and Expanding Visiting Opportunities

Although there is mixed evidence for the impacts that visits with incarcerated parents have on child well-being, child-friendly visits or those that occur as part of a parenting intervention appear to be consistently positive regarding supporting children, clarifying children's feelings of ambiguous loss, bonding with the parent, and making plans for when the parent reenters the community (Poehlmann et al., 2010; Poehlmann-Tynan & Pritzl, 2019). However, visits—especially those that occur behind glass or involve extensive security procedures—may also be negative in that they could institute feelings of secondary prisonization or possibly retraumatize children (Arditti, 2003; Comfort, 2003). These findings have real implications for correctional administrators, community partners, and advocates to identify and remove barriers to positive contact and communication between incarcerated parents and their families, especially because contact has implications for the mental health and recidivism of incarcerated parents (see chapter 7).

To facilitate positive parent-child communication during a parental jail stay, we recommend implementation of child-friendly visits whenever possible, especially as an extension of parenting programs offered in prisons and jails. Young children appear confused by visits that occur behind glass, and they seem to react most negatively to long wait times followed by long visits. Thus, corrections administrators could offer more face-to-face contact visits and decrease wait times, while families could be mindful of how to prepare children for different types of visits or even when to bring or not bring young children for visits.

We also recommend that parents and children stay in touch between in-person visits through video (preferably remote video so that children can connect from the comfort of home), phone calls, and letters or emails. Supported remote video visits can be a helpful way for children and families to connect when there are barriers to in person visits or phone calls because of family circumstances, cost, or children's developmental capacities (Charles et al., 2021; Kerr et al., 2022).

Whether it is in person or remote—such communication can build family relationships and help alleviate some feelings of ambiguous loss. Just think back to chapter 3 and our discussion of children's drawings conducted at home and in the jail. The drawings that were made during a visit to the incarcerated parent in jail, such as those created by Armoni, were more likely to depict the whole family and show signs of happiness compared to the drawings made by the same children when at home. Although visiting is not possible for all families, when it is a supported and positive experience, children and their families can benefit.

Because children's caregivers often report negative aspects related to visits, in part because the financial burdens of visiting and calls are placed on them and they must manage children's behaviors and emotional reactions on a day-to-day basis, it is important to provide support to caregivers around visiting. It can also be helpful to assist caregivers in seeing the situation from the child's perspective and focusing on the possible benefits, as well as challenges, to parent–child contact during incarceration.

### Reducing Costs of Visits and Phone Calls

Offering free or reduced-cost communication should be a goal whenever possible, as then low-income families are not further stressed beyond their means. Some corrections facilities offered free phone calls or video visits to incarcerated individuals during the COVID-19 pandemic (Dallaire et al., 2021), and some facilities continued this practice even as other forms of visiting resumed. Because more visits and other forms of incarcerated parent-child contact are associated with less recidivism for incarcerated parents along with better integration into their families following release (see, e.g., La Vigne et al., 2005; McKay et al., 2019), reducing the cost of communication, or offering free phone calls and video visits, may be a good investment for communities.

Beyond decreasing recidivism and improving reintegration of individuals returning to their communities, there may also be intergenerational implications of supporting positive parent-child communication for children with incarcerated parents. Thus, more children should have the same opportunity as Meekah to hug and connect with an incarcerated parent in a positive way.

# "Da-Da Gonna Play with Me Soon!"

As WE WALK UP to the cement driveway to the front porch of the small Midwestern, rural home, Katie opens the door to greet us. The 30-year-old White woman, wearing black yoga pants and a black zip-up hooded sweatshirt with a pink tank top sticking out underneath, smiles and looks eager to take time out of her relaxing Saturday afternoon to meet with our team. She is wearing a thick headband with the rest of her dark blonde hair pulled into a ponytail that leans slightly toward one side as she holds the door open with her body for us to enter. Her demeanor matches the energy of the greeting—calm and collected. Katie lets us know that she has been looking forward to our visit, what she describes as a cathartic experience to reflect on how the last few months have gone caring for her three-year-old daughter, Miley, while her 23-year-old Native American boyfriend and Miley's father, Damian, has been in jail, and how excited she is for him to be released in the coming days.

We squeeze past her and nearly run into the couch that is placed directly in front of the doorway. The main living space feels tight and cramped. The fabric couch is navy blue with a plaid pattern that covers it entirely, yet the design gets almost lost amidst the piles of laundry and blankets that are stacked on top of the seating space. The floor is cluttered with toys, and many colorful books are stacked along the wall. The room feels dark with the blinds closed, relying on one sole floor lamp to light the space which casts shadows on the wood-paneled wall behind the couch. Even still, it is clear that Katie has made her home a safe space for Miley to learn and grow, making sure that she has ample access to books, puzzles, musical instruments, and toys. It is also evident that she has made it a point to keep Damian present in Miley's mind with family pictures on the walls and bookshelves as well as written letters hung by colorful magnets on the kitchen refrigerator alongside some of Miley's drawings. In these letters to Miley, Damian writes about how excited he is to see Miley soon and lists out all of her favorite activities that they can do together again, like drawing with sidewalk chalk on their paved driveway, chasing butterflies around their big backyard, and building a snowman this winter.

As we settle into the living room and begin clearing space to unpack our bags, Miley runs out of a back room to meet us. The biracial White and Native American little girl has short brown curly hair that flies freely in the air, and she is wearing a red-and-blue polka-dot hoodie that has a big panda face on the front, matched with a pair of jeans that are cuffed at the ankle. She is a smiley girl with pierced ears and an inviting presence. Miley lets out a high-pitched giggle, yelling "Puppy!" with her squeaky voice as she runs to help our research team members unpack the red-and-white stuffed dog from our bag of toys. Grabbing the puppy by the ear, Miley runs it across the room to Katie, now seated on the plaid couch. On route, she scoots past the framed family pictures of her and her parents set on the entertainment center, seemingly unphased by the standing reminders of the separation from her father. Fortunately, the happy triad standing behind these glass frames will soon be reunited once Damian is released from the county jail in just under two weeks.

After just a few seconds, Miley sets down the puppy that had enraptured her and it quickly becomes clear that she is a chatty girl, excitedly making comments about every new toy that she lays her eyes on. We see clear evidence about how, at home, her mom encourages her to learn the names of colors, patterned speech, spatial relationships, numbers, and words—but she is still working on her language development after experiencing early language delay, as seen in her simple, yet boisterous, remarks about the toys. Her youthful joy and genuine sense of discovery remain evident as she demonstrates these lessons by, for example, counting "one . . . two . . . three . . ." as we unpack toy cars and yelling "YELLOW!" when she sees the Matchbox school bus. As we play, she giggles with us, sits close to us, and is quick to share her toys. Katie tells us that she is pleasantly surprised at how Miley's demeanor has improved a bit, saying that she had been more sad, angry, anxious, depressed, and lonely than normal since her dad was arrested. She is hopeful that this will continue to improve when her dad comes home but is not sure if that will actually be the case. Actually, Katie tells us that this has been a big point of conversation in her phone calls with Damian recently. Damian says that once he is home, he is excited to use Miley's chatterbox personality to his advantage to talk her through her feelings about him being away and now coming back, promising that—no matter what—she will always have him in her life.

The behavioral problems that Katie alluded to are something we became more aware of as we played with Miley throughout the day. For instance, Miley lets out an angry shriek as she struggles to slip the remaining blocks through the half-zipped bag we brought along with us when we clean up and move to a new activity. Her mom readily attends to the signal, used to the frustration that her daughter loudly expresses when she cannot find a toy. From that point forward, the two play together in a way that shows that this set of interactions seems to play on repeat. When Miley gets frustrated, she screams very suddenly and loudly, but Katie is calm and provides a positive, calm presence and engages in reaffirming reciprocal play that seems to center her daughter during an outburst. When this happens, Miley quickly recovers and continues to play with her mom. Once focused and calm, Miley embodies strong determination. For instance, she began stacking the blocks as high as she could, expressing excitement when she eventually accomplished the task, shouting "Ta-da!"—a stark contrast to her bursts of anger exhibited just minutes (if not seconds) prior.

When we met with Damian at the jail, he told us about these outbursts, too, opening up about how Miley has recently been exhibiting more frequent and significant signs of distress—emotions that he commits himself to helping her work through together once he is physically back in her life. He tells us that he really hopes that once he is released from the county jail, his active presence and increased involvement can help curb some of these stressors. In fact, Damian thinks that their reunification will be really positive for the two of them, describing to us his plans for some of those same activities that he wrote to Miley about, such as reading books, playing in the yard, and taking her fishing (something his dad did with him when he was growing up but which he has not yet had the opportunity to do with his daughter). He wonders, though, how much Miley's interests may have changed since he has been away. Although he has only been incarcerated for a couple of months, he feels as though this has been a big chunk of his three-year-old's life. For instance, Katie was recently telling him about how Miley has gotten so obsessed with a new Disney movie that came out while he has been gone, saying that she constantly sings the songs and wants everything from its line of toys. Although he finds it hard to relate to Miley about this movie right now, he is he is excited for her to be able to show it to him in the coming days and looks forward to all of their new (and old) adventures together. When we asked Damian what he was most looking forward to back in the community, he told us without hesitation: "Just being a dad, waking up and seeing Miley every day."

While we do not know exactly what the reunification process looked like for Miley and her dad, if the environment we left her and her mom in is any indication, then we have cause for optimism. Miley and Katie maintained thoughtful play amidst the living space for quite some time while our research team took a back seat and observed. Throughout our time together, it became clear that Katie was in sync with her daughter's needs, tuning herself in to different strategies to effectively help Miley regain her calm, be it singing those Disney songs, telling nursery rhymes, or becoming mutually absorbed in one of their many favorite picture books about butterflies. These were precisely the types of books lining the wall that caught our attention when we first walked in. Scanning the room once more, we are reminded of all the ways in which Miley's parents have set up the space to support her—both before, during, and likely after her dad's time in jail. Hanging above the clothes-covered plaid couch is a framed family picture of Miley, Katie, and Damian that looks over the dyad as they play. Toward the end of our visit, Miley points to the picture and says, "Da-Da gonna play with me soon." And she is right—in just under two weeks from when we sat with them in their living room, the happy family depicted on the wall finally would be allowed to resume in reality; a long-awaited reunion where smiley Miley, her patient mom, and her dedicated dad would all be able to play together on what would hopefully be relaxing afternoons together, much like the one on this day.

### Reentry and Family Reunification

In just a few days—because of her father's reentry into the community—Miley will join the millions of other children who do not currently, but have at some point in their young lives, had a parent in jail or prison. For many children, the release of their parents is almost inevitable because the vast majority of those incarcerated (nearly 95 percent) eventually are released (Hughes & Wilson, 2003). For instance, in 2019 alone, state and federal prisons released more than 600,000 people (Carson, 2020). That said, given the high rates of arrest and admissions to jail coupled with relatively short sentences for misdemeanor convictions, jails see more individuals walk out of their doors than prisons, with an estimated 9 million people released from jails each year (Beck, 2006). Some of these individuals will be released free from criminal legal system oversight, but many will remain on community supervision, contributing to the largest share of those under criminal legal surveillance—a total of 4.4 million people in 2017 (Kaeble & Alper, 2020). Included in these statistics are large shares of parents who are returning to community life, some of whom resume living together with their children. This means that millions of U.S. children, just like Miley, must navigate the complex experiences of family reunification after a parental jail stay.

The postrelease period, when parents and all those previously incarcerated come home, is commonly referred to as "reentry" or, even better, "reintegration" (R. J. Miller, 2021). Yet importantly, reintegration is not a discrete experience that begins and ends on the day of release; rather, it is an ongoing process that can bring with it any number of challenges, such as

trying to find employment and housing, changes of residence or even homelessness, struggling to keep material hardship and food insecurity at bay,
health concerns, addiction and recovery, exposure to violence, strained and
complicated family relationships, and possibility rearrest or reincarceration
(Western, 2018). In fact, first-person accounts of incarceration and reentry
(e.g., Hinton & Hardon, 2018; Senghor, 2016) intimately describe the
trauma and healing that can occur postrelease. While a growing body of
literature has begun describing the inherent difficulties in navigating family
reunification after incarceration, characterizing parent-child relationships
postrelease as "mending broken fences" (Charles et al., 2019), scholars are
only beginning to amass enough evidence to make claims about how parental reentry may be experienced by children.

Reentry and family reunification processes are particularly challenging
for children, given the risks experienced while parents are in jail, many of
which have been discussed in this book. For children, the incarceration of
a parent may happen very quickly and seemingly out of thin air. Perhaps their
parent made them breakfast that morning before school but was nowhere to
be found when they returned home that afternoon. Some children may have
contact with their parent throughout the incarceration, whereas others may
be in the dark for the duration of the sentence, left wondering if it is their
own fault that mom or dad is gone and if they will ever come back home.
What happens both before and during the incarceration matters for how
children make sense of the reunification process. Much of this sense-making
process is driven by context as well as personal and family characteristics.

### Children's Postrelease Social Emotional Well-Being

Changes in children's emotional regulation and behaviors are common
while parents are in jail, and Miley's mom's concern over a continuation of
these issues postrelease may be warranted, given what we know about how
other children in her situation fare following parents' incarceration and
reentry. Though the literature in this area is still slim and scholars are trying
to make sense of trends that they observe in children's behaviors after their
parents return home or to the community after being in jail, we see indications that children's challenges may persist even after parents are released.
For instance, in other samples of children with previously incarcerated parents, emotional problems still seem to be present, at least in some capacity,
postrelease. One study interviewed a group of college students and asked
them to reflect on what it was like to have a parent incarcerated during their
childhood, some of whom discussed experiences of reentry for those who
had been released. Across the board, these now young adults reflected on a
number of emotional challenges, such as grief, anxiety, and worry, that they

continued to experience during childhood, even after their parents came back home (Zhang & Flynn, 2020). Other work with young adults has asked them to think back to what reentry felt like for them as children when their parents were released, identifying damaged trust and low confidence in relationships as particularly persisting consequences (Young & Smith, 2019). Children in this position may also experience increased self-doubt, anger, regret, and sadness—often tied to stigma (Young & Smith, 2019). It is interesting to think about the mechanisms behind these more internalized and emotional responses that children experience. Although the behaviors being exhibited (e.g., the loneliness and anxiety that Miley is experiencing) may be similar after parental incarceration as they are during the time parents are away, the underlying reason may differ. Maybe it is damaged trust that co-occurs with rebuilding parent-child bonds postrelease that leads to feelings of loneliness, or perhaps it is the stigma of having a previously incarcerated parent back in one's physical presence in the home or community that leads to feelings of anxiety. Or maybe even it is worry that the incarceration and separation could happen again.

We are just beginning to unpack some of the nuances behind these qualitative findings using quantitative methods with larger samples of parents and children. For example, work that uses a sample of nearly a thousand families and children has tried to parse out some of the differences that we see across groups (Yaros et al., 2018). The researchers found that older children, as opposed to younger children (like Miley and the others we came to know in our study), experience more internalizing behaviors upon their parents' release than during the incarceration, which are further exacerbated when parents have substance use issues back home (Yaros et al., 2018). Compared to older children, children's young age and corresponding language, cognitive, and emotional development may have protective effects on their coping when parents return to the community. However, this does not mean that poor outcomes are out of the question just because a child is young at the time of a parent's release. Indeed, a recent review suggests that when parental incarceration occurs when children are young, the effects can be larger and magnify as children grow older (Poehlmann-Tynan & Turney, 2021). Pointedly, the finding in Yaros and colleagues' (2018) study that parents' substance use can be linked to children's behavioral adjustment during reentry has important implications for family-level strategies that can help support children's well-being across the continuum of criminal legal system involvement. Evidence that children's compromised emotional states may continue after incarceration and even be linked to new challenges strongly demonstrates the need to support families and children touched by the criminal legal system when a parent comes home from jail or prison. This shows just how much reintegration is an ongoing process that unfolds over time.

Miley's increased internalizing behavior problems were not the only concern of her parents. In fact, Katie told us about her increased anger and other externalizing behaviors that have spiraled since Damian went to jail, and which we saw off and on throughout their play. However, she is not alone; this is something other studies have begun to examine in children following the release of a parent from jail or prison. As with internalizing behaviors, there may be reason to think that Miley may continue to struggle even when her dad comes home. That is, externalizing behavior problems, including actions such as aggression or disobedience, seem to be a continued risk for children with recently released parents. One analysis that used data from the Fragile Families and Child Wellbeing Study measured "reentry" as *previously* but not *currently* having a parent incarcerated (Craigie et al., 2018). Though this conceptualization limits our ability to make sense of certain experiences of reentry (such as when it happened and how long it has been since it happened), the study highlights important trends in a sample of more than 2,000 urban kids. These findings suggest that reentry does not pause challenges to children's externalizing behaviors, but rather may heighten them, particularly for boys and children of color (Craigie et al., 2018). On average, these behavioral consequences are chronic and persist for years after release, increasing over time, on average (Craigie et al., 2018). Another project that includes children with parents who have been, but are not currently, incarcerated in a population-based sample finds that even compared to those with a currently incarcerated parent, adolescents with a parent who has been released report higher rates of particular externalizing behaviors, such as lying and difficulty paying attention (Ruhland et al., 2020).

All that said, other quantitative work with more nuanced measures has identified some protective factors for children that occur during parental reentry. For instance, children's externalizing behavioral responses seem to improve when they have positive relationships with their recently released parents and if they co-reside with them following incarceration (Yaros et al., 2018). These findings highlight the intervening role of positive and supportive relationships as potentially stabilizing processes during a uniquely destabilizing period for children's behavior. For children experiencing difficulty adjusting before, and maybe even following, their parent's release, aspects of family support may curb further poor outcomes and help children overcome previous adversity. These insights mean that children like Miley, who have positive relationships with both parents and are excitedly awaiting their parent's return home, may see less environmental risk for further behavioral adjustment than children who do not have these opportunities.

*Postrelease Parent-Child Involvement*

Findings around postrelease co-residence remain a bit of a paradox in the field, for young men (Arditti & Parkman, 2011) and others. Damian, for instance, is planning to live with Miley and Katie upon his release, but this is not always the case when parents are released back to the community from prison or jail. We know that significantly fewer children live with their parents after release from prison than did before the incarceration, but children who are younger, have more contact, and whose parents are married are more likely to live with their parent both prior to incarceration and following release (McKay et al., 2018). Meanwhile, parents who do not live with their children prior to incarceration are likely to remain nonresident even after they return to the community (Western et al., 2004).

Children who co-reside with their parents postrelease are not guaranteed to have the easiest adjustments. For instance, a recent study examining paternal recidivism found the greatest effect sizes for children who did not reside with their fathers following release (Muentner, 2022). This may be because co-resident children often experience many day-to-day challenges during the reentry period, such as renegotiating norms and roles, altering expectations, coping with changes in guardianship or allocation of resources, possibly different forms of discipline and communication, and managing stigma, all while parents navigate their own complexities that the first few months of reentry bring. In their study of previously incarcerated fathers, Yaros and colleagues (2018, p. 156) further discuss co-residence as being a complex phenomenon, finding that strained father-child relationships increase children's behavior problems when they live together postrelease and commenting that "how much a child is exposed to his or her father helps to determine the influence the father–child relationship has on the child's well-being." Because reentry is most smooth for children when it does not disrupt their regular routines (Smith & Young, 2017), it may be that shifts in household functioning prevent co-resident children from improving in the same ways as non–co-resident children who go about this transition without such immediate exposures.

Regardless of residential status, reentering parents often have the opportunity to become involved with their children through a number of other interactions. For Damian, he envisioned such interactions including reading, playing outside, fishing, and movie watching with Miley. We know from other research that the loss of quality time during incarceration deeply affects children and parents, and many parents and children anxiously await an increase in involvement after the parent's release (Yocum & Nath, 2011; Young & Smith, 2019). This can include prosocial activities such as playing ball, helping with homework, going on outings, and laughing (Kiczkowski,

2011) or through emotional connection, communication, and dialogue (Yocum & Nash, 2011). While a parent is incarcerated, children like Miley lose a role model, confidant, and loved one, and reintegration provides an opportunity where they can potentially get these back, thus adding strong value to a parent's presence upon release (Kiczkowski, 2011). Overall, however, the frequency of these parent-child activities tends to decline from pre-incarceration to postrelease among fathers who were incarcerated (McKay et al., 2018). Exceptions to this are in the cases of younger children, where bonds are reportedly easier to rebuild (Crandell-Williams & McEvoy, 2017), as well as when there was more frequent contact during incarceration and when parents have strong co-parent relationships, particularly for nonresidential parents (McKay et al., 2018). Given such findings, it is likely that Miley will benefit from being so young during the reunion period. Opportunities for connection postrelease often depend on who has been caring for the child during the incarceration, especially when children are young. Much has been written about the gatekeeping roles of children's caregivers, including access to phone calls and visits during incarceration, and involvement in the child's life during release (see, e.g., Arditti et al., 2005; Tasca, 2016).

On top of these activities, when parents are released, they often resume some sort of financial responsibility for their children. Older children are more aware of the economic strain that incarceration brings to the home than younger children, and they often include financial support as a nonnegotiable expectation of parents upon release from prison or jail (Yocum & Nash, 2011). Despite these expectations, we know that financial support for children is significantly lower postrelease than before incarceration, for a variety of reasons (McKay et al., 2018). In fact, children's household economic situations remain depleted when parents return home and many families continue to rely on welfare and public housing support (Smith & Young, 2017). There is variation in financial responsibility, though; for instance, younger children with more frequent contact with their fathers during incarceration have higher odds of receiving financial support upon reentry (McKay et al., 2018), perhaps owing to resumption of child support payments, securing employment, or distribution from other public sources.

Reentry can be a critical time for parents to feel empowered in their role to shape positive life outcomes for their children, calling specifically on their own strength, confidence, and resilience (Charles et al., 2019). Many children find this particularly meaningful, expressing desire for involvement during reentry both in instances of positive and strained preincarceration relationships. When children see their parents seek support, they are more likely to remain hopeful and encouraged by their parents' success (Yocum & Smith, 2011). Nevertheless, there is variation in these responses. Some young ones take more of a "wait and see" approach in regard to how they allow themselves to open up to the family reunification. For instance, parents who have been away for longer and have therefore missed a number of children's developmental milestones and rites of passage report a potentially more difficult time reconnecting with their children (Muentner & Charles, 2022).

### Risk and Protective Factors

The mechanisms by which children's compromised well-being persists in reentry are less clear. It is thought that changes in household structure (Rodriguez, 2016) and changes in caregiving arrangements (Wakefield et al., 2016) both induce stress in children, which makes them more vulnerable to socioemotional strife. The release of a parent may also force the child to revisit traumatic experiences associated with the parent's arrest or incarceration (e.g., witnessing their arrest; having negative visit experiences; feeling ashamed, embarrassed, or even feeling at fault for what happened; or receiving little information about what happened). In fact, what details about the parent's incarceration are shared with children has recently been linked to the child's postrelease well-being, finding fewer social emotional problems once parents return home for more informed younger children (Muentner & Eddy, 2021).

Other vulnerabilities may be at play, too. For instance, the disproportionality of incarceration rates within low-income communities of color may create a cumulative disadvantage. A Black child, for example, may be affected both by systemic racism and having an incarcerated parent—an experience in which multiple conditions may make it harder to cope with a parent's incarceration and return and accompanying stigma, all of this on top of racism and discrimination experienced unrelated to their parent's criminal legal system involvement. In Miley's case, her father is Native American, which may also make them the subject of racism or discrimination. Additionally, boys have been found to be more vulnerable to disruption than girls, perhaps because often social and cultural expectations are placed on boys to emphasize toughness and discourage emotional expression, and because boys experience more risk for developing mental health challenges than girls, with the exception of depression (Zahn-Waxler et al., 2008). Other incarceration-related risk factors may also play a role, such as the number of prior incarcerations and releases, the nature and severity of the crime, and the length of time that the parent was removed from the child's life.

Talking with Miley's dad gave us more insight on his reflections as he counted down the days to coming home. On top of his overt excitement was a tone of nervousness. Damian has been incarcerated more than 20 times throughout his life for a variety of charges, and he credits his dependence on substances partly for his recidivism and reintegration challenges.

Both untreated substance use and mental health concerns are significant predictors of a destabilized reentry experience and elevated risk for recidivism (Katsiyannis et al., 2018). As mentioned earlier, parental substance use in the home following prison—and presumably untreated mental health issues—may significantly worsen children's states of well-being (Yaros et al., 2018), calling into question the extent to which this and other parent-level risks may be present for children in our study. In a previously published paper, we examined mental health and substance use issues in our sample of parents, most of which were untreated (see Milavetz et al., 2021). To measure these challenges, we used the Adult Self-Report (ASR), a standardized self-report questionnaire for adults aged 18 to 59 years that asks about behavioral, social, and emotional problems and strengths, including mental health, substance use, and adaptive functioning. Each problem item is rated 0 (not true), 1 (somewhat true), or 2 (very true), based on the past six months. Scores in the clinical range are higher than scores reported by 97 percent of the national normative sample (Rescorla & Achenbach, 2004). (See appendix B for more information on our measures).

We examined the frequency of jailed parents scoring in the clinical range and then calculated the probability of them experiencing significant mental health concerns relative to the ASR's standardization sample. Descriptively, depression and thought problems were the most commonly reported mental health problems, with 17 percent of jailed parents falling into a clinical range on the thought problems scale and 16 percent scoring in that range for depression. Indeed, jailed parents had significantly higher odds of mental health problems relative to the standardization sample for thought problems, depression, and attention deficit/hyperactivity disorder (ADHD), with 3.7 to 5.7 times the odds of normal rates of clinically significant symptoms. Additionally, 54.6 percent of jailed parents reported past or recent alcohol abuse, and 62.7 percent reported past or recent drug abuse. In short, our sample of incarcerated parents struggled significantly with both ongoing mental health issues and substance use—both known predictors of subsequent instability postrelease.

Approximately 53 percent of jailed parents (41 percent of fathers, 92 percent of mothers) self-reported prior mental health diagnoses, with depression and anxiety as the most common, followed by bipolar disorder, ADHD, and posttraumatic stress disorder. However, only 17.4 percent of the total sample indicated that they had received mental health treatment in the past. When asked about treatment for alcohol abuse and drug abuse, roughly two-thirds reported prior treatment but only 10 percent reported current treatment in the jail. Notably, incarcerated mothers reported more depression, anxiety, ADHD, and drug abuse than fathers. This warrants a particular level of support for mothers who are reintegrating into the household, especially.

While untreated mental health and substance use can potentially destabilize parents' ability to reintegrate into the community following jail, there are also developmental challenges potentially present. For instance, later in our interview with Damian, he looked somberly into our eyes as he recounted Katie telling him of some of Miley's challenges as of late, particularly her recent routine of pleading "We have to go find Da-Da!" almost daily. You can tell that this weighs heavily on Damian, making his upcoming release feel more urgent. What Damian is alluding to is an important point that contributes to variation in family reunification responses, which may depend upon the child's age and developmental skills. It may be that while younger children like Miley are confused about aspects of the separation (shown in her efforts to "go find Da-Da") and reunification, they are more inclined to welcome parents back into their lives with joy (Crandell-Williams & McEvoy, 2017). In contrast, older children may be more likely to feel resentful of their previously incarcerated parent, reluctant to accept their authority, and doubtful that they will remain in the community for good (McKay et al., 2018), perhaps due to previous instances of recidivism or breaking of trust (Yocum & Nash, 2011). Indeed, although rebuilding relationships with young children postrelease is not guaranteed to be easy, it may have many positive aspects. There is often difficulty in rebuilding strong attachments with children who are younger because relationships are contingent upon gatekeepers (Crandell-Williams & McEvoy, 2017), meaning that caregivers or co-parents hold the power to maintain or cut off relationships during the incarceration and oftentimes even after release. Damian feels fortunate that Katie is welcoming him back into Miley's life with open arms. Yet for fathers in opposite situations to Damian, who are perhaps nonresidential or do not have positive relationships with their children's mother or caregiver, being able to see their children postrelease and navigate this reunification process might be quite complicated. Once again we see how positive co-parenting relationships can affect children's well-being during and following parental incarceration, helping to facilitate resilience processes.

### Recidivism and Desistance for Incarcerated Parents

As made clear throughout this chapter, reentry is an ongoing process, and just because a parent is released does not necessarily mean they will stay home for good. As parents reintegrate back into the community, they may experience chronic ins and outs of incarceration—the frequency of such situations adversely complicates children's adjustment processes. Indeed, a study that examined this directly with nearly 550 kids within the first year and a half of their father's release found that stable reentry was associated with lessened problem behaviors postrelease, that each count of recidivism related to additional behavior challenges for children, and that each additional month that fathers remained in the community was associated with less behavior problems (Muentner, 2022). Additionally, instances of reincarceration have been found to be adversely associated with parent-child relationship quality and youth's mentalities toward the criminal legal system (Few-Demo & Arditti, 2014; Smith & Young, 2017).

Notably, once parents like Damian are released back to the community, their risk for recidivism remains high. Estimates from prison populations suggest that 68 percent recidivate within three years of release, 77 percent within five years, and 83 percent within nine years; one-third of recidivisms occur within the first six months of release and more than half by the end of that first year (Alper et al., 2018). Risk is not a certainty, however. Given structural and programmatic differences between prison and jail, recidivism data may vary significantly across these types of institutions. Though limited work has studied this in jail populations and thus statistics are overwhelmingly inconclusive, one study measured a return-to-incarceration rate of 36.7 percent within the first year after release from jail alone (Jung et al., 2010). Although we were unable to follow up with Miley, Katie, and Damian directly to see how the reunification processes played out for them due to the study design, we were able to administratively track instances of rearrest or reincarceration for Damian and the other parents in our study. With this incarceration being Damian's "20th-something" time behind bars, he knows the churning process all too intimately, but this is precisely what makes jail incarceration and recidivism data so unique and so important to study.

To look at this in our sample, we asked parents when we met with them in the jail if they had lived with their child right before coming to jail and if they planned to co-reside again after release. We also asked them if their child had visited them in jail and what their reunification plans were, recording responses as close to verbatim as possible. After this initial interview, we administratively tracked their current and subsequent cases in the following year by using the state's open-access circuit court system (with participants' permission), which contains public records of citations, convictions, and incarcerations, and used new convictions as a measure of recidivism. These findings are included in a recently published article that focuses on children with an incarcerated father (A. Thomas et al., 2022), as summarized below. Although study constraints prevented us from longitudinally assessing children's postrelease well-being, the findings describe some important aspects regarding what family life may have looked like for our participants once they left the jail and returned home.

We were able to find public information on 84 of the 86 parents a year after we did our home visits (we think that the remaining two parents may have been relocated). We found that more than one-third of the parents had reoffended. Almost 10 percent more had an open criminal case and about that same percentage were reincarcerated. Though fewer than half of parents successfully desisted from future criminal involvement, 44 percent remained on some type of community-based correctional oversight (parole or probation) within this first year, most of which included home monitoring with an ankle bracelet. In these instances, about half were related to the original conviction that brought them to jail when we first met with them, but the other half were related to new charges. The proportions were nearly identical for fathers and mothers who were originally incarcerated when we first met them.

For the group of Black incarcerated fathers, coauthor Julie Poehlmann—along with her colleagues Alvin Thomas from the University of Wisconsin-Madison and David Pate Jr. from the University of Wisconsin-Milwaukee—estimated a series of quantitative models to understand potential predictors of desistance in this year after jail (see A. Thomas et al., 2022). We found that parents who were employed at any point in the year prior to their time in jail more successfully reintegrated into the community and refrained from future rearrest and reincarceration. This may be because employment prior to incarceration makes it easier to find a job following release, thus creating prosocial networks, a supportive community, and additional means to support their parenting—all of which may ultimately reduce risk of recidivism. Additionally, parents who planned to live with their child following release and who had the highest level of contact with their kids while in jail were more likely to desist than those with lower levels of contact. However, planning to live with children postrelease versus planning to live elsewhere did not directly link to lower likelihoods of desistance. These initial results show that parents who overcome barriers to communication during the most difficult parts of incarceration may be more adept at successful reunification and reintegration processes postrelease. Based on qualitative analysis of interviews with incarcerated parents, we found that reuniting with their children provided an important motivation for desistance (A. Thomas et al., 2022).

In many ways, these findings complement what we know about reentry and recidivism in prison populations. Newly extending them to studies of parents departing jail, we now know that the ways in which jailed parents stay in contact with young children during incarceration depends largely on third-party adults (often the other parent, caregiver, or extended family). Thus, having positive, supportive family members is critical for postrelease outcomes, given how increased contact during jail increases opportunity for postrelease parental involvement. And even when parents do not plan to live with children postrelease, support from family can help manage parenting expectations, handle potential gatekeeping they face, and aid in their rebuilding of trust with children.

In many cases, this reintegration into family life is one of the most sought-after things parents looked forward to after their release. For many parents in these situations, these more mundane or routine opportunities for involvement are of top priority given the major milestones missed in children's lives while they were incarcerated and sadness over returning to find children developmentally different than when they left. Events such as birthdays, first steps or words, potty training, or initial enrollment in school are big and important milestones in young children's lives, and many incarcerated parents long to be a part of such milestones again. Those who miss these experiences because of incarceration may use it as personal encouragement to remain in the community, and thus in the child's life, following their release so as to never miss another celebration (Charles et al., 2019).

Based on our time spent with Damian and review of the administrative records, we know that he was one of those 44 percent of parents who were released on an electronic monitoring bracelet. Once released, he planned to return to home with Miley and Katie, in the same place he lived before he was arrested and incarcerated. Since this sentence, no new criminal records were opened against Damian in the year following his release. In fact, individuals who are released into the community and rejoin their families—like Damian—are less likely to recidivate than those who do not rejoin their families (Visher & Courtney, 2007). Formerly incarcerated individuals often report that family support is the most important thing keeping them out of prison; many add that seeing their children is the biggest reason for avoiding crime and rearrest (Visher & Courtney, 2007). Thus, attending to issues of family reunification when preparing parents for release from jail can not only help to set parents up for success, but also may bolster outcomes for young children now adjusting to life with their loved one back home.

## How Can We Help?

Throughout this chapter we demonstrate how collateral consequences of incarceration do not necessarily subside the moment a parent is released from jail. Rather, there are a significant number of challenges that await children once parents come home. These findings point to two ways in which we can help families involved in the criminal legal system and ease reunification processes, first by funding reentry support services and second by advocating for alternatives to incarceration.

### Reentry Support Services

On the practice front, perhaps the most direct way to combat adversity that children experience postrelease is to adequately prepare parents and children for and continue to assist them upon release. The primary goal of any institution's reentry planning should be to stabilize individuals in preparation for release; however, minimal services exist and availability is inconsistent, especially in jails. Ideally, reentry planning begins at the time of intake or admission and extends as a continuum of support after a parent returns to the community to promote long-term postrelease success. This reintegration planning typically includes, at a minimum, an individualized assessment and a recording of primary needs upon release, including anticipating problems that may occur outside the institution. With specific attention to children in mind, sending parents out of prison or jail with a plan that leverages the support of families may have positive consequences for all members of the system. Including children's needs in a parent's reentry plan would help anticipate and intervene on potential adjustment challenges. Advocating that state and federal Department of Corrections provide these formalized services may better promote equity and postrelease success for all individuals under their supervision.

Once the parent is back in the community, it may prove advantageous to offer a continuum of care to both the parent and their children. Such care would mean continuing intervention and prevention services parents were receiving while incarcerated but now in a community-based setting, including children as is appropriate. At a minimum, the state Department of Corrections or local jail could provide all exiting individuals with a release handbook listing community resources. Ideally, however, this continuum of care would directly connect parents with the necessary services and programming that attend to identified needs in the individualized reentry plan. There is also an urgency for multifaceted support for released parents that bolsters socioeconomic, social, and self-care needs but, importantly, has a family focus. Commonly referred to as multimodal, these services cater to the diversity of needs across these domains and not only have the potential to strengthen the development of parenting skills but also may reduce contextual challenges that induce challenges for children. Practice strategies that recognize the importance of multimodal services will be more likely to strengthen a family across all spheres, improve a returning parent's chance of success, and attend to children's needs.

*Advocating for Alternatives to Incarceration*

Shifts toward rehabilitation are embedded in nearly all proposals for criminal legal system reform, many of which include pushes to "decarcerate" or even abolish correctional facilities altogether. Overall, expanding access to services that increase one's likelihood of postrelease success in employment, housing, education, and substance abuse and mental health treatment is a key pillar of rehabilitative approaches that begin to redress disparities among those who have been incarcerated. Such strategies may have the added potential to improve outcomes for children whose parents are involved in the system. For instance, since recidivism postrelease is linked to children's socioemotional problems, a parent's access to rehabilitative services that strengthen their capacity for postrelease success would serve to benefit children, as well as parents, and thus society. As the field continues to rewrite policy that lessens its reliance on institutions, reduces sentence length, and defers to alternatives to incarceration, it not only takes steps toward abolishing detrimental components of the criminal legal system but also fosters an incarcerated individual's potential, the consequences of which likely affect the family unit and ease children's adjustment processes.

Increased policy attention has more recently been placed on alternatives to incarceration for parents involved in the criminal legal system, specifically. While these distinct programs have yet to be rigorously tested for effectiveness, many show initial promise for fiscal responsibility and humanitarian focus. Probation (community-based supervision often in lieu of incarceration) stands as the most used and well-known alternative to incarceration; yet its structural barriers may elevate risk for revocation and reincarceration, which ultimately induces risk for child and family well-being and parent-child relationships. That said, because this form of legal system oversight is less expensive and allows for greater family and community engagement, well-supported probation may be a mutually beneficial option for parents and children compared to incarceration. Alternatively, community-based services—such as drug treatment or in-/out-patient mental health programs—may directly intervene on parental hardship and household dysfunction with positive spillovers for children, and certain states serve as models for what this can look like for parents. For example, the state of Washington has enacted both the Family and Offender Sentencing Alternative and the Community Parenting Alternative (Washington State Department of Corrections, n.d.), which make certain parents eligible for mandated treatment programming by way of either community supervision or co-residence with an approved sponsor—both of which open up the door to more involvement with children (relative to involvement during incarceration). These policy levers may mitigate against the adversity that children experience when a parent is incarcerated and reduce challenges with reunification processes postrelease, since parents largely remain in the community for their rehabilitative treatment.

CHAPTER 8

# Opportunities for Growth

RESILIENCE AND ITS IMPLICATIONS
FOR INTERVENTION AND POLICY

AT THE BEGINNING OF THIS BOOK, we defined resilience as the process of developing competence and positively adapting despite experiencing significant risks, including the strengths that each child and family hold on to or develop despite the challenges associated with having an incarcerated parent. In the chapters that followed, we opened the doors to the lives of seven children and their families to see how they were balancing their various individual, family, and community assets with newfound and ongoing hardship. Take, for instance, Lincoln, who was introduced in chapter 1: despite his recent move into a new home and his mom's mental health issues, he found respite and support in his relationship with his sister. This form of deep connection and social support is an aspect of resilience. Chapter 4 introduced Jasmyne, whose health concerns, delayed development, and recent regressions were troublesome to her parents, but the undeniably strong relationship between her and her mom, along with the dedicated support of her dad, created a space for Jasmyne to ultimately thrive. These relational and involvement factors contribute to Jasmyne's resilience. And, finally, recall Meekah's positive temperament and family support while visiting with her dad in jail, which was detailed in chapter 6. This opportunity for constructive and affirmative contact with her incarcerated father aids in her coping, ultimately bolstering elements of resilience.

We saw these indisputable processes in every single child, caregiver, and incarcerated parent that we met over the course of our study. These characteristics fall within the concentric resilience model of children with parents involved in the carceral system that was introduced in chapter 1. Each strength maps on to contexts emphasized herein, spanning individual child-level attributes, dyadic and family relationships, proximal contexts within nearby environments, and community and system qualities which shape the world in which a child lives and grows. In our study, we note significant diversity in children's ability to thrive despite any number of risks and hardships.

That is, across the various levels of influence described in the conceptual model, children experience multiple co-occurring networks that can bring challenges but also opportunities for growth and resilience.

### Resilient Families, Resilient Kids

By now we have made it clear that the findings from our study contribute to a body of research suggesting that, on average, parental incarceration harms children (see, e.g., Wakefield & Wildeman, 2018). Nearly across the board, this is the answer to a question that has been posed over the past decade mostly by sociologists but recently by a multidisciplinary field of scholars, practitioners, and advocates. The small proportion of children who may benefit from a parent's incarceration are those who have experienced maltreatment or severe parental substance abuse (Poehlmann-Tynan & Turney, 2021). For the most part, children who have experienced the incarceration of a parent are exposed to a host of disadvantages and risks for negative outcomes compared to their peers who have never experienced parental incarceration (see, e.g., Poehlmann-Tynan & Turney, 2021; Turney & Haskins, 2019). Thus, parental incarceration undoubtedly increases children's risk for a number of deleterious outcomes at the population level, as we have seen in our study.

Increased risk is not equivalent to certainty, however. Although children with incarcerated parents may be twice as likely to develop behavior problems or five times more likely to experience other trauma than children who have not experienced parental incarceration, many if not most children—as we saw with Lincoln, Jasmyne, and Meekah—develop competencies and thrive despite the risks. *That* is resilience. Each child and family unit comes with their own unique set of strengths and challenges—arising from within the family or outside of it—that may make them more or less at risk for instability, more or less adept at employing coping strategies, more or less likely to live in a supportive context, or some combination thereof. Carlos's family, introduced in chapter 5, provides him with close, positive relationships: his mom, his aunt and uncle, and his grandparents all help support him financially, and they all live under the same roof. Carlos has a dad who is willing to talk to him openly about his incarceration; and his family and school provide opportunities for bilingual language development. All of these factors support Carlos's growth and well-being as he copes with the stress and sadness he feels because he is separated from his dad, evidenced by his elevated behavioral and emotional problems relative to his peers who may not be experiencing such adversity.

Recognizing and trying to understand the full range of adaptation to parental incarceration helps us learn from families who are doing well so we can apply that knowledge to help children and families who are not doing as well. This lens offers a personal perspective on how losing a parent to incarceration, even if it is temporary, may affect individual children and their families, thereby creating space to see particular families who have contact with the criminal legal system within the wider context of on-average research trends.

A strengths-based resilience perspective provides evidence for the ways in which children overcome adversity and function well despite challenges and disruption in their lives. Oftentimes caregiving quality and self-regulation are thought of as uniquely powerful resources and assets to children who experience adversity, including children of incarcerated parents (Masten, 2014). This can be seen in Miley's family (chapter 7), as she is growing up in a safe environment that gives her room to play and grow in a supported way. When caregivers provide a safe and loving environment, demonstrate parental involvement and supervision, and offer high-quality family interactions along with open communication, children exhibit more positive outcomes. Likewise, children who employ more successful self-regulation strategies embody resilient characteristics that are missed by focusing primarily on deleterious outcomes.

The current study incorporated a number of measures that assess risk and uncover protective and promotive factors, including coded recordings of sensitive parenting interactions with children, positive home environments, supportive interactions with extended family and friends, and indications of child self-regulation, along with available resources in communities. These indicators provided evidence as to how the children we met illustrate variations in resilience. With these families as examples of how children can be supported to thrive, strengths within (and outside of) families affected by parental incarceration are presented in ways that most of the literature rarely discusses. Providing evidence of self-regulation, high-quality caregiving environments, supportive extended families and communities, and other aspects of family life that contribute to strength and resilience processes uncovers potential targets for interventions to bolster when promoting the well-being of children with incarcerated parents.

To situate patterns of resilience for children presented in the case studies in this book, we created a series of outcome profiles to compare indicators of resilience processes. (Please note that we did not include Lincoln in these maps because he only appeared in chapter 1 and thus readers did not get a chance to learn more about his family nor specifics about his coping amidst the range of child outcomes.) Children's scores across a broad set of measures (detailed further in appendix B) were compared against the sample's mean to map out where each child falls relative to the rest of our sample, further depicting areas of strength (i.e., resilience) and areas of risk. Figure 8.1 details how children like Meekah, Carlos, and Miley are resilient on one,

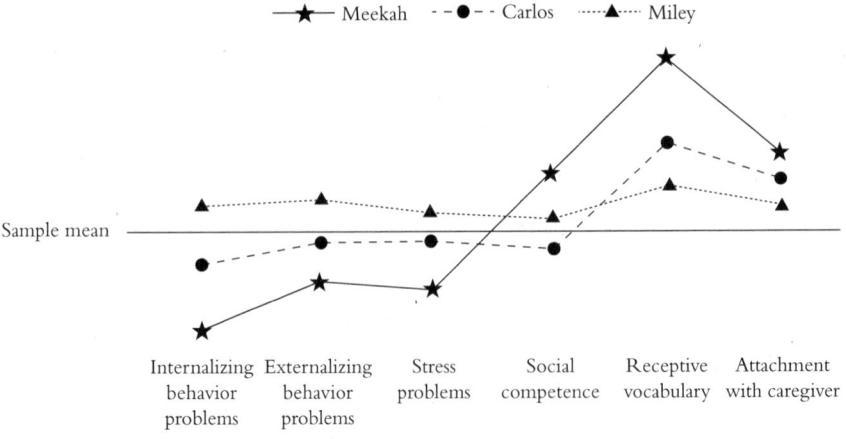

Figure 8.1. Children demonstrating strongly resilient profiles (above).

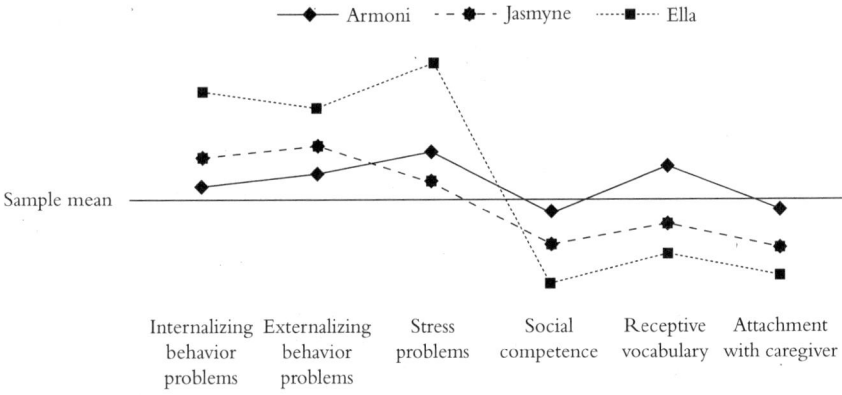

Figure 8.2. Children demonstrating "at risk" profiles (above).

many, or all of the measures that we used. Figure 8.2 includes scores from the children who, like Ella, Armoni, and Jasmyne, appear to be struggling across several or all areas that we measured. In these figures, the items toward the left, including internalizing and externalizing behavior problems and stress problems, are negative indicators of resilience. That is, when such problems are low, children are more likely to be exhibiting resilience. In the figures, the items toward the right, including social competence, receptive vocabulary, and secure attachments with caregivers, are considered positive indicators of resilience. This means that when such scores are high—reflecting more social competence, higher than average vocabulary, and secure attachments—children are more likely to exhibit resilience.

Resilience in children can be examined in at least two different ways: (1) looking at groups of children (a "person-focused" resilience analysis) and

(2) looking at how different variables relate to each other across families (a "variable-focused" resilience analysis). In her dissertation, Cynthia Burnson (2016) conducted both types of analyses to examine resilience in children with incarcerated parents in our study. In chapter 3, when discussing children's family relationships, we presented the "variable-focused" analysis that identified high quality caregiver-child interactions as a key protective factor, or buffer, for children with jailed parents.

For the "person-focused" analysis, Burnson identified three groups of children based on their level of behavior problems and social competence. To create the groups, scores were calculated for children based on (a) whether or not they exhibited borderline clinical or clinical levels of total behavior problems on a standardized behavior checklist (the Child Behavior Checklist; Achenbach & Rescorla, 2000, 2007) and (b) whether or not they scored in the top third of the sample in social competence. Of the 86 children in the study, 28 had low levels of behavior problems (less than subclinical) and high social competence (top third of the sample) and were therefore considered resilient. The 22 children who had high behavior problems (subclinical or clinical levels) and lower social competence (bottom third) were considered "at risk." The 36 other children were the "middle" group. Meekah is one of the children who falls in the resilient group (figure 8.1) because she shows few behavior problems and a high level of social competence, evident in how her mom spoke so highly of her ability to share and play with other children at school, her politeness with her brother, and positive interactions with family members. We saw this at the jail visit, too. She kept a calm demeanor, despite visits being potentially confusing or stressful for young children, as well as a respectfully playful demeanor with her brother in the visiting area; she also showed secure attachment behaviors with her mom at home and during the visit, going through security procedures and waiting, having the visit, and then saying goodbye to her father.

For the children presented in the case studies, Meekah is actually the only one who falls within this top "resilient" category. In fact, the majority of children (like Carlos, Miley, and Armoni) fall into what Burnson conceptualizes as the middle group. That leads to Jasmyne, whose health problems and developmental delays amount to cumulative disadvantage, and Ella, whose poor attachment processes and significant aggression and other behavior problems fall into the most "at risk" category. For the children in the middle group, many of their characteristics leave them teetering between aspects that reflect how they are truly thriving in addition to the areas that may situate them at higher risk levels. So, while some children show more resilience in the area of behavior problems, like Miley, or in vocabulary, like Carlos, other kids tend to struggle across the board. The areas where children struggle are precisely the realms that intervention and prevention services should target. Take, for instance, Armoni—with whom we met only a hand-ful of weeks after the traumatic experience of witnessing his mom's arrest (detailed in chapter 2). Despite having higher vocabulary skills than most kids in our study, in addition to amazing drawing skills, he also has heightened stress and elevated behavior problems (figure 8.2). Trauma-informed services that capitalize on his learning, language skills, and creativity while targeting his socioemotional concerns would serve to more holistically foster aspects of resilience. Or consider Jasmyne, whose low vocabulary and social compe-tence scores come coupled with close-to-average internalizing behavior prob-lems, even with the loving and supportive care that her mother gives her. Given her frequent doctor's appointments, screening tools could be utilized to identify developmental needs and appropriate interventions to improve her learning outcomes, capitalizing on her strong emotional bandwidth and generally positive relationship with her mother, potentially bolstering her resilience.

To emphasize factors that are associated with the functioning of the resil-ient group, Burnson dichotomized group membership into "resilient" and "not resilient" (the latter comprising both the "at risk" and "middle" groups) and analyses were conducted to examine what factors were associated with group membership. A model was constructed by entering control variables like who the child's caregiver was (e.g., grandparent, mother, etc.), the child's age and gender, their jailed parent's and caregiver's gender and race, as well as any instances of previous caregiving disruption (such as separations from care-givers); four risk variables (caregiver parenting stress, stressful life events, poor co-parenting alliance, and low caregiver education and income); and two pro-tective factors: high-quality caregiver-child interaction as measured by the Early Relational Assessment (ERA; Clark, 1999) subscales and child effortful control, a type of temperament-based behavior also referred to as emerging self-regulation. Effortful control is a child's ability to suppress an impulsive response in order to exhibit a more appropriate or controlled response, and it can reflect a child's temperament and early self-regulation abilities (Rothbart et al., 1994). Studies conducted with other children have shown that effortful control is an important factor in school success in addition to contributing to a child's developing regulation of emotions and attention. For example, among young children attending Head Start, effortful control and the inhibi-tory aspect of executive function measured in preschool related to math ability and letter knowledge during kindergarten (Blair & Razza, 2007). In addition, Valiente et al. (2008) found that effortful control was positively related to school grades and negatively related to school absences among children aged 7 to 12 years.

Our results indicated that the two protective factors and a risk variable predicted who was in the resilient group: a caregiver-child interaction subscale and child effortful control on the positive side, and level of caregiver perceived parenting stress on the negative side. For every standard deviation decrease in observed caregiver negative affect and behavior in the home, children were 3.5 times more likely to be resilient. For each one standard deviation increase in child effortful control ratings, children were more than three times as likely to be considered resilient. In contrast, caregiver perceived parenting stress significantly predicted non-resilient group status; for each one standard deviation increase in the caregiver parenting stress scale, children were 0.61 times less likely to be considered resilient. None of the control variables significantly predicted resilience in this group of children with incarcerated parents.

What these models demonstrate, then, is how children who have supportive and positive caregivers who are also less stressed out—as well as those children who have more positive self-regulation skills—are more likely to be resilient. Again, consider Meekah, who demonstrated these trends. She showed significant self-soothing tendencies in addition to having a mother who cares for her endlessly and feels supported in her own right (e.g., having Carla's help in transporting them to the jail for the visit and offering additional childcare helps to reduce Jade's parenting stress). Meekah's parents worked together to facilitate visits and co-parenting was not a significant source of parenting stress either. Conversely, consider Ella, who falls into the most "at risk" level of resilience of any child introduced throughout the book. Her heightened behavior problems may reflect her challenges with self-regulation and effortful control that, when coupled with frequent changes in her caregiving situation that result in a less involved parental figure and a family arrangement full of stress, significantly reduce resilience processes. The constant conflict between Ella's parents also contributes to parenting stress.

In young children with jailed parents, children who are on a developmental pathway toward resilience like Carlos and Miley are those who show more regulated behavior and attention, who get along with others including family members and peers, and who have repeatedly experienced positive interactions with their caregivers in the home. These two children may not be adjusting and coping as seemingly exceptionally as Meekah, but they demonstrate significant resilience across many domains—impressive outcomes considering the circumstances.

Often the processes that affect and are reflected in families are also reflected in children: in other words, resilient families are often raising resilient kids. As detailed in chapter 5, many caregivers have overcome obstacles to engage in positive parenting and sensitive responsive interactions with children in their care despite the financial hardship, residential instability, stigma, and lack of support that ensue following the incarceration of a co-parent. For example, Jasmyne's mother Tanisha overcame the experience of her own father's incarceration to be an involved, positive, and sensitive mother, although she struggles with open communication regarding her partner's incarceration, as detailed in chapter 4. She also engages in positive co-parenting with Jasmyne's father, which helps maintain harmony and feelings of security in the home. The resilient caregivers have fostered secure attachments with children in their care so that the children can internalize positive family relationships and environments, as we saw with Miley (chapter 7). In our home observations, the many educational toys and countless books that her mom Katie made accessible for her were increasingly evident. This likely plays into the higher receptive vocabulary scores Miley achieved compared to some of the other children we got to know. Resilient incarcerated parents take advantage of opportunities to learn and stay in touch with their children during their incarceration, as was the case for Miley's family, and to leave substance abuse and alcoholism behind, just as Miley's dad Damian was striving to do, thereby staying on a positive path following release into the community. As they grow older, the children who have parents with these protective qualities and behaviors are more likely to do well academically and socially, and they are also more likely to stay healthy and cope with stress better (Masten, 2014). Resilient families also recognize when children need assistance and seek out supports and services, such as Jasmyne's family's regular use of health services and Carlos's family's participation in dual-language learning education. However, we also recognize that there are many barriers to getting services and supports for children in need, as well as their caregivers, such as living in an area where such resources are not readily available.

## How to Help More Children with Incarcerated Parents Opportunities to Develop Resilience

More children with incarcerated parents need opportunities and support to develop resilience as they grow up. Indeed, preventing the negative effects of parental incarceration on young children is urgently needed in several areas related to parental jail incarceration. In the previous chapters, we have provided findings that argue for the importance of (1) protecting children during parental arrest; (2) supporting caregivers of children during parental incarceration, especially in the areas of poverty prevention, parenting, and mental health; (3) supporting children so that they can have positive family relationships during parental incarceration, including secure attachments with their caregivers and positive contact with their incarcerated parents; and (4) facilitating reintegration, reentry, and family reunification for incarcerated parents and their families.

**Protecting children during parental arrest.** Although there are protocols developed by law enforcement for safeguarding children during parental arrest, they are often not applied or only applied in limited circumstances. Because of young children's proximity to their parents in daily life, young children are likely to be exposed to parental crime and arrest, with potentially devastating consequences. This book documents trauma exposure in young children exposed to parental arrest, including extreme distress and blunted cortisol reactivity that may have lasting effects on children's developing brains. Implementing model safeguarding practices that are customized by local law enforcement is one way to protect children and ensure that fewer children are traumatized by witnessing the arrest of a parent. If children are traumatized by witnessing a parent's arrest, it is important to help them heal. Connecting them to mental health professionals and providing support at home and in school are good ways to help children recover from potentially traumatic experiences.

**Supporting caregivers of children during parental incarceration, especially in the areas of poverty prevention, parenting, and mental health.** When a parent goes to jail or prison, children's caregivers are responsible for child and family well-being, including economic factors, physical environment and safety, emotional context, and educational facets of family life. Positive caregiving environments for young children during parental incarceration are essential. However, very few interventions exist for caregivers of children with incarcerated parents. Once a family experiences parental incarceration, they may be eligible for poverty prevention efforts and benefits (e.g., food stamps, support for childcare, work programs, etc.), but many families do not know this, and others are stressed beyond capacity. Additional efforts are needed to help connect families to tangible resources in their communities. Moreover, additional programs are needed to help at-home caregivers with parenting and mental health (including substance misuse) during the parental incarceration period so that caregivers can foster child well-being to the best of their ability.

**Supporting children so that they can have positive family relationships during parental incarceration, including secure attachments with their caregivers and positive contact with their incarcerated parents.** Corrections and community programs that work together to provide child-friendly visits and other forms of positive family relationship connections are critical for family relationships and children's emotional well-being during parental incarceration. Parenting programs for caregivers are rare but could facilitate positive family relationships (Makariev & Shaver, 2010), such as the Strengthening Families program (A. L. Miller et al., 2013, 2014) or attachment-based interventions such as the Circle of Security (Cassidy et al., 2010), Attachment and Biobehavioral Catchup (Dozier & Bernard,

2017), or Triple P: Positive Parenting Program (Sanders, 2008; R. Thomas & Zimmer-Gembeck, 2007) interventions. More access to these programs is essential for the well-being of children affected by parental incarceration. Young children internalize their family environments, and provision of positive home and family environments is a key method for promoting resilience in children affected by parental incarceration. Learning how to talk with young children about parental incarceration is important as well, and Sesame Workshop's Little Children, Big Challenges: Incarceration initiative can help in this area. The materials are available online or in the app store for free and they have been rigorously evaluated.

**Facilitating reentry and family reunification for incarcerated parents.** Finally, although most efforts regarding supporting incarcerated parents in corrections have focused on offering parenting classes in prisons, we argue that increased emphasis on reentry and family reunification is needed, especially in jails because it is the most common form of incarceration. Such programming, when implemented during and following a jail incarceration, may prevent longer incarcerations and the type of "parental churning" in and out of jail that is often experienced by families involved in the criminal legal system. When children experience repeated separations from their parents and caregivers, it can stress their developing systems too much and make them vulnerable for developing problems with health, mental health, and learning. Assisting with reentry from jail, during community supervision, and with the process of family reunification may be protective for young children.

Taken together, the chapters in this book augment a burgeoning literature on the collateral consequences of parental incarceration for children. The exploration of a rich mixed method dataset with young children and families impacted by incarceration, and a deep-dive case study approach provides a multidimensional and holistic perspective that hopefully impacts how the reader sees young children in vulnerable families. We hope that this book provides you with a crucial foundation for understanding individual-level, family-level, and community-level risk and resilience processes that may serve as points of policy or practice intervention moving forward. Indeed, providing a humanizing perspective to families caught up in the carceral system sends a call out to policy makers, practitioners, and researchers to understand how children and parents may be aligned with or differ from aggregate trends, which can result in more effective intervention and prevention strategies. Indeed, over-focus on the on-average trends can dismiss the heterogeneity of children, experiences, and contexts surrounding parental incarceration. An approach rooted in dignity and self-determination provides one effective response for those who want to support children's well-being and allows for equitable treatment of those who bear the brunt of the unintended consequences of mass incarceration and the unequal distribution of disadvantage that plagues the U.S. criminal system.

Researchers, practitioners, and policy makers using a resilience framework to understand and help children with incarcerated parents must work toward the complementary goals of promoting resilience processes in children in addition to preventing the risk of having an incarcerated parent in the first place. Uniquely situated to address some of the pressing needs of children with incarcerated parents, a developmental resilience perspective highlights important areas for intervention at multiple levels. However, challenges remain.

Working with children affected by parental incarceration can be difficult, both when doing interventions and when doing research. We must improve methodological sophistication and develop a full range of evidence-based interventions for children and their families, as well as strong advocacy efforts. Beyond methodological sophistication, we simply lack a data infrastructure that allows us to track parental status as they move in and out of the criminal legal system (although such efforts could have unintended surveillance effects if not thoughtfully designed). Yet the positives often outweigh the disadvantages of learning about vulnerable kids, and thus we conclude with what the children in our study have taught us: a resilience perspective remains a compelling and compassionate approach for researchers, interventionists, and policy-makers regarding young children affected by their parent's incarceration. Together we can try to address some of young children's difficult questions with open communication, compassion, and care, such as when they ask their incarcerated parents "When are you coming home?"

# Study Methods

## SAMPLE

Although the seven families presented in this book provide insight into the experiences of young children who have experienced parental incarceration, it is also important to examine the experiences of a larger group of children and families. To gain a more holistic perspective of the situation, we interviewed a total of 165 jailed parents with children aged 2–6 years of age. In addition, 86 children and their caregivers participated in the study. Of the 165 jailed parents who participated in the study, 140 (84.8 percent) identified as fathers, and 25 (15.2 percent) identified as mothers; the proportion of men and women was consistent with estimates for jails across the United States (Zeng & Minton, 2021). Consistent with statistics on racial disparities in mass incarceration (Wakefield & Wildeman, 2013), 45.7 percent of jailed parents indicated that they were Black, 33.9 percent White, 7.4 percent Latino, and 13 percent multiple or other races. Incarcerated parents ranged in age from 18 to 49 years, with a mean of 29 years (SD = 5.83). More than one-third of jailed parents had the equivalent of a high school diploma, and another third continued their education after high school. About one-quarter had less than a high school education. Most individuals were employed prior to their current incarceration, and nearly half received public assistance. Almost all jailed parents had been arrested before ($n$ = 155, 96.9 percent). The average length of the time that the jailed participants had spent in jail for their current incarceration was just over two months (SD = 153.4 days). Jailed parents were incarcerated for drug-related charges (15 percent), probation violations (21 percent), battery/violence (13 percent), nonpayment of child support (15 percent), domestic dispute/domestic violence (17 percent), DUI or DWI (11 percent), and other crimes (theft, property damage) (8 percent). The majority of parents lived with their children prior to the current incarceration. Eighty percent of jailed parents reported recent drug abuse and 55 percent reported recent alcohol abuse, with incarcerated mothers scoring higher than incarcerated fathers on the number of days using drugs and tobacco but not alcohol.

Children's caregivers in the sample—the adults who cared for children on a day-to-day basis in the community—were primarily women (93 percent), and the majority were the child's mother ($n = 64$, 79 percent), with other relations including fathers ($n = 4$, 4.7 percent), grandmothers ($n = 10$, 11.6 percent), and other extended family members ($n = 3$, 3.6 percent). Those in the caregiver sample had higher levels of education than the incarcerated parents; 80 percent of caregivers reported high school graduation or more education. The majority of caregivers were White ($n = 42$, 48.8 percent), and roughly one-third were Black ($n = 33$, 38.4 percent). More than half of the caregivers were currently employed and most were receiving public assistance.

Focal children ranged from two to six years of age, with an average of four years (SD = 1.31). Children in this age range were selected because they are among the most common group of children affected by parental incarceration (Glaze & Maruschak, 2008; Murphey & Cooper, 2015). Moreover, it is an important time for families to influence children's development, especially as children who experience parental incarceration when they are young appear to be particularly affected as they grow older (Poehlmann-Tynan & Turney, 2021). Of the children studied, 42 (48.8 percent) were boys and 44 (51.2 percent) were girls. Thirty-three children were Black, 24 White, 10 were Latinx, and 19 were of mixed or other race(s).

Of the 165 jailed parents in the study, 86 (52 percent) caregivers of their children completed home visits, 33 (20 percent) refused, 44 (27 percent) were unable to be contacted, and 3 (2 percent) were ineligible for various reasons (e.g., they lived in another state, jailed parent was not the parent of the child). Reasons for caregivers' refusal included a lack of time, wanting to "put it all behind them," and anger toward the jailed parent. Caregivers who were unable to be contacted had disconnected phones, did not respond to voicemails or mailings, or the jailed parent was unable to provide complete contact information for them. The caregiver participation rate of 52 percent is comparable to other studies of children with an incarcerated parent and a previous study of children with jailed parents (48 percent; Dallaire & Wilson, 2010) but slightly lower than a study of children with imprisoned mothers (63 percent; Poehlmann, 2005b).

In order to examine whether child and caregiver participation was associated with any jailed parent variables, a series of analyses were conducted. Jailed parents of children who participated in the study did not differ from those whose children did not participate on parent race, age, gender, education, type of offense, whether or not the parent was employed prior to incarceration, whether this was the parent's first arrest or first incarceration, whether the child lived with the jailed parent prior to incarceration, child age, or child gender. However, children with jailed fathers were more likely to participate in the study compared to children with jailed mothers, and children who participated were more likely to visit their jailed parents than children who did not participate.

## STUDY DESCRIPTION AND PROCEDURES

All of the parents, children, and families in this book come from a mixed-methods short-term longitudinal study that sought to explore the extent to which having a parent in jail impacts young children and family well-being. The study was funded by the Eunice Kennedy Shriver National Institute of Child Health and Human Development (protocol: Young Children of Jailed Parents, R21HD068581, 1/05/2012–12/31/2016, Principal Investigator Julie Poehlmann). The study and all of its procedures and measures were approved by the University of Wisconsin-Madison's Institutional Review Board (protocol: Young Children of Jailed Parents, SE-2010-0812) and a National Institutes of Health Certificate of Confidentiality was used. We also complied with the ethical codes of the Society for Research in Child Development and the American Psychological Association.

Three jails participated in this research study, which occurred from 2012 to 2016 in a Midwestern state. The first jail is located in a large urban community with racial disparities in arrest and incarceration rates. Although 86 percent of people in the county are White, approximately half of the jail inmates are Black; for example, of the total 9,276 inmates who spent time in the county jail in 2012, 47 percent were Black. The facility has an 823-bed capacity, with an average daily population of 788 inmates (79 percent men and 21 percent women). At the time of our study, visits occurred through a Plexiglas barrier in a secure section of the jail or through video visitation in a nonsecure section of the jail.

The second jail is located in an urban community and holds a mix of individuals from urban and rural locations. The jail holds 972 beds total (754 beds for men and 188 beds for women). In the year of 2015, the jail population was 52,229 men (30 percent Black and 47 percent White—although 21 percent of the data was missing) and 14,144 women (37 percent Black, and 61 percent White). At the time of our study, visits occurred through a Plexiglas barrier in a secure section of the jail or through face-to-face visitation in a secure section of the jail, or in a nonsecure section of the jail-diversion housing unit.

The third jail is located in a rural county. The jail has a 458-bed capacity, and in 2009 the jail had a daily count of 277 inmates (90 percent men, 10 percent women), although the daily count declined during the study period. During the study period, visits occurred through closed circuit TV in a nonsecure part of the jail. This third location was ultimately dropped from recruitment due to low numbers of intake soon after the recruitment efforts were initiated in the study. All three jail systems that participated in this research were run by county sheriff's departments. The sheriff's departments were in charge of both law enforcement and jails in their counties.

Recruitment efforts began with the jailed parent. Research staff consulted with jail administrators to identify potential participants for interviews, based on jail intake data (parental status and child age were added to the jail intake form for the purposes of this study). Identified incarcerated individuals then participated in a brief initial screening with a trained researcher to determine if they met research criteria indicating that they (1) were at least 18 years old, (2) had a child who lived with kin within the county in which the inmate was serving time (or an adjacent county), (3) had retained legal rights to the child and had not committed a crime against the child, (4) had cared for the child at least part of the time prior to incarceration, (5) could understand and read English, and (6) had already been sentenced to serve jail time or were accused of committing a misdemeanor crime that would result in jail (rather than prison) time. If the incarcerated individual had more than one child in the age range, one child was randomly selected for participation in the study (termed "focal child").

If an incarcerated individual met the eligibility criteria, the researcher described the procedures in detail to them and read aloud all sections of the consent forms, ultimately asking for and answering any questions they had about the study. The consent form indicated that participation is voluntary and could be ended without any negative consequences at any time. It also said that the participants could skip any questions that make them uncomfortable and that the research had no effect on their sentence or parole eligibility. Because of potential literacy issues, the consent forms were written at a fifth-grade reading level, and the jailed parents were asked to sign for their own participation in an interview.

Eligible incarcerated parents were interviewed in a private area within the cell block, with security staff stationed nearby, as agreed to by the jails. We asked jailed parents about their demographics (age, education, race/ethnicity, number of children, preincarceration employment), children's living arrangements prior to and following incarceration (i.e., caregiving stability), children's experience of incarcerated-related events (e.g., witnessing the parent's crime, arrest, sentencing), and previous and current contact with children and children's caregivers. We also administered a picture vocabulary test to assess jailed parents' receptive vocabulary, and self-report questionnaires focusing on alcohol and substance use prior to incarceration, adult mental health problems, the child's developmental status, and the parent-caregiver relationship.

During interviews with jailed parents, researchers also asked the incarcerated individual for the contact information of the child's caregiver; to sign a consent form for the child's participation and for the observed jail visit; to sign release forms to contact the child's caregiver; and to send a questionnaire to the child's teacher or day-care provider. Because of jail regulations, we were unable to compensate jailed parents for their participation in the study. Following the interview, researchers looked up jailed parents' length of sentence, current offense, and number of prior arrests and incarcerations on the Public Records of the Consolidated Court Automation Programs (CCAP) database. The vast majority of records are available to the public (except juvenile offenses, which are not available in CCAP).

Children's caregivers were then contacted by telephone, letter, or in person, depending on what information the incarcerated parent provided. We felt as though it was important to keep each of these options open for this population because of reasons such as frequent telephone disconnections and residential relocations. Once in touch, the study was described by the researcher using a script. If the caregiver was interested in participating in the study, a home visit was scheduled in addition to a jail visit observation, if possible. In the home, the caregiver was described the study in detail (the consent form was read out loud to them because of potential literacy issues). The consent form, again written at a fifth-grade reading level, stated that participation in the research was voluntary and that they may withdraw at any time with no negative consequences. The consent form also stated that caregivers may skip answering any questions that make them uncomfortable. Finally, children were asked to give verbal assent because of their young age.

At least two researchers conducted each home visit, which typically lasted about three hours, sometimes longer. One researcher interviewed the caregiver and the other assessed the child, with additional research team members offering childcare supervision as needed for other children in the home. This was to ensure that children did not overhear sensitive material about their parent's incarceration and were provided adequate supervision and high-quality care. One researcher conducted an interview with the caregiver to assess the quality of the home environment, the child's and caregiver's contact with the jailed parent, children's living arrangements prior to and following the parent's incarceration (i.e., caregiving stability), and the child's experience of incarceration-related events. Self-report questionnaires were also administered to caregivers to assess children's behaviors (in general and in response to visits at the jail) and the parent caregiver relationship. Because some caregivers may have had trouble reading the questionnaires due to literacy or eyesight issues, the researcher read aloud the items on questionnaires to the caregivers.

During this time, the other researcher conducted standardized assessments of the child's receptive vocabulary and cognitive skills in a different area of the home. The researchers then observed the caregiver and child interacting during a free play session. Additionally, researchers obtained a small hair sample from the children (about the size of the tip of a pencil) which was cut with stainless steel scissors from four sampling areas on the scalp within the child's posterior vertex to assess physiological stress hormones (i.e., cortisol and cortisone). Caregivers were paid $50 following the home visit and children were given an age-appropriate book.

In addition to the jailed parent interviews and home visits with caregivers and children, researchers inquired about the possibility of observing a jail visit. If agreed upon by both adults and scheduled, researchers collected data in the jail visiting areas. During the jail observations, which typically lasted about 30–90 minutes, caregivers completed a developmental screening and the child's visit with the jailed parent was observed and rated. Children were accompanied to the jail visit by their caregiver, whom the researchers met in the jail waiting area. After the caregiver completed the study forms, the researcher accompanied the caregiver and child to the visiting area. The observer was not able to hear or interact with the jailed parent, although the jailed parent knew that the observer was present and was previously provided written consent for this observation. The observer was able to see and hear the child, and thus focused on rating the child's experience of and emotional/behavioral reactions to the visit. Caregivers were paid $50 following the jail visit. Because we were not able to audio or video record in the jail, all of the information was handwritten in the form of a running record and the Jail-Prison Observation Checklist was completed (see Measures in appendix B).

Because participating children came from numerous school districts and childcare centers, preschool teachers and day-care providers were also contacted by mail rather than obtaining school district consent for each child. In the present study, we sent teachers an explanatory cover letter, a teacher consent form, a copy of the signed parental and caregiver releases, a child behavior questionnaire, and a stamped return address envelope. Teacher participation took about 15 minutes per child, and teachers received a $15 gift card in the mail once forms were received by the researchers. If the child was enrolled in the study during the summer, then we mailed materials to the previous year's teacher at the beginning of the next school year. Teachers were not informed that the child's parent was in jail; rather, for confidentiality purposes, teachers were simply told that the child was participating in research.

### Case Study Approach

In order to provide a multi-faceted understanding of parental incarceration, we paired our quantitative methodology with a case study mode of inquiry—a qualitative method for exploring individuals' experiences within multiple bounded systems (i.e., children and families affected by parental incarceration) through detailed, in-depth data collection (e.g., observations, interviews, audiovisual material, documents, and reports). The intent of presenting case studies is to ground our on-average, or quantitative, findings (that are presented throughout this book) in the lived experiences of children and families, providing a humanizing look into the experience of parental incarceration as it plays out in reality for different families. A hallmark of including case studies in this format is to understand the variability of effects that incarceration has for different children and families. Indeed, what may be a detrimental risk or challenge to family functioning in one case may be experienced as an opportunity for growth in another.

Within case study research, the process of approaching data analysis differs from selecting families for statistical analysis. In this situation, our case studies were bounded by families within our larger sample. Seven families were selected from the study on the basis of creating a diverse and data-rich subsample of both boys and girls across the entire age range of the study (ages 2–6), with both incarcerated fathers and mothers. We also made sure that we had all of the study data on the families, including jailed parent interviews, caregiver interviews, home visits, observations of play and caregiver-child interactions, child assessments, teacher reports, and jail visit observations. For each of the families chosen for case study analysis, we identified themes that represent particular aspects of parental incarceration, as highlighted in each chapter. In doing so, we applied two specific analytic approaches. First, we provided a rich description of each case and introduced readers to the context of these families, which is called within-case analysis. Second, throughout the book, we presented cross-case analyses to discuss assertions and interpretations of the meaning of the topic for each child and family. In this process, parental incarceration, its precursors, and its outcomes are unveiled through the eyes of those with lived experiences, a social justice–oriented approach that amplifies the voices of the participants in our study and emphasizes the dignity and worth of each person. The seven children and their families selected for our case study approach represent only a few perspectives on the real-life complexities that they, and the other 10 million U.S. children just like them, face in regard to parental incarceration. Please note that we use pseudonyms for the children and families and we changed certain demographic information and descriptions to protect their identities.

### Study Limitations

As with any study, our investigation has a number of important limitations that should be kept in mind when interpreting our findings.

We focused on a relatively small sample of children with jailed parents (not imprisoned parents). The sample is not nationally representative, and the study did not include children who did not experience the incarceration of a parent. A matched comparison group could have provided an opportunity to address questions about whether parental incarceration is potentially causally related to the outcomes that we observed in young children; however, many of the variables we examined would not have been relevant for a comparison group (e.g., child witnessing their parent's crime or arrest; child visiting their parent in a corrections setting). The young children in our study had experience living with the parent at some point prior to the parent's confinement in jail and hence the study is not generalizable to children in other circumstances.

Not all arrests lead to incarceration, and our study does not represent families that experienced arrest without incarceration. Further, our exclusion criteria prevented us from including incarcerated parents who were arrested for criminal charges against the child or the family. We collected a limited amount of information about the incarcerated parent's criminal arrest and criminal charges. Future research would ideally include measures aimed at exploring how one's criminal charges (i.e., violent vs. nonviolent) may or may not be associated with parent and child well-being. In addition, the incarcerated parents and children's caregivers who declined to participate in our study may have differed in significant ways from those that consented and ultimately participated in the study.

We set out to collect new data using unique measures and approaches that have only been used rarely or not at all in the existing literature on children of jailed parents. Our study utilized a unique approach to collecting data in that we had multiple informants contributing to our study. Many of the families had multiple adults involved in children's care, and we only interviewed one of the children's caregivers. Further, our study relied heavily on parent and caregiver report information, but we also supplemented this with reports from teachers or day-care providers as well as observations. It may have been challenging for incarcerated parents and caregivers to disclose some of the difficult aspects of their lives, given the structural constraints, stress, and stigma they may have been experiencing, so social desirability bias may have been present.

We were unable to assess preincarceration development and learning in children. We asked incarcerated parents and caregivers to rate various emotional symptoms within the last six months and the measure of physiological stress that we used captured stress across the past several months. Longitudinal panel designs with representative samples that begin prior to the parent's arrest are needed. Please see Wildeman et al. (2018) and Poehlmann-Tynan and Eddy (2019) for a more detailed description of our vision for future research on children with incarcerated parents and their families.

# Study Measures

A list of measures and their associated descriptions are included below, as organized by chapter and alphabetized therein. Table B.1 organizes each measure by respondent and methodology.

### CHAPTER 2

**Caregiver interview.** Caregivers were asked questions about both their own and their child's adjustment with incarceration-related experiences. Additionally, they offered their own background demographics (as well as that of their child) in addition to family-related characteristics, such as income, household structure, and communication with the incarcerated individual. Of particular relevance for this book, caregivers reported on children's witnessing and distress toward a parent's crime, arrest, and sentencing; previous care placements; health and developmental histories and concerns; what information was shared with children about the incarceration; any additional caregivers; and whether the child had visited or would visit the parent in jail. Data obtained via this instrument were either coded into quantitative variables or left as qualitative, depending on the nature of the question and the method of analysis.

**Child Behavior Checklist (CBCL).** Both jailed parents and caregivers reported on children's behavior problems over the last six months using either the preschool (1.5–5 years) or school-age (6–18 years) forms (Achenbach & Ruffle, 2000). Both forms contain a list of problem behaviors that adults rated on a three-point scale: not true (=0), somewhat or sometimes true (=1), or often or very true (=2). Responses map onto broadband scales used to reflect children's externalizing (1.5–5: Cronbach's $\alpha$ [hereafter called $\alpha$] = 0.94, 6–18: $\alpha$ = 0.94) and internalizing (1.5–5: $\alpha$ = 0.91; 6–18: $\alpha$ = 0.93) behavior problems, as well as subscales including stress-related (1.5–5: $\alpha$ = 0.79; 6–18: $\alpha$ = 0.91) behaviors. In previous studies, the CBCL has shown adequate internal consistency ($\alpha$ = 0.78–0.97) and has often been used with children of incarcerated parents (Craigie, 2011; Geller et al., 2009; Geller et al., 2012; Perry & Bright, 2012; Wildeman, 2010). To account for the difference in the

TABLE B.1
*Study measures by respondent and method*

| | Child | Caregiver | Jailed parent |
|---|---|---|---|
| **Observational** | ■ Attachment Q-Sort<br>■ Early Relational Assessment<br>■ Jail-Prison Observation Checklist | ■ Attachment Q-Sort<br>■ Early Relational Assessment<br>■ Home Observation for Measurement of the Environment<br>■ Jail-Prison Observation Checklist | ■ Jail-Prison Observation Checklist |
| **Direct assessment** | ■ Attachment Story Completion Task<br>■ Child Stress Hormones<br>■ Family drawings<br>■ Peabody Picture Vocabulary Test<br>■ Stanford Binet | | |
| **Participant report** | | ■ Caregiver interview<br>■ Center for Epidemiological Studies Depression<br>■ Child Behavior Checklist<br>■ Children's Behavior Questionnaire<br>■ Confusion, Hubbub, and Order Scale<br>■ Inventory of Family Feelings<br>■ Life Events–Short Form Questionnaire<br>■ Parenting Alliance Measure<br>■ Parents' Evaluation of Developmental Status: Developmental Milestones<br>■ Social Competence Scale | ■ Adult Self-Report<br>■ Child Behavior Checklist<br>■ Inventory of Family Feelings<br>■ Jailed parent interview<br>■ Parenting Alliance Measure<br>■ Residential Time–Line Follow-Back Inventory |
| **Administrative data** | | | ■ Court records |

number of problem behaviors listed on the two different forms, T-scores were used rather than raw scores in this study's analyses.

**Child stress hormones.** Children's scalp hair was analyzed for cortisol and cortisone concentrations, conceptualized as retrospective biomarkers of physiological stress hormone secretion over approximately three months (Stalder et al., 2012). Using a collection method created in collaboration with researchers at the University of Wisconsin-Madison's School of Human Ecology and colleagues at the Wisconsin National Primate Research Center, approximately one cubic centimeter was measured and divided into four sampling areas within the child's posterior vertex, the area of the scalp with the most consistent hair growth rates (Pragst & Balikova, 2006). Hair was measured and up to three centimeters most proximal to the scalp, cut with stainless steel scissors, and stored in aluminum foil at room temperature for analysis. The scissors are wiped with ethanol swabs before and immediately following each sample to diminish cross-contamination (Vaghri et al., 2013).

The hair samples were then assayed for cortisol and cortisone using a liquid chromatography-tandem mass spectrometry approach at the Wisconsin National Primate Research Center (Kapoor et al., 2014). Hair samples were placed into tubes and washed twice with 2-propanol. Solvent was collected from the wash steps to determine steroid loss before being dried, ground into a fine powder using a ball mill, and precisely weighed. These substances were then placed into a glass culture tube and stored in the dark at room temperature until extraction where methanol and internal standard was added to the tube of ground hair and incubated overnight. After incubation, the tubes were vortexed and centrifuged, and the supernatant was removed and run through solid-phase, followed by liquid-phase, extraction. The organic phase was placed in a clean test tube, evaporated to dryness and then resuspended in mobile phase. All samples were analyzed using a QTRAP 5500 quadrupole linear ion trap mass spectrometer (AB Sciex, Framingham, MA). Chromatographic separation was performed using a Kinetex C18 column (Phenomenex, Torrance, CA). All data were processed with Analyst software (AB Sciex). Intra- and inter-assay coefficients of variation for this method are 4.3 and 9.2 and 3.7 and 11.3 for cortisol and cortisone, respectively.

Although a relatively new method for assessing retrospective cumulative hormone secretion, evidence indicates acceptable validity and reliability (Stalder et al., 2012). Animal models reveal strong positive correlations between hair cortisol concentration and salivary cortisol, fecal samples, and salivary cortisol (Accorsi et al., 2008; Bennett & Hayssen, 2010; Davenport et al., 2006). In humans, validity studies have confirmed significant associations between these biomarkers and traditional methods of physiological stress measurement, such as saliva and urine (D'Anna-Hernandez et al., 2011; van Holland et al., 2012; Xie et al., 2011). Within adult samples, discriminant validity has been established in studies of adults (Manenschijn et al., 2012; Stalder et al., 2010; Thomson et al., 2010) and predictive validity with child samples (Palmer et al., 2013; Vaghri et al., 2013).

**Jailed parent interview.** Interviews were conducted with incarcerated parents in the jail. Jailed parents were asked about demographics, relationship status, family life, previous criminal activity, substance abuse, and previous trauma. Incarcerated parents also answered questions pertaining to their children, which included their demographic information, current living situation, details of parent-child contact, and concerns about the children. Additionally, they provided insight into their lives and those of their families both before and during the incarceration, including regarding children's exposure to their crime, arrest, or sentencing; visiting experiences; their own trauma histories; and details of their incarceration history (such as how many times, for how long, and in what setting). Responses were either coded into quantitative variables or left as qualitative data, depending on the nature of the question and analytic approach.

CHAPTER 3

**Attachment Story Completion Task (ASCT).** This attachment measure was designed to elicit responses reflecting the attachment relationship between a child and parental figure (Bretherton et al., 1990). It has proven effective for preschool and school-aged children, with successful assessment by researchers in home and lab environments (Goodman et al., 1998). The ASCT includes four increasingly stressful story prompts: (a) parental figure as authority (spilled juice), in which a child accidentally spills their juice at dinner; (b) parental figure as comforter (hurt knee), in which a child falls off a rock and hurts their knee while walking with his/her family in the park; (c) parental figure as protector (monster in bedroom), in which a child calls for the parental figure, thinking they saw a monster when going to bed; and (d) separation of the child from the parental figure as they leave for a trip and reunite the next day (separation-reunion). For the current study, we focused on the first three story stems.

Thematic codes drawn from previous coding manuals (e.g., Golby et al., 1995) and a review of the literature resulted in a coding scheme of the (a) content and (b) structure of children's narratives. Content codes include positive attachment or caregiving behaviors (e.g., hugging, kissing, close proximity, comforting; $\alpha = 0.77$), parental or family vulnerability (e.g., exposing figures to the possibility of being hurt; $\alpha = 0.89$), and violence (e.g., themes related to death, destruction, injury, or aggression; $\alpha = 0.85$). Structure/process codes include coherence (e.g., the story follows a logical progression with clear elements and characters; $\alpha = 0.73$), bizarre actions (e.g., uninterpretable behaviors; $\alpha = 0.75$), and family chaos (e.g., overall disorganization and representation of the family or home is random; $\alpha = 0.65$). After reviewing each of the three story stems, each content code domain was coded in a binary fashion and then summed so that children's scores ranged from 0 (present in none of the stems) to 3 (present in all of the stems). In the current study, interrater reliability ranged from 0.64 to 0.86, which is considered acceptable to high agreement.

**Attachment Q-Sort.** The Attachment Q-Sort, version 3.0, is an attachment measure that is based on observations of children typically aged 1–5 years but up to age 6 in special populations (Vaughn & Waters, 1990; Waters, 1995). The Q-Sort is an ipsative rather than a normative measure, meaning it captures how much a child engages in some behaviors compared to other possible behaviors (in contrast, a normative measure would compare an individual child's behaviors to that of other children's). With this method, researchers observe children naturally interacting with their caregivers or parents in the home for a range of attachment-related behaviors across 90 items (including secure base behaviors, safe haven behaviors, exploration, emotional responses, and social cognitions). These items are then sorted into a fixed distribution (10 piles of nine items) based on how much children engage in positive or negative attachment behaviors relative to other behaviors and then compared to a validated "ideally secure" profile (Waters & Deane, 1985). A security score is calculated as the correlation between the child's Q-profile and the Criterion Security Q-Sort (the composite of attachment experts' sorts). The Q-Sort has been found to be a reliable measure in other studies (Cadman et al., 2018; van IJzendoorn et al., 2004). In our lab, Q-Sort scores received an intraclass correlation coefficient of 0.72, reflecting good interrater reliability.

**Caregiver interview.** This measure is described in detail under Chapter 2 above.

**Early Relational Assessment (ERA).** In an effort to capture children's interactions with caregivers during play and structured tasks, we video recorded 15 minutes of caregiver-child play during home visits and coded the recordings with the ERA (Clark, 1985). The ERA is a global rating instrument used to capture positive (e.g., warm tone of voice, positive affect, cheerful mood, positive physical contact) and negative (e.g., hostile tone of voice, withdrawn mood, criticism, rigidity) behavioral and affective relationship quality in parent-child dyads. Sixty-five items comprise the ERA: 29 parent items that span 6 domains (i.e., tone of voice, affect, mood, attitudes, involvement, and parenting style); 28 child items across 4 domains (i.e., mood, behavioral abilities, activity level, communication); and 8 dyadic items that map onto 2 constructs (quality and mutuality of involvement). The ERA has demonstrated acceptable discriminant validity (Black et al., 1994; Teti et al., 1991).

In the present study, children and caregivers were given a standard bag of toys and instructed to play for 15 minutes while a researcher video recorded the interactions. Because of early terminated play and technical issues, only the first five minutes of play were used in coding. These segments were watched repeatedly and coded across the three domains covering all 65 items. Each item was rated on a five-point scale assessing interactional quality with 1–2 indicating an area of concern, 3 indicating an area of somewhat concern, and 4–5 indicating an area of strength. Interrater reliability was established at the subscale level, obtaining intraclass correlations of 0.70 or higher on 20 percent of the total sample with a master coder. Intraclass correlation coefficients ranged from 0.70 to 0.93, with a mean of 0.82. We used the ERA subscales originally validated by factor analysis—positive affective involvement and verbalization; negative affect and behavior; and intrusiveness, insensitivity, and inconsistency (Clark, 1985). Higher scores indicate more adaptive behavior across all subscales. Thus, for the subscales focusing on negative caregiving behavior, higher scores indicated higher-quality caregiving. Final subscales scores were averaged by dividing the composite score by the number of items in each subscale.

**Family drawings.** This attachment measure allows for the examination of parent-child relationships as displayed in the overall emotional tone of children's family drawings (Fury et al., 1997). During home visits, research assistants systematically laid out a standard set of eight colored markers and an 8.5″ × 11″ sheet of white paper and asked children to draw them any picture; this original illustration was used as a "warm up." Following this, the researcher laid out a fresh sheet of paper and asked the child to draw them a picture of their family, again using any color marker. Children were able to take their time and go into as much detail or structure as they chose to do. These procedures were followed again at the jail.

The research team then took the drawings back to the lab and coded them across eight dimensional categories using a seven-point scale ranging from 1 (extremely low) to 7 (extremely high). These categories include (1) vitality and creativity: elaboration and completeness of drawing including color, imagination and energy; (2) family pride and happiness: signs of positive emotion, completeness and organization of figures, and background detail; (3) vulnerability: size, proximity, and placement of figures in relationship to others, and exaggeration of body parts; (4) emotional distance and isolation: placement of child in relation to adult(s) and expression of emotion; (5) tension and anger: rigidity of figures, lack of color and background world, constricted figures; (6) role reversal: size distinction between adult(s) and child; (7) bizarreness and dissociation: presence or absence of unusual signs; morbid, dark, or aggressive quality; angry scribbling or facial features; and (8) global pathology: omissions, false starts, color and size of figures, rigidity or relaxed nature in the figures and completion of figures.

**Inventory of Family Feelings (IFF).** The IFF (Lowman, 1980) addresses interpersonal affect between family members. Consisting of 38 questions, the IFF asks about positive and negative feelings toward another family member currently. The IFF is well suited to address parent-child and parent-caregiver relationships and has been used previously in a variety of relationship contexts, including between incarcerated parents, at-home caregivers, and children (Poehlmann, 2005b; Poehlmann et al., 2008). Jailed parents and caregivers each completed the IFF in relation to each other and to the target child. In the current study, Cronbach's alpha for jailed parent's report was 0.796 and for caregivers it was 0.838.

**Life Events Questionnaire.** To measure stressful events that children experienced over the past year, caregivers completed the Life Events–Short Form Questionnaire (Herbers, 2011). Respondents reported Yes (=1) or No (=0) for 30 personal or family events, 24 of which were deemed potentially stressful or even traumatic ($\alpha = 0.69$). Example items include "The family was evicted from a house or apartment during this past year" and "During this past year a parent had trouble with alcohol or drugs." Results were then summed, with higher scores denoting more stressful events.

CHAPTER 4

**Caregiver interview.** This measure is described in detail under Chapter 2 above.

**CBCL.** This measure is described in detail under Chapter 2 above.

**Child stress hormones.** This measure is described in detail under Chapter 2 above.

**Life Events Questionnaire.** This measure is described in detail under Chapter 3 above.

**Parents' Evaluation of Developmental Status: Developmental Milestones (PEDS:DM).** The PEDS:DM (Glascoe et al., 2006) is a widely used screening measure for children's developmental milestones from birth to 11 years of age. This assessment allows for either parent report (in the context of young children) or direct administration to children (for those old enough to read and self-report) across 6–8 developmental milestones. These items span a number of developmental domains, including fine and gross motor skills, expressive and receptive language, self-help behaviors, and social-emotional skills. Respondents report whether or not children pass an item; not passing an item indicates difficulties in that domain, with cutoffs at the 16th percentile and below. Children are considered to have missed a developmental milestone if they do not pass one or more of the items on each scale. The PEDS:DM has sensitivity and specificity between 70 percent and 97 percent across ages and developmental domains, finding strong correlations with other standardized assessments and in diverse samples (Halle et al., 2011; Schmeer et al., 2020).

**Peabody Picture Vocabulary Test (PPVT).** The PPVT-4 (Dunn et al., 2003) measures the vocabulary of children and adults by evaluating comprehension of spoken words in standard English. In administering the test, researchers examine participants' achievement in acquiring vocabulary. The test consists of two parallel forms, each containing 228 test items with four full-color pictures arranged on a page. The 228 items in each form are grouped into 19 sets of 12 items and are arranged in order of increasing difficulty so that the examiner can easily administer only the sets appropriate for the examinee's vocabulary level. The PPVT-4 age norms are based on a representative sample of 3,540 people aged 2.5 years through 90 years and older from across the United States (Dunn et al., 2003). With its added items for the youngest ages and its ease of administration, the PPVT test is useful in assessing vocabulary in early childhood, an important indicator of a children's cognitive development and school readiness.

**Stanford Binet.** The Stanford Binet Intelligence Scale (Roid & Barram, 2004; Roid & Pomplun, 2012) is a widely used, individually administered standardized test of verbal and nonverbal cognitive skills for children aged from two years old up to adulthood. It focuses on children's developing cognitive capacities. In this study, five subsets were administered: vocabulary, comprehension, pattern analysis, copying, and memory for sentences. Children's responses were scored and then compared to composite values that have a mean of 100 and standard deviation of 16. The assessment is used in assessing developmental delays and cognitive disabilities and planning for interventions, including individual family and education plans.

CHAPTER 5

**Adult Self-Report (ASR).** Jailed parents and caregivers completed the ASR (Achenbach et al., 2003), a standardized self-report measure of mental and behavioral health questions that has been normed on samples of adults between the ages of 18 and 59. On this measure, respondents report on their own socioemotional and behavioral health in the previous six months, including mental health, substance use, adaptive function, and various strengths. They also report on elements of their personal life such as employment, education, and family relationships. Across each set of items, jailed parents and caregivers rated items on a scale of 0 to 2 (ranging from not true to very true). Scores reported in the 97th percentile or higher fall within the clinical range (Achenbach et al., 2003). Previous studies show high internal consistency for the ASR, with Cronbach's alphas of 0.93 and 0.89 for the internalizing and externalizing scores, respectively. In the present sample, the proportions of jailed parents falling at or above the clinical level for the internalizing and externalizing behavior composites were 10.8 percent and 10.8 percent, respectively, and for caregivers, 13.6 percent and 4.9 percent, respectively.

**Caregiver interview.** This measure is described in detail under Chapter 2 above.

**Center for Epidemiological Studies Depression (CESD).** This measure of adult depressive symptoms was administered to both caregivers and jailed parents. It contains 20 items that have been previously validated to measure distress and symptoms associated with depression, including lack of appetite, restless sleep, and feeling lonely. Across these questions, respondents report whether they experienced the symptoms rarely or none of the time (=0), some or little of the time (=1), or most or all of the time (=3) during the past week. Responses were then summed to create a range of depressive symptoms from 0 to 60. Previous research has found this scale to be validated in general and clinical populations (Radloff, 1977), and it yielded very good internal consistency (>.80) in this study as well.

**Confusion, Hubbub, and Order Scale (CHAOS).** Family disruption is determined by summing 21 items on the CHAOS scale (Evans et al., 2005; Matheny et al., 1995) and three items regarding caregiver instability (Vernon-Feagans et al., 2010), as reported by the caregiver themselves. Together these 24 items reflect three subscales: residential instability (e.g., number of changes in child's primary caregiver), lack of routine and ritual (e.g., "Target child does not go to bed at a regular time"); and environmental stimulation and confusion (e.g., "You can't hear yourself think in our home"). Each of these constructs has shown adequate reliability and/or validity in previous studies with $\alpha = 0.76$ for residential instability (Vernon-Feagans et al., 2010), $\alpha = 0.77$ for home routine and rituals (Evans et al., 2005), and $\alpha = 0.76-0.79$ for environmental stimulation and confusion (Bridgett et al., 2013; Matheny et al., 1995). Additionally, the constructs have been found to be significantly correlated with observer-rated measures of the physical home environment (e.g., noise and crowding) (Matheny et al., 1995). These trends hold in the current study as well, where summary indexes demonstrate sound internal consistency ($\alpha = 0.83$).

**Home Observation for Measurement of the Environment (HOME).** We evaluated the quality of the home environment by observing children when they were awake and interacting with others in caregivers' homes, as well as using a structured interview based on Caldwell and Bradley's (2001) HOME (Early Childhood version). The HOME is a standardized checklist, with each item scored in a binary fashion. It is designed to systematically assess a child's environment through both interviews and observations. We combined the items on the scale to create a total HOME score for each child ($\alpha = 0.85$). Two trained researchers independently coded the homes of 10 families in the study, with a mean of 0.87, reflecting high interrater reliability.

**Parenting Alliance Measure (PAM).** To measure perceptions of co-parenting and co-parenting relationship quality, parents and caregivers each completed the PAM (Abidin & Konold, 1999) in relation to each other. The PAM consists of 20 questions about the other person, regarding perceptions of the co-parent's relationship with the child, parenting style, the relationship between caregivers, and alignment between parenting styles. The PAM has been used previously with incarcerated fathers and mothers with minor children, with word changes to fit the context (e.g., replacing "child's other parent" with "child's caregiver") (Loper et al., 2014). Items are summed to calculate a total score. Higher scores indicate parenting alliances with more respect, communication, and teamwork, with scores of 20 or higher falling within the normal range, 19–15 within marginal, 14–6 within problematic, and scores less than 5 within the dysfunctional range. In this sample, Cronbach's alphas for the total sum score for jailed parent report and caregiver report were 0.947 and 0.955, respectively.

**Residential Time-Line Follow-Back (RTLFB) Inventory.** This measure was used to index jailed parents' autobiographical memory of housing instability in the year before jail, including their number of transitions, bouts of homelessness, and previous incarcerations (Tsemberis et al., 2007). In our interviews with jailed parents, we used an interviewing method that included a calendar and visual and verbal memory cues. Going through the 12 months leading up to the incarceration together on the calendar, the researcher asked the jailed parent to recall where their primary residence had been at biweekly intervals, highlighting transitions made from one form of residence to the next. At each transition, the incarcerated individual provided information about the living environment (house/apartment, incarceration, homeless, or recovery center), living arrangements (alone, with family, with roommates, with partner, with children), whether or not and how many of their children were with them, and the reason for leaving each living situation.

### Chapter 6

**CBCL.** This measure is described in detail under Chapter 4 above.

**Jailed parent interview.** This measure is described in detail under Chapter 2 above.

**Jail-Prison Observation Checklist (JPOC).** The JPOC is an observational rating scale for researchers to use in jail or prison settings starting from when a child enters the corrections facility for a visit until the time they leave. Codes for children's affect and behavior toward the incarcerated parent during the visit included visual attention, listening, verbal and nonverbal responding, avoiding, paying attention to other visits, happy, excited, loving, sad, angry, whining, fearful, confused, somber. In addition, codes for children's affect and behavior toward the caregiver during the visit included proximity seeking, sitting on lap, holding hands, clinging, avoiding, hitting or pushing, happy, excited, sad, angry, whining, fearful, confused, somber. Interrater reliability for items on the JPOC was established between two independent observers across 15 observed jail visits as part of the larger study. Interrater reliability (intraclass correlation coefficients) for Child's Affect and Behavior toward Incarcerated Parent during the Visit ranged from 0.65 to 1.0 (mean = 0.87), and Child's Affect and Attachment Behavior toward Caregiver during the Visit ranged from 0.65 to 1.0 (mean = 0.82).

# CHAPTER 7

**ASR.** This measure is described in detail under Chapter 5 above.

**Court records.** To track recidivism and desistance in our sample, we extracted publicly available court data from a Circuit Court Access system of criminal convictions and incarcerations. Jailed parents consented for our research team to follow along with their ongoing or subsequent legal involvement over the course of the year following the study. We used the publicly available database to look up parents at the time of study enrollment to determine their offense and then one year following their release from jail. We used new convictions as the measure of recidivism, coding the variable of desistance as 1 if they have a new or open case and recidivism as 0 if there were no new reports in the database following their release. In addition, we recorded new incarcerations and community supervision.

**Jailed parent interview.** This measure is described in detail under Chapter 2 above.

**Caregiver interview.** This measure is described in detail under Chapter 2 above.

**CBCL.** This measure is described in detail under Chapter 4 above.

**Children's Behavior Questionnaire-Very Short Form (CBQ).** As a measure of children's ability to self-regulate, we asked caregivers to complete the CBQ (Putnam & Rothbart, 2006; Rothbart et al., 2001). The current analyses rely on the effortful control scale from the form where caregivers rated children on a seven-point scale ranging from 1 (extremely untrue of your child) to 7 (extremely true of your child). In total, the CBQ consists of 36 items, 12 of which make up the effortful control scale from which the study draws. Example items include statements such as "My child is good at following instructions" or "[My child] sometimes becomes absorbed in a picture book and looks at it for a long time." Other studies have used the scale in samples of similar demographics (e.g., Harris et al., 2007) and internal consistency in the present study was good ($\alpha = 0.65$).

**ERA.** More information is detailed under Chapter 3 above.

**Jailed parent interview.** This measure is described in detail under Chapter 2 above.

**Social Competence Scale (SCS).** Caregivers completed the SCS to report on children's social competence across the domains of prosocial behaviors, self-control, and communication skills (Conduct Problems Prevention

Research Group, 1995). The instrument asks caregivers to rate 12 items on a five-point scale based on how well the item describes their child, ranging from "Not at All" to "Very Well." Sample items include "Your child shares things with others" and "Your child can calm down when excited or all wound up." The SCS has been used in children at high risk for behavior problems (Gouley et al., 2008) and internal consistency in the current study was good ($\alpha = 0.88$).

# Acknowledgments

This research was supported by a grant from the Eunice Kennedy Shriver National Institute of Child Health and Human Development (R21HD068581, Principal Investigator Julie Poehlmann) as well as a center grant from the National Institutes of Health (NIH) that funds the Waisman Center at the University of Wisconsin-Madison (P30HD03352, Principal Investigator was Marsha Mailick at the time of the study). The content is solely the responsibility of the authors and does not necessarily represent the official views of the NIH. Special thanks to participating counties' sheriff's offices and jail staff for their support of the project; to colleagues from University of Wisconsin-Extension for their work on the project; to numerous undergraduate students for assistance with data collection and coding; and to the families who participated in this research. The study was approved by the Institutional Review Board of the University of Wisconsin (Young Children of Jailed Parents; ID: SE-2010-0812) and an NIH Certificate of Confidentiality was used.

# Glossary

**Alternatives to incarceration.** After a conviction, sometimes a person is sentenced to a penalty that does not include being locked in prison or jail. This could include house arrest (i.e., wearing an ankle bracelet to monitor one's activity, often with the person only able to travel between home and work), community service, or community supervision.

**Ambiguous loss.** Pauline Boss introduced the concept of ambiguous loss in the 1970s to describe loss that is more confusing and open-ended than the usual experience, because there is no confirmation or certainty that the person will come back or return to their lives in the way they used to be. Scholars and professionals have applied this concept to families' experiences of losing someone to incarceration.

**Arrest.** When law enforcement agents apprehend a person and then take them into custody. This typically occurs because the individual is suspected of committing an act that breaks a law.

**Attachment.** In the child development literature, attachment is the relationship that forms between a child and an adult who cares for the child. It can also refer to the close emotional bond that forms between adults in intimate relationships.

**Caregiving.** In the child development literature, caregiving is the adult side of the child's attachment relationship. Adults form caregiving bonds with children in their care.

**Child-friendly visits.** Children's in-person visits with incarcerated parents are described as child-friendly when they meet certain criteria, including preparing children and adults for the visit, reducing security procedures when children enter the facility; allowing physical contact between children and parents throughout the visit; offering developmentally appropriate play, craft, and/or reading activities for children and their parents to engage in during the visit; allowing freedom of movement for children and parents in the space; having snacks or meals available for children and their parents to share together; having supportive staff dressed in plain clothes present; and facilitating positive parent–child contact between visits.

**Chronic stress.** When significant stressors occur repeatedly over time, they can lead children or adults to feel overwhelmed, negatively affecting health, development, and learning.

**Community supervision.** Community corrections offers programs that monitor people who have been convicted of crimes, the most common of which are probation and parole. People on community supervision are monitored in the community rather than spending time in prison or jail.

**Co-parenting.** When two or more people work together to raise a child. Co-parenting can occur when the people live together or when they do not live together.

**Coping.** Coping refers to how children and adults deal with the stressors in their lives.

**Cortisol.** Cortisol is a type of glucocorticoid hormone made by the adrenal cortex (on the top of the kidneys). Cortisol works with parts of the brain to regulate or control mood, motivation, and fear, and is involved in how we react to stressors.

**Cortisone.** Cortisone is another type of glucocorticoid hormone made by the adrenal cortex (on the top of the kidneys). It has a close relation to cortisol, as cortisone easily forms from or is converted to cortisol in the blood.

**Criminal legal system.** The criminal legal system is the entire process that occurs when someone is accused of or has committed a crime. We prefer to use the phrase "criminal legal system" rather than the "criminal justice system" because we think that the system is often unjust, and there is evidence that it is fraught with racial and economic disparities.

**Decarceration.** Decarceration is a movement to decrease the number of people in prison or jail, either by releasing people in custody or limiting who is sent to prison or jail.

**Department of Corrections.** A state or federal agency in the United States that is in charge of overseeing people who have been convicted of crimes.

**Desistance.** In the context of the criminal legal system, desistance refers to not committing crimes.

**Developmental delay.** A developmental delay occurs when a child does not meet expected developmental milestones.

**Developmental milestones.** We refer to skills such as reaching for objects, walking, saying first words, and pointing as developmental milestones. Children reach such milestones in their speaking, playing, learning, behaving, and moving as they grow older.

**Developmental regressions.** A reduction in ability or loss of a child's previously accomplished developmental milestone.

**Disparity.** A significantly differing, disproportionate, or unequal distribution of an experience for a certain group compared to another group or groups.

**Early intervention.** Supportive programs, policies, resources, or services that target a growing and developing child and their family, either early in life or at the forefront of an emerging issue or problem, often in the case of developmental concerns or with particularly vulnerable groups.

**Externalizing behaviors.** Reactions to situations or stressors that are exerted outward of oneself and toward one's environment, such as aggression, disobedience, defiance, and overactivity.

**Gatekeeping.** A relational response between a child's caregiver and parent such that the caregiver may control the child's access to the other person. This involves providing opportunities, limits, or possibly even cutting off the other parent's contact, communication, and information with the child.

**Hypercortisolism.** A rise or elevation in one's cortisol levels, often as a result of the body's response to stressful situations.

**Hypocortisolism.** The body's response to stress resulting in the production of an insufficient amount or otherwise dramatic reduction, depletion, or inactivation of cortisol levels, resulting in a "blunted stress response."

**Internalizing behaviors.** Attitudes, responses, or reactions that are directed inward toward oneself (as opposed to lashing out at others), such as anxiety, distress, withdrawal, depression, loneliness, guilt, or fear.

**Jail.** A locally operated correctional or carceral facility that is under the authority of a regional jurisdiction, such as a sheriff's office or city or county administrator or law enforcement agency. These institutions often hold people who are awaiting trial, conviction, or sentencing; people who are sentenced for one year or less for often nonviolent or misdemeanor offenses; people readmitted on probation, parole, or bail violations; or individuals who are awaiting transfer to a different institution.

**Mass incarceration.** The United States' current response to crime and punishment, which has resulted in skyrocketing rates of jailing and imprisonment.

Driven by policy change as opposed to upticks in crime, this period is also referred to as the prison boom, mass imprisonment, or hyperincarceration and began during the 1970s and remains ongoing in modern day.

**Meta Analysis.** A systematic review of existing research used to examine and describe that body of research as a whole.

**Parole.** A form of community supervision that allows an individual to be conditionally released from prison and serve the remainder of their sentence outside of an institution. This often occurs after an individual has completed a predetermined portion of their sentence or otherwise due to consistent compliance while incarcerated. Once released to the community, those on parole often regularly report to parole officers, fulfill specific conditions, adhere to rules of conduct, and pay certain fees.

**Plexiglas visit.** A form of noncontact visits at a correctional facility that takes place with an incarcerated individual separated from their visitors by a barrier, often a sheet of thick glass or plastic. This partition prevents physical touch and oftentimes requires individuals to communicate through listening and speaking devices that resemble a telephone receiver.

**Postrelease.** The period of time following jail or prison resulting from an individual's completed sentence (and thus exit to community life) or shift to community supervision. See also Reentry and Reintegration.

**Prison.** A long-term confinement facility, often either state or federally operated, which detains individuals serving sentences of greater than one year and oftentimes for more serious offenses, such as felony convictions.

**Probation.** A form of community supervision that is court ordered, oftentimes in the place of incarceration. Although some instances of probation include a short-term jail or prison sentence (i.e., a "split sentence"), this primarily community-based alternative often requires an individual to report regularly to a probation officer, comply with rules of conduct, and fulfill certain conditions (such as paying fines and fees, participating in treatment programs, undergoing regular drug testing, and/or seeking employment).

**Probation officer/Parole officer.** A staff member who supervises individuals who have been released from incarceration and are on a form of community supervision, such as probation or parole. This individual is responsible for supporting those previously or alternatively incarcerated throughout their release and ensuring they are meeting the conditions of their release, such as attending required programming. Colloquially referred to as a "P.O."

**Promotive factors.** In the child development literature, promotive factors are those behaviors or experiences that support positive child development across the vast majority of children.

**Protective factors.** In the child development literature, protective factors are those behaviors or experiences that support positive child development in the face of risk. An analogy is often used comparing protective factors to a seat belt—although it is present in a car, it is only activated when there is a negative event, like a fast stop or crash. Similarly, protective factors are often "activated" and become useful during adversity.

**Psychological stress.** Psychological stress refers to a mental or emotional state of reacting to adversity or stressors.

**Psychopathology.** In the child development literature, psychopathology refers to when children experience significant dysfunction in their emotions or behaviors. This is best understood in the context of typical child development.

**Qualitative research.** Qualitative studies focus on involve collecting and analyzing nonnumerical data to describe and understand patterns.

**Quantitative research.** Quantitative studies involve collecting and analyzing numerical data to understand patterns; the numerical data are used to calculate averages, make predictions, test relations among variables or groups, and generalize results to broader populations.

**Recidivism.** When an individual who is convicted of a crime and has served their sentence reengages in criminal activity or is arrested or incarcerated again, depending on the definition used.

**Reentry.** The process of an individual returning to the community after confinement; often referred to as reintegration.

**Rehabilitation.** In the criminal legal literature, rehabilitation refers to the process of removing an individual from their environment to stop criminal behavior while providing programing and training to improve overall safety and wellness.

**Reintegration** In the criminal legal field, reintegration refers to the process of reentering into the community. This process can include connecting individuals to resources such as programing and community services to ensure a successful reentry process, including reconnecting with family.

**Residential mobility.** The process of changing households or living arrangements.

**Resilience.** The process of developing competence despite significant adverse experiences.

**Revocation.** In the criminal legal literature, revocation refers to revoking or canceling a decision, such as one's probation or parole. Revocation can occur because of new criminal behavior or because of technical violations (such as not showing up for a P.O. appointment or fulfilling other technical requirements of probation or parole), which results in the person returning to confinement.

**Risk factors.** Characteristics that may increase vulnerability for negative experiences or outcomes.

**Self-regulation.** The act of modifying one's emotions, thoughts, and/or behavior, which begins to develop during the infancy and toddler period and continues throughout life.

**Sentencing.** The legal process of determining a person's punishment after they have been convicted of a crime.

**Standard deviation.** A statistical term used to describe a distribution or dispersion of values in relation to the average or mean.

**Stigma.** Social stigma is the disapproval of, or discrimination against, a person based on perceived characteristics (including social, physical, or psychological attributes).

**Toxic stress.** The body's response to prolonged stress without the ability for the body to recover.

# References

Abidin, R. R., & Konold, T. R. (1999). *PAM: Parenting Alliance Measure: Professional manual*. Psychological Assessment Resources.

Accorsi, P. A., Carloni, E., Valsecchi, P., Viggiani, R., Gamberoni, M., Tamanini, C., & Seren, E. (2008). Cortisol determination in hair and faeces from domestic cats and dogs. *General and Comparative Endocrinology, 155*(2), 398–402. https://doi.org/10.1016/j.ygcen.2007.07.002.

Achenbach, T. M., Dumenci, L., & Rescorla, L. A. (2003). *Ratings of relations between DSMIV diagnostic categories and items of the Adult Self-Report (ASR) and Adult Behavior Checklist (ABCL)*. https://aseba.org/wp-content/uploads/2019/02/dsm-adultratings.pdf.

Achenbach, T. M., & Rescorla, L. A. (2000). *Manual for the ASEBA preschool forms and profiles*. University of Vermont, Research Center for Children, Youth, & Families.

Achenbach, T. M., & Rescorla, L. A. (2007). Achenbach System of Empirically Based Assessment. *Mental Measurements Yearbook*. EBSCO. https://www.ebsco.com/products/research-databases/mental-measurements-yearbook.

Achenbach, T. M., & Rescorla, L. A. (2014). The Achenbach system of empirically based assessment (ASEBA) for ages 1.5 to 18 years. In *The use of psychological testing for treatment planning and outcomes assessment* (pp. 179–214). Routledge.

Achenbach, T. M., & Ruffle, T. M. (2000). The Child Behavior Checklist and related forms for assessing behavioral/emotional problems and competencies. *Pediatrics in Review, 21*(8), 265–271. https://doi.org/10.1542/pir.21.8.265.

Ainsworth, M. D. S., Blehar, M. C., Waters, E., & Wall, S. (1978). *Patterns of attachment: A psychological study of the strange situation*. Hillside. NJ: Erlbaum.

Alper, M., Durose, M. R., & Markman, J. (2018). *2018 update on prisoner recidivism: A 9-year follow-up period (2005–2014)*. NCJ 250975. U.S. Department of Justice, Office of Justice Programs, Bureau of Justice Statistics. https://bjs.ojp.gov/content/pub/pdf/18upr9yfup0514.pdf.

Anda, R. F., Felitti, V. J., Bremner, J. D., Walker, J. D., Whitfield, C. H., Perry, B. D., Dube, Sh. R., & Giles, W. H. (2006). The enduring effects of abuse and related adverse experiences in childhood. *European Archives of Psychiatry and Clinical Neuroscience, 256*(3), 174–186. https://doi.org/10.1007/s00406-005-0624-4.

Arditti, J. A. (2003) Locked doors and glass walls: Family visiting at a local jail. *Journal of Loss & Trauma, 8*(2), 115–138. https://doi.org/10.1080/15325020305864.

Arditti, J. A. (2012). Child trauma within the context of parental incarceration: A family process perspective. *Journal of Family Theory & Review, 4*(3), 181–219. https://doi.org/10.1111/j.1756-2589.2012.00128.x/.

Arditti, J. A. (2016). A family stress-proximal process model for understanding the effects of parental incarceration on children and their families. *Couple and Family Psychology: Research and Practice, 5*(2), 65. https://doi.org/10.1037/cfp0000058.

Arditti, J. A., Lambert-Shute, J., & Joest, K. (2003). Saturday morning at the jail: Implications of incarceration for families and children. *Family Relations, 52*(3), 195–204. https://doi.org/10.1111/j.1741-3729.2003.00195.x.

Arditti, J. A., & Parkman, T. (2011). Young men's reentry after incarceration: A developmental paradox. *Family Relations, 60*(2), 205–220. https://doi.org/10.1111/j.1741-3729.2010.00643.x.

Arditti, J. A., & Savla, J. (2015). Parental incarceration and child trauma symptoms in single caregiver homes. *Journal of Child and Family Studies, 24*(3), 551–561. https://doi.org/10.1007/s10826-013-9867-2.

Arditti, J. A., Smock, S. A., & Parkman, T. S. (2005). "It's been hard to be a father": A qualitative exploration of incarcerated fatherhood. *Fathering: A Journal of Theory, Research & Practice about Men as Fathers, 3*(3), 267–288. https://doi.org/10.3149/fth.0303.267.

Beck, A. J. (2006). *The importance of successful reentry to jail population growth.* Urban Institute Jail Reentry Roundtable.

Bennett, A., & Hayssen, V. (2010). Measuring cortisol in hair and saliva from dogs: Coat color and pigment differences. *Domestic Animal Endocrinology, 39*(3), 171–180. https://doi.org/10.1016/j.domaniend.2010.04.003.

Bevans, K., Cerbone, A., & Overstreet, S. (2008). Relations between recurrent trauma exposure and recent life stress and salivary cortisol among children. *Development and Psychopathology, 20*(1), 257–272. https://doi.org/10.1017/S0954579408000126.

Bevans, K., Cerbone, A. B., & Overstreet, S. (2009). The interactive effects of elevated midafternoon cortisol and trauma history on PTSD symptoms in children: A preliminary study. *Psychoneuroendocrinology, 34*(10), 1582–1585. https://doi.org/10.1016/j.psyneuen.2009.04.010.

Black, M. M., Hutcheson, J. J., Dubowitz, H., & Berenson-Howard, J. (1994). Parenting style and developmental status among children with nonorganic failure to thrive. *Journal of Pediatric Psychology, 19*(6), 689–707. https://doi.org/10.1093/jpepsy/19.6.689.

Blair, C., & Raver, C. C. (2016). Poverty, stress, and brain development: New directions for prevention and intervention. *Academic Pediatrics, 16*(3), S30–S36. https://doi.org/10.1016/j.acap.2016.01.010.

Blair, C., & Razza, R. P. (2007). Relating effortful control, executive function, and false belief understanding to emerging math and literacy ability in kindergarten. *Child Development, 78*(2), 647–663. https://doi.org/10.1111/j.1467-8624.2007.01019.x.

Bocknek, E. L., Sanderson, J., & Britner, P. A. (2009). Ambiguous loss and posttraumatic stress in school-age children of prisoners. *Journal of Child and Family Studies, 18*(3), 323–333. https://doi.org/10.1007/s10826-008-9233-y.

Boss, P. (2006). *Loss, trauma, and resilience: Therapeutic work with ambiguous loss.* W. W. Norton & Company.

Boss, P. (2007). Ambiguous loss theory: Challenges for scholars and practitioners. *Family Relations, 56*(2), 105–110. http://www.jstor.org/stable/4541653.

Boudin, C., Stutz, T., & Littman, A. (2013). Prison visitation policies: A fifty-state survey. *Yale L. & Pol'y Rev., 32*, 149. https://heinonline.org/HOL/P?h=hein.journals/yalpr32&i=154.

Bowlby, J. (1973). *Attachment and loss: Vol. 2. Separation.* Basic Books.

Bowlby, J. (1982). Attachment and loss: Retrospect and prospect. *American Journal of Orthopsychiatry, 52*(4), 664–678. https://doi.org/10.1111/j.1939-0025.1982.tb01456.x.

Bowlby, J. (1982). *Attachment and loss: Vol. 1. Attachment* (2nd ed.). Basic Books.

Braungart-Rieker, J., Courtney, S., & Garwood, M. M. (1999). Mother- and father-infant attachment: Families in context. *Journal of Family Psychology, 13*(4), 535–553. https://doi.org/10.1037/0893-3200.13.4.535.

Bretherton, I. (1985). Attachment theory: Retrospect and prospect. *Monographs of the Society for Research in Child Development, 50*(1–2), 3–35. https://doi.org/10.2307/3333824.

Bretherton, I. (1995). A communication perspective on attachment relationships and internal working models. *Monographs of the Society for Research in Child Development, 60*(2–3), 310–329. https://doi.org/10.2307/1166187.

Bretherton, I., Ridgeway, D., & Cassidy, J. (1990). Assessing internal working models of the attachment relationship: An attachment story completion task for 3-year-olds. In M. T. Greenberg, D. Cicchetti, & E. M. Cummings (Eds.), *Attachment in the preschool years: Theory, research, and intervention* (pp. 273–308). University of Chicago Press.

Bridgett, D. J., Burt, N. M., Laake, L. M., & Oddi, K. B. (2013). Maternal self-regulation, relationship adjustment, and home chaos: Contributions to infant negative emotionality. *Infant Behavior and Development, 36*(4), 534–547. https://doi.org/10.1016/j.infbeh.2013.04.004.

Bronfenbrenner, U., & Ceci, S. J. (1994). Nature-nurture reconceptualized in developmental perspective: A bioecological model. *Psychological Review, 101*(4), 568–586. https://doi.org/10.1037/0033-295x.101.4.568.

Brown, M., & Bloom, B. (2009). Reentry and renegotiating motherhood: Maternal identity and success on parole. *Crime & Delinquency, 55*(2), 313–336. doi:10.1177/0011128708330627.

Buckley, D. (2021). "Daddy, if I come see you, will I have to be locked up, too?" *The Marshall Project.* https://www.themarshallproject.org/2021/07/01/daddy-if-i-come-see-you-will-i-have-to-be-locked-up-too.

Burnson, C. (2016). *Resilience in young children of jailed parents* [Unpublished doctoral dissertation]. University of Wisconsin-Madison.

Cadman, T., Diamond, P. R., & Fearon, P. (2018). Reassessing the validity of the attachment Q-sort: An updated meta-analysis. *Infant and Child Development, 27*(1), e2034. https://doi.org/10.1002/icd.2034.

Caldwell, B. M., & Bradley, R. H. (2001). *HOME inventory and administration manual* (3rd ed.). University of Arkansas for Medical Sciences and University of Arkansas at Little Rock.

Carlson, E. A., Hostinar, C. E., Mliner, S. B., & Gunnar, M. R. (2014). The emergence of attachment following early social deprivation. *Development and Psychopathology, 26*(2), 479–489. https://doi.org/10.1017/S0954579414000078.

Carson, E. A. (2020). *Prisoners in 2019.* NCJ 255155. U.S. Department of Justice, Office of Justice Programs, Bureau of Justice Statistics. https://bjs.ojp.gov/content/pub/pdf/p19.pdf.

Cassidy, J., Ziv, Y., Stupica, B., Sherman, L. J., Butler, H., Karfgin, A., Cooper, G., Hoffman, K. T., & Powell, B. (2010). Enhancing attachment security in the infants of women in a jail-diversion program. *Attachment & Human Development, 12*(4), 333–353. https://doi.org/10.1080/14616730903416955.

Celinska, K., & Siegel, J. A. (2010). Mothers in trouble: Coping with actual or pending separation from children due to incarceration. *The Prison Journal, 90*(4), 447–474. doi:10.1177/0032885510382218.

Charles, P., Kerr, M., Wirth, J., Jensen, S., Massoglia, M., & Poehlmann-Tynan, J. (2021). Lessons from the field: Developing and implementing an intervention for jailed parents and their children. *Family Relations, 70*(1), 171–178. https://doi.org/10.1111/fare.12524.

Charles, P., Muentner, L., Jensen, S., Packard, C., Haimson, C., Eason, J., & Poehlmann-Tynan, J. (2021). Incarcerated during a pandemic: Implications of COVID-19 for jailed individuals and their families. *Corrections: Policy, Practice and Research.* https://doi.org/10.1080/23774657.2021.2011803.

Charles, P., Muentner, L., & Kjellstrand, J. (2019). Parenting and incarceration: Perspectives on father-child involvement during reentry from prison. *Social Service Review, 93*(2), 218–261. https://doi.org/10.1086/703446.

Christian, J. (2005). Riding the bus: Barriers to prison visitation and family management strategies. *Journal of Contemporary Criminal Justice, 21*(1), 31–48. https://doi.org/10.1177/1043986204271618.

Christian, J., Mellow, J., & Thomas, S. (2006). Social and economic implications of family connections to prisoners. *Journal of Criminal Justice, 34*(4), 443–452. https://doi.org/10.1016/j.jcrimjus.2006.05.010.

Clark, R. (1985). *The Parent-Child Early Relational Assessment (PCERA): Instrument and manual.* University of Wisconsin Medical School, Department of Psychiatry.

Clark, R. (1999). The parent-child early relational assessment: A factorial validity study. *Educational and Psychological Measurement, 59*(5), 821–846. https://doi.org/10.1177/00131649921970161.

Clark, R. (2015). *The Parent-Child Early Relational Assessment: Instrument and Manual.* University of Wisconsin Medical School, Madison.

Clark S., & Symons, D. (2000). A longitudinal study of Q-sort attachment security and self-processes at age five. *Infant and Child Development, 9,* 91–104. https://doi.org/10.1002/1522-7219(200006)9:2<91::AID-ICD218>3.0.CO;2-O.

Comfort, M. L. (2003). In the tube at San Quentin: The "secondary prisonization" of women visiting inmates. *Journal of Contemporary Ethnography, 32*(1), 77–107. https://doi.org/10.1177/0891241602238939.

Comfort, M. (2008). *Doing time together: Love and family in the shadow of prison.* University of Chicago Press.

Comfort, M., McKay, T., Landwehr, J., Kennedy, E., Lindquist, C., & Bir, A. (2016). The costs of incarceration for families of prisoners. International Review of the Red Cross, 98(903), 783–798. https://doi.org/10.1017/S1816383117000704.

Conduct Problems Prevention Research Group. (1995). Social Competence Scale (Parent Version) [Unpublished instrument].

Correa, N. P., Hayes, A. K., Bhalakia, A. M., Lopez, K. K., Cupit, T., Kwarteng-Amaning, V., Keefe, R. J., Greeley, C. S., & Van Horne, B. S. (2021). Parents' perspectives on the impact of their incarceration on children and families. *Family Relations, 70*(1), 162–170. https://doi.org/10.1111/fare.12529.

Costello, E. J., Angold, A., Burns, B. J., Stangl, D. K., Tweed, D. L., Erkanli, A., & Worthman, C. M. (1996). The Great Smoky Mountains Study of Youth: Goals, design, methods, and the prevalence of DSM-III-R disorders. *Archives of General Psychiatry, 53*(12), 1129–1136. https://doi.org/10.1001/archpsyc.1996.01830120067012.

Coyl, D. D., Roggman, L. A., & Newland, L. A. (2002). Stress, maternal depression, and negative mother–infant interactions in relation to infant attachment. *Infant Mental Health Journal, 23*(1–2), 145–163. https://doi.org/10.1002/imhj.10009.

Craigie, T.-A. L. (2011). The effect of paternal incarceration on early child behavioral problems: A racial comparison. *Journal of Ethnicity in Criminal Justice, 9*(3), 179–199. https://doi.org/10.1080/15377938.2011.594349.

Craigie, T.-A., Pratt, E., & McDaniel, M. (2018). Father reentry and child outcomes. Low-Income Working Families Initiative/Urban Institute.

Cramer, L., Goff, M., Peterson, B., & Sandstrom, H. (2017). Parent-child visiting practices in prisons and jails. Urban Institute.

Crandell-Williams, A., & McEvoy, A. (2017). Fathers on parole: Narratives from the margin. *Journal of Men's Studies, 25*(3), 262–277. https://doi.org/10.1177/10608265 16676840.

Dallaire, D. H., Ciccone, A., & Wilson, L. C. (2012). The family drawings of at-risk children: Concurrent relations with contact with incarcerated parents, caregiver behavior, and stress. *Attachment & Human Development, 14*(2), 161–183. https://doi .org/10.1080/14616734.2012.661232.

Dallaire, D. H., Shlafer, R. J., Goshin, L. S., Hollihan, A., Poehlmann-Tynan, J., Eddy, J. M., & Adalist-Estrin, A. (2021). COVID-19 and prison policies related to communication with family members. *Psychology, Public Policy, and Law, 27*(2), 231–241. https://doi.org/10.1037/law0000297.

Dallaire, D. H., & Wilson, L. C. (2010). The relation of exposure to parental criminal activity, arrest, and sentencing to children's maladjustment. *Journal of Child and Family Studies, 19*(4), 404–418. https://doi.org/10.1007/s10826-009-9311-9.

D'Anna-Hernandez, K. L., Ross, R. G., Natvig, C. L., & Laudenslager, M. L. (2011). Hair cortisol levels as a retrospective marker of hypothalamic–pituitary axis activity throughout pregnancy: Comparison to salivary cortisol. *Physiology & Behavior, 104*(2), 348–353. https://doi.org/10.1016/j.physbeh.2011.02.041.

Davenport, M. D., Tiefenbacher, S., Lutz, C. K., Novak, M. A., & Meyer, J. S. (2006). Analysis of endogenous cortisol concentrations in the hair of rhesus macaques. *General and Comparative Endocrinology, 147*(3), 255–261. https://doi.org/10.1016/j .ygcen.2006.01.005.

Davis, L., & Shlafer, R. J. (2017). Mental health of adolescents with currently and formerly incarcerated parents. *Journal of Adolescence, 54*(1), 120–134. https://doi .org/10.1016/j.adolescence.2016.10.006.

De Graaf, I., Speetjens, P., Smit, F., de Wolff, M., & Tavecchio, L. (2008). Effectiveness of the Triple P Positive Parenting Program on behavioral problems in children: A meta-analysis. *Behavior Modification, 32*(5), 714–735. https://doi.org/10 .1177/0145445508317134.

De Haan, B. D., Mienko, J. A., & Eddy, J. M. (2019). The interface of child welfare and parental criminal justice involvement: Policy and practice implications for the children of incarcerated parents. In J. M. Eddy & J. Poehlmann-Tynan (Eds.) *Handbook on Children with Incarcerated Parents* (2nd edition, pp. 279–294). Springer, Cham.

De Wolff, M. S., & van Ijzendoorn, M. H. (1997). Sensitivity and attachment: A meta-analysis on parental antecedents of infant attachment. *Child Development, 68*(4), 571–591. https://doi.org/10.1111/j.1467-8624.1997.tb04218.x.

Dowling, W. D. (1991). Learning disabilities among incarcerated males. *Journal of Correctional Education, 42*(4), 180–185.

Dozier, M., & Bernard, K. (2017). Attachment and biobehavioral catch-up: Addressing the needs of infants and toddlers exposed to inadequate or problematic caregiving. *Current Opinion in Psychology, 15*, 111–117. https://doi.org/10.1016/j.copsyc .2017.03.003.

Dunn, L. M., Dunn, D. M., & Bulheller, S. (2003). *Peabody Picture Vocabulary Test: PPVT.* Swets Test Services.

Durtschi, J. A., Soloski, K. L., & Kimmes, J. (2017). The dyadic effects of supportive coparenting and parental stress on relationship quality across the transition to parenthood. *Journal of Marital and Family Therapy*, *43*(2), 308–321. https://doi.org/10.1111/jmft.12194.

Duwe, G., & McNeeley, S. (2020). Just as good as the real thing? The effects of prison video visitation on recidivism. *Crime and Delinquency*. Advance online publication. https://doi.org/10.1177/0011128720943168.

Eddy, J. M., Kjellstrand, J. M., Martinez, C. R., Newton, R., Herrera, D., Wheeler, A., Shortt, J. W., Schumer, J. E., Burraston, B. O., & Lorber, M. F. (2019). Theory-based multimodal parenting intervention for incarcerated parents and their children. In J. M. Eddy & J. Poehlmann-Tynan (Eds.), *Handbook on children with incarcerated parents* (2nd ed., pp. 219–235). Springer. https://doi.org/10.1007/978-3-030-16707-3_15.

Eddy, J. M., Martinez, C. R., Schiffmann, T., Newton, R., Olin, L., Leve, L., . . . & Shortt, J. W. (2008). Development of a multisystemic parent management training intervention for incarcerated parents, their children and families. *Clinical Psychologist, 12*(3), 86–98. https://doi.org/10.1080/13284200802495461.

Eddy, J. M., & Poehlmann-Tynan, J. (Eds.). (2019). *Handbook on children with incarcerated parents* (2nd ed.). Springer. https://doi.org/10.1007/978-3-030-16707-3.

Eddy, J. M., Reid, J. B., & Fetrow, R. A. (2000). An elementary school-based prevention program targeting modifiable antecedents of youth delinquency and violence: Linking the Interests of Families and Teachers (LIFT). *Journal of Emotional and Behavioral Disorders*, *8*(3), 165–176. https://doi.org/10.1177/106342660000800304.

Enns, P. K., Yi, Y., Comfort, M., Goldman, A. W., Lee, H., Muller, C., Wakefield, S., Wang, E. A., & Wildeman, C. (2019). What percentage of Americans have ever had a family member incarcerated?: Evidence from the Family History of Incarceration Survey (FamHIS). *Socius: Sociological Research for a Dynamic World*, *5*, 237802311982933. https://doi.org/10.1177/2378023119829332.

Evans, G. W., Eckenrode, J., & Marcynyszyn, L. A. (2010). Chaos and the macrosetting: The role of poverty and socioeconomic status. In G. W. Evans & T. D. Wachs (Eds.), *Chaos and its influence on children's development: An ecological perspective* (pp. 225–238). American Psychological Association. https://doi.org/10.1037/12057-014.

Evans, G. W., Gonnella, C., Marcynyszyn, L. A., Gentile, L., & Salpekar, N. (2005). The role of chaos in poverty and children's socioemotional adjustment. *Psychological Science*, *16*(7), 560–565. https://doi.org/10.1111/j.0956-7976.2005.01575.x.

Fanning, K. (2018). Lighthouse in the storm: A comparative case study of challenges and resilience processes for children experiencing homelessness and parental incarceration. Unpublished master's thesis, University of Wisconsin-Madison.

Federal Bureau of Investigation (2020). 2019 crime in the United States. https://ucr.fbi.gov/crime-in-the-u.s/2019/crime-in-the-u.s.-2019/topic-pages/tables/table-29.

Felitti, V., Anda, R., Nordenberg, D., Williamson, D., Spitz, A., Edwards, V., & Marks, J. (1998). Childhood trauma tied to adult illness. *American Journal of Preventive Medicine*, *14*(6), 245–258. https://doi.org/10.1016/S0749-3797(98)00017-8.

Ferraro, K. F., Schafer, M. H., & Wilkinson, L. R. (2016). Childhood disadvantage and health problems in middle and later life: Early imprints on physical health? *American sociological review*, *81*(1), 107–133. doi:10.1177/0003122415619617.

Few-Demo, A. L., & Arditti, J. A. (2014). Relational vulnerabilities of incarcerated and reentry mothers: Therapeutic implications. *International Journal of Offender Therapy and Comparative Criminology*, *58*(11), 1297–1320. https://doi.org/10.1177/0306624X13495378.

Fontaine, J., Cramer, L., & Paddock, E. (2017). Encouraging Responsible Parenting among Fathers with Histories of Incarceration. Washington, DC: Urban Institute.

https://www.urban.org/sites/default/files/publication/89771/responsible
_parenting_brief_0.pdf.

Foster, H., & Hagan, J. (2007). Incarceration and intergenerational social exclusion. *Social Problems, 54*(4), 399–433. https://doi.org/10.1525/sp.2007.54.4.399.

Foster, H., & Hagan, J. (2009). The mass incarceration of parents in America: Issues of race/ethnicity, collateral damage to children, and prisoner reentry. *Annals of the American Academy of Political and Social Science, 623*(1), 179–194. https://doi.org/10.1177/0002716208331123.

Foster, H., & Hagan, J. (2017). Maternal imprisonment, economic marginality, and unmet health needs in early adulthood. *Preventive Medicine, 99*, 43–48. https://doi.org/10.1016/j.ypmed.2017.01.018.

Fury, G., Carlson, E. A., & Sroufe, A. (1997). Children's representations of attachment relationships in family drawings. *Child Development, 68*(6), 1154–1164. https://doi.org/10.2307/1132298.

Garavan, H., Bartsch, H., Conway, K., Decastro, A., Goldstein, R. Z., Heeringa, S., Jernigan, T., Potter, A., Thompson, W., & Zahs, D. (2018). Recruiting the ABCD sample: Design considerations and procedures. *Developmental Cognitive Neuroscience, 32*, 16–22. https://doi.org/10.1016/j.dcn.2018.04.004.

Geller, A., Cooper, C. E., Garfinkel, I., Schwartz-Soicher, O., & Mincy, R. B. (2012). Beyond absenteeism: Father incarceration and child development. *Demography, 49*(1), 49–76. https://doi.org/10.1007/s13524-011-0081-9.

Geller, A., & Curtis, M. A. (2011). A sort of homecoming: Incarceration and the housing security of urban men. *Social science research, 40*(4), 1196–1213. https://doi.org/10.1016/j.ssresearch.2011.03.008.

Geller, A., Garfinkel, I., Cooper, C. E., & Mincy, R. B. (2009). Parental incarceration and child well-being: Implications for urban families. *Social Science Quarterly, 90*(5), 1186–1202. https://doi.org/10.1111/j.1540-6237.2009.00653.x.

Ghandour, R. M., Jones, J. R., Lebrun-Harris, L. A., Minnaert, J., Blumberg, S. J., Fields, J., Bethell, C., & Kogan, M. D. (2018). The design and implementation of the 2016 National Survey of Children's Health. *Maternal and Child Health Journal, 22*(8), 1093–1102. https://doi.org/10.1007/s10995-018-2526-x.

Gifford, E. J., Eldred Kozecke, L., Golonka, M., Hill, S. N., Costello, E. J., Shanahan, L., & Copeland, W. E. (2019). Association of parental incarceration with psychiatric and functional outcomes of young adults. *JAMA Network Open, 2*(8), e1910005. https://doi.org/10.1001/jamanetworkopen.2019.10005.

Gjelsvik, A., Dumont, D. M., Nunn, A., & Rosen, D. L. (2014). Adverse childhood events: Incarceration of household members and health-related quality of life in adulthood. *Journal of Health Care for the Poor and Underserved, 25*(3), 1169–1182. https://doi.org/10.1353/hpu.2014.0112.

Glascoe, F. P., Macias, M. M., & Wegner, L. M. (2006). Screening in primary care: Validation of Parents' Evaluation of Developmental Status: Developmental Milestones (PEDS-DM). *Journal of Developmental & Behavioral Pediatrics, 27*(5), 446–447. https://doi.org/10.1097/00004703-200610000-00068.

Glaze, L. E., & Maruschak, L. M. (2008). Parents in prison and their minor children. NCJ 222984. U.S. Department of Justice, Office of Justice Programs, Bureau of Justice Statistics, Washington, D.C. https://bjs.ojp.gov/content/pub/pdf/pptmc.pdf.

Grinstead, O., Faigeles, B., Bancroft, C., & Zack, B. (2001). The financial cost of maintaining relationships with incarcerated African American men: A survey of women prison visitors. *Journal of African American Men, 6*, 59–69. https://www.jstor.org/stable/41819418.

Glaze, L. E., & Maruschak, L. M. (2016). *Parents in prison and their minor children.* NCJ 252645. U.S. Department of Justice, Office of Justice Programs, Bureau of Justice Statistics. https://bjs.ojp.gov/content/pub/pdf/pptmcspi16st.pdf.

Glick, J. E., King, V. & McHale, S. M. (Eds.) (2022). *Causes and consequences of parent-child separations: Pathways to resilience.* Springer. https://doi.org/10.1007/978-3-030-87759-0.

Golby, B., Bretherton, I., Winn, L., & Page, T. (1995). *Coding manual for the attachment story completion task* [Unpublished manuscript]. University of Wisconsin-Madison.

Goodman, G., Aber, J. L., Berlin, L., & Brooks-Gunn, J. (1998). The relations between maternal behaviors and urban preschool children's internal working models of attachment security. *Infant Mental Health Journal, 19*(4), 378–393. https://doi.org/10.1002/(SICI)1097-0355(199824)19:4<378::AID-IMHJ2>3.0.CO;2-J.

Gouley, K. K., Brotman, L. M., Huang, K. Y., & Shrout, P. E. (2008). Construct validation of the social competence scale in preschool-age children. *Social Development, 17*(2), 380–398. https://doi.org/10.1111/j.1467-9507.2007.00430.x.

Grieb, S.M.D., Crawford, A., Fields, J., Smith, H., Harris, R., & Matson, P. (2014). "The stress will kill you": Prisoner reentry as experienced by family members and the urgent need for support services. *Journal of Health Care for the Poor and Underserved, 25*(3), 1183–1200. https://doi.org/10.1353/hpu.2014.0118.

Hagan, J., & Foster, H. (2012). Children of the American prison generation: Student and school spillover effects of incarcerating mothers. *Law & Society Review, 46*(1), 37–69. https://doi.org/10.1111/j.1540-5893.2012.00472.x.

Hail-Jares, K., Vichta-Ohlsen, R., Butler, T., & Dunne, A. (2021). Psychological distress among young people who are couchsurfing: An exploratory analysis of correlated factors. *Journal of Social Distress and Homelessness*, 1–5. https://doi.org/10.1080/10530789.2021.1967647.

Hairston, C. F. (2007). Focus on children with incarcerated parents: An overview of the research literature. Annie E. Casey Foundation. https://repositories.lib.utexas.edu/bitstream/handle/2152/15158/aecasey_children_incparents.pdf?sequence=2.

Halle, T., Zaslow, M., Wessel, J., Moodie, S., & Darling-Churchill, K. (2011). *Understanding and choosing assessments and developmental screeners for young children ages 3–5: Profiles of selected measures.* OPRE Report No. 2011-23. U.S. Department of Health and Human Services, Administration for Children & Families.

Hanlon, T. E., Carswell, S. B., & Rose, M. (2007). Research on the caretaking of children of incarcerated parents: Findings and their service delivery implications. *Children and Youth Services Review, 29*(3), 348–362. https://doi.org/10.1016/j.childyouth.2006.09.001.

Harris, R. C., Robinson, J. B., Chang, F., & Burns, B. M. (2007). Characterizing preschool children's attention regulation in parent–child interactions: The roles of effortful control and motivation. *Journal of Applied Developmental Psychology, 28*(1), 25–39. https://doi.org/10.1016/j.appdev.2006.10.006.

Haskins, A. R. (2014). Unintended consequences: Effects of paternal incarceration on child school readiness and later special education placement. *Sociological Science, 1*, 141–158. https://doi.org/10.15195/v1.a11.

Haskins, A. R. (2016). Beyond boys' bad behavior: Paternal incarceration and cognitive development in middle childhood. *Social Forces, 95*(2), 861–892. https://doi.org/10.1093/sf/sow066.

Haskins, A. R., & McCauley, E. J. (2019). Casualties of context? Risk of cognitive, behavioral and physical health difficulties among children living in high-incarceration neighborhoods. *Journal of Public Health, 27*(2), 175–183. https://doi.org/10.1007/s10389-018-0942-4.

Heard-Garris, N., Winkelman, T. N., Choi, H., Miller, A. K., Kan, K., Shlafer, R., & Davis, M. M. (2018). Health care use and health behaviors among young adults with history of parental incarceration. *Pediatrics, 142*(3), e20174314. https://doi.org /10.1542/peds.2017-4314

Herbers, J. E. (2011). *Parent-child relationships in young homeless families: Co-regulation as a predictor of child self-regulation and school adjustment* [Unpublished doctoral dissertation]. University of Minnesota.

Hinton, A. R., & Hardin, L. L. (2018). *The sun does shine: How I found life and freedom on death row*. St. Martin's Press.

Hiolski, K., Eisenberg, M. E., & Shlafer, R. J. (2019). Youth self-reported health and their experience of parental incarceration. *Families, Systems, & Health, 37*(1), 38–45. https://doi.org/10.1037/fsh0000394.

Hirschi, T. (1969). The causes of delinquency. Berkeley: The University of California Press.

Hughes, T. A., & Wilson, D. J. (2003). *Reentry trends in the United States*. U.S. Department of Justice, Office of Justice Programs, Bureau of Justice Statistics. https://bjs .ojp.gov/content/pub/pdf/reentry.pdf.

International Association of Chiefs of Police. (2014). *Safeguarding children of arrested parents*. U.S. Department of Justice, Bureau of Justice Assistance. https://bja.ojp .gov/sites/g/files/xyckuh186/files/Publications/IACP-SafeguardingChildren.pdf.

Jackson, D. B., & Vaughn, M. G. (2017). Parental incarceration and child sleep and eating behaviors. *Journal of Pediatrics, 185*, 211–217. https://doi.org/10.1016/j.jpeds .2017.03.026.

Jacobsen, W. C. (2019). The intergenerational stability of punishment: Paternal incarceration and suspension or expulsion in elementary school. *Journal of Research in Crime and Delinquency, 56*(5), 651–693. https://doi.org/10.1177/0022427819829794.

Jaffee, S. R., McFarquhar, T., Stevens, S., Ouellet-Morin, I., Melhuish, E., & Belsky, J. (2015). Interactive effects of early and recent exposure to stressful contexts on cortisol reactivity in middle childhood. *Journal of Child Psychology and Psychiatry, 56*(2), 138–146. https://doi.org/10.1111/jcpp.12287.

Johnson, E. I., Planalp, E. M., & Poehlmann-Tynan, J. (2022). Parental arrest and child behavior: Differential role of executive functioning among racial subgroups. *Journal of Child and Family Studies*, 1–14. https://doi.org/10.15154/1520776.

Johnson, E. I., & Waldfogel, J. (2002). Parental incarceration: Recent trends and implications for child welfare. *Social Service Review, 76*(3), 460–479. https://doi.org /10.1086/341184

Johnson, R. C. (2009). Ever-increasing levels of parental incarceration and the consequences for children. In S. Raphael & M. A. Stoll (Eds.), *Do prisons make us safer? The benefits and costs of the prison boom* (pp. 177–206). Russell Sage Foundation.

Jung, H., Spjeldnes, S., & Yamatani, H. (2010). Recidivism and survival time: Racial disparity among jail ex-inmates. *Social Work Research, 34*(3), 181–189. https://doi .org/10.1093/swr/34.3.181.

Kaeble, D., & Alper, M. (2020). *Probation and parole in the United States, 2017–2018*. NCJ 252072. U.S. Department of Justice, Office of Justice Programs, Bureau of Justice Statistics. https://bjs.ojp.gov/content/pub/pdf/ppus1718.pdf.

Kaeble, D., & Cowhig, M. (2018). *Correctional populations in the United States, 2016*. NCJ 251211. U.S. Department of Justice, Office of Justice Programs, Bureau of Justice Statistics. https://bjs.ojp.gov/library/publications/correctional-populations -united-states-2016.

Kam, D. (2021, June 23) Plan to digitize prison mail sparks outcry among inmates' families, advocates. *Pensacola News Journal*. https://www.pnj.com/story/news/2021

/06/23/florida-prison-mail plan-sparks-outcry-among-inmates-families-advocates /5320779001/

Kampfner, C. J. (1995). Post-traumatic stress reactions in children of imprisoned mothers. In K. Gabel & D. Johnston (Eds.), *Children of incarcerated parents* (pp. 89–100). New York: Lexington Books.

Kapoor, A., Lubach, G., Hedman, C., Ziegler, T. E., & Coe, C. L. (2014). Hormones in infant rhesus monkeys' (*Macaca mulatta*) hair at birth provide a window into the fetal environment. *Pediatric Research, 75*(4), 476–481. https://doi.org/10.1038/pr .2014.1.

Kapoor, A., Schultz-Darken, N., & Ziegler, T. E. (2018). Radiolabel validation of cortisol in the hair of rhesus monkeys. *Psychoneuroendocrinology, 97*, 190–195. https:// doi.org/10.1016/j.psyneuen.2018.07.022.

Katsiyannis, A., Whitford, D. K., Zhang, D., & Gage, N. A. (2018). Adult recidivism in the United States: A meta-analysis 1994–2015. *Journal of Child and Family Studies, 27*(3), 686–696. https://doi.org/10.1007/s10826-017-0945-8.

Kerr, M. L., Charles, P., Massoglia, M., Jensen, S., Wirth, J., Fanning, K., Holden, K., Poehlmann-Tynan, J. (2022). Development and implementation of an attachment-based intervention to enhance visits between children and their incarcerated parents. In Krysik, J. & Rodriguez, N. (Eds), *Children of Incarcerated Parents: From Understanding to Impact*. Springer. https://doi.org/10.1007/978-3-030-84713-5_7.

Kiczkowski, U. H. (2011). Successful community reentry after incarceration: Exploring intangible aspects of social support during the reintegration process. *Columbia Social Work Review, 9*(1), 73–85. https://doi.org/10.7916/cswr.v9i1.1955.

Kjellstrand, J. M., Reinke, W. M., & Eddy, J. M. (2018). Children of incarcerated parents: Development of externalizing behaviors across adolescence. *Children and Youth Services Review, 94*, 628–635. https://doi.org/10.1016/j.childyouth.2018.09.003.

Klein, P. S., Shohet, C., & Givon, D. (2017). A mediational intervention for sensitizing caregivers (MISC): A cross-cultural early intervention. In *Handbook of applied developmental science in sub-Saharan Africa* (pp. 291–312). Springer, New York, NY. https://doi.org/10.1007/978-1-4939-7328-6_16.

Kobak, R., Zajac, K., & Madsen, S. D. (2016). Attachment disruptions, reparative processes, and psychopathology: Theoretical and clinical implications. In J. Cassidy & P. R. Shaver (Eds.), *Handbook of attachment: Theory, research, and clinical applications* (3rd ed., pp. 25–39). Guilford Press.

Lane, J. (2020). An overview: What we know about incarcerated women and girls. *Women and Prison*, 1–13. https://doi.org/10.1007/978-3-030-46172-0_1.

Lang, J. M., Bory, C. T., & Marshall, T. (2013, March). *Supporting children following a parent's arrest: Development of a collaborative model for law enforcement, health, and child welfare* [Paper presentation]. 26th Annual Children's Mental Health Research & Policy Conference, Tampa, FL.

Langan, P. A., & Levin, D. J. (2002). *Recidivism of prisoners released in 1994*. NCJ 193427. U.S. Department of Justice, Office of Justice Programs, Bureau of Justice Statistics. https://bjs.ojp.gov/content/pub/pdf/rpr94.pdf.

La Vigne, N. G., Naser, R. L., Brooks, L. E., & Castro, J. L. (2005). Examining the effect of incarceration and in-prison family contact on prisoners' family relationships. *Journal of Contemporary Criminal Justice, 21*(4), 314–335. https://doi.org/10 .1177/1043986205281727.

Lee, R. D., Fang, X., & Luo, F. (2013). The impact of parental incarceration on the physical and mental health of young adults. *Pediatrics, 131*(4), e1188–e1195. https:// doi.org/10.1542/peds.2012-0627.

Lewis, N., & Lockwood, B. (2019a). Can you hear me now? *The Marshall Project.* https://www.themarshallproject.org/2019/12/19/can-you-hear-me-now.

Lewis, N., & Lockwood, B. (2019b). The hidden cost of incarceration. *The Marshall Project.* https://www.themarshallproject.org/2019/12/17/the-hidden-cost-of-incar ceration.

Lindquist, C., Steffey, D., McKay, T., Comfort, M., & Bir, A. (2018). The multisite family study on incarceration, partnering, and parenting: Design and sample. *Journal of Offender Rehabilitation, 57*(2), 83–95. https://doi.org/10.1080/10509674.2018.1441211.

Loeber, R., Farrington, D. P., & Stallings, R. (2011). The Pittsburgh Youth Study. In R. Loeber & D. P. Farrington (Eds.), *Young homicide offenders and victims* (pp. 19–36). Springer. https://doi.org/10.1007/978-1-4419-9949-8_2.

Loper, A. B., Carlson, L. W., Levitt, L., & Scheffel, K. (2009). Parenting stress, alliance, child contact, and adjustment of imprisoned mothers and fathers. *Journal of Offender Rehabilitation, 48*(6), 483–503. https://doi.org/10.1080/10509670903081300.

Loper, A. B., Phillips, V., Nichols, E. B., & Dallaire, D. H. (2014). Characteristics and effects of the co-parenting alliance between incarcerated parents and child caregivers. *Journal of Child and Family Studies, 23*(2), 225–241. https://doi.org/10 .1007/s10826-012-9709-7.

Loper, A. B., & Tuerk, E. H. (2010). Improving the emotional adjustment and com- munication patterns of incarcerated mothers: Effectiveness of a prison parenting intervention. *Journal of Child and Family Studies, 20*(1), 89–101. https://doi.org/10 .1007/s10826-010-9381-8.

Lowman, J. (1980). Measurement of family affective structure. *Journal of Personality Assessment, 44*(2), 130–141. https://doi.org/10.1207/s15327752jpa4402_3.

Makariev, D. W., & Shaver, P. R. (2010). Attachment, parental incarceration and pos- sibilities for intervention: An overview. *Attachment & Human Development, 12*(4), 311–331. https://doi.org/10.1080/14751790903416939.

Manenschijn, L., Spijker, A. T., Koper, J. W., Jetten, A. M., Giltay, E. J., Haffmans, J., Hoencamp, E., & van Rossum, E.F.C. (2012). Long-term cortisol in bipolar disor- der: associations with age of onset and psychiatric co-morbidity. *Psychoneuroendo- crinology, 37*(12), 1960–1968. https://doi.org/10.1016/j.psyneuen.2012.04.010.

Maruschak, L. M., Bronson, J., & Alper, M. (2021). *Parents in prison and their minor children: Survey of Prison Inmates, 2016.* NCJ 252645. U.S. Department of Justice, Office of Justice Programs, Bureau of Justice Statistics. https://bjs.ojp.gov/content /pub/pdf/pptmcspi16st.pdf.

Maruschak, L. M., Glaze, L. E., & Mumola, C. J. (2010). Incarcerated parents and their children: Findings from the Bureau of Justice Statistics. In J.M. Eddy & J. Poehlmann (Eds) *Children of incarcerated parents: A handbook for researchers and prac- titioners,* pp 33–54. Urban Institute Press.

Masten, A. S. (2014). *Ordinary magic: Resilience in development.* Guilford Press.

Masten, A. S. (2018). Resilience theory and research on children and families: Past, present, and promise. *Journal of Family Theory & Review, 10*(1), 12–31. doi:10.1111/ jftr.12255.

Masten, A. S., & Garmezy, N. (1985). Risk, vulnerability, and protective factors in developmental psychopathology. In *Advances in clinical child psychology* (pp. 1–52). Springer, Boston, MA. doi:10.1007/978-1-4613-9820-2_1.

Matheny Jr., A. P., Wachs, T. D., Ludwig, J. L., & Phillips, K. (1995). Bringing order out of chaos: Psychometric characteristics of the confusion, hubbub, and order scale. *Journal of Applied Developmental Psychology, 16*(3), 429–444. https://doi.org /10.1016/0193-3973(95)90028-4.

McClure, H. H., Shortt, J. W., Eddy, J. M., Holmes, A., Van Uum, S., Russell, E., Koren, G., Sheeber, L., Davis, B., Snodgrass, J. J., & Martinez, C. R. (2015). Associations among mother–child contact, parenting stress, and mother and child adjustment related to incarceration. In J. Poehlmann-Tynan (Ed.), *Children's contact with incarcerated parents* (pp. 59–82). Springer. https://doi.org/10.1007/978-3-319-16625-4_4.

McEwan, A. G. (2009). New insights into the protective effect of manganese against oxidative stress. *Molecular Microbiology, 72*(4), 812–814. https://doi.org/10.1111/j.13652958.2009.06700.x.

McEwen, B. S. (2012). Brain on stress: How the social environment gets under the skin. *Proceedings of the National Academy of Sciences, 109*(Suppl. 2), 17180–17185. https://doi.org/10.1073/pnas.1121254109.

McGonagle, K. A., Schoeni, R. F., Sastry, N., & Freedman, V. A. (2012). The panel study of income dynamics: Overview, recent innovations, and potential for life course research. *Longitudinal and Life Course Studies, 3*(2). https://doi.org/10.14301/llcs.v3i2.188.

McHale, J. P., Kuersten-Hogan, R., & Rao, N. (2004). Growing points for coparenting theory and research. *Journal of adult development, 11*(3), 221–234. doi:1068-0667/04/0700-0221/0.

McKay, T., Comfort, M., Lindquist, C., & Bir, A. (2019). *Holding on: Family and fatherhood during incarceration and reentry.* University of California Press. https://doi.org/10.2307/j.ctvp2n5h7.

McKay, T., Feinberg, R., Landwehr, J., Payne, J., Comfort, M, Lindquist, C. H., Kennedy, E. K., & Bir, A. (2018). "Always having hope": Father-child relationships after reentry from prison. *Journal of Offender Rehabilitation, 57*(2), 162–187. https://doi.org/10.1080/10509674.2018.1441206.

Milavetz, Z., Pritzl, K., Muentner, L., & Poehlmann-Tynan, J. (2021). Unmet mental health needs of jailed parents with young children. *Family Relations, 70*(1), 130–145. https://doi.org/10.1111/fare.12525.

Miller, A. L., Perryman, J., Markovitz, L., Franzen, S., Cochran, S., & Brown, S. (2013). Strengthening incarcerated families: Evaluating a pilot program for children of incarcerated parents and their caregivers. *Family Relations, 62*(4), 584–596. https://doi.org/10.1111/fare.12029.

Miller, A. L., Weston, L. E., Perryman, J., Horwitz, T., Franzen, S., & Cochran, S. (2014). Parenting while incarcerated: Tailoring the Strengthening Families Program for use with jailed mothers. *Children and Youth Services Review, 44*, 163–170. https://doi.org/10.1016/j.childyouth.2014.06.013.

Miller, R. J. (2021). *Halfway home: Race, punishment, and the afterlife of mass incarceration.* Hachette UK.

Mitchell, O., & Caudy, M. S. (2015). Examining racial disparities in drug arrests. *Justice Quarterly, 32*(2), 288–313. https://doi.org/10.1080/07418825.2012.761721.

Muentner, L. (2021). *Reentry and family reunification: Examining children's well-being after incarcerated parents are released from prison* [Unpublished doctoral dissertation]. University of Wisconsin-Madison.

Muentner, L. (2022). Churning through the system: Implications of fathers' reentry and recidivism after prison for children's well-being. *Crime & Delinquency.* Advance online publication. https://doi.org/10.1177/00111287221087956.

Muentner, L., & Charles, P. (2022). Family reunification after fathers are released from prison: Perspectives on children's adjustment. *Family Relations.* Advance online publication. https://doi.org/10.1111/fare.12739.

Muentner, L., & Eddy, J. M. (2021). *What they don't know won't hurt them? Linking children's knowledge of parental incarceration to post-release child well-being.* School of Social Work, University of Wisconsin-Madison.

Muentner, L., Holder, N., Burnson, C., Runion, H., Weymouth, L., & Poehlmann-Tynan, J. (2019). Jailed parents and their young children: Residential instability, homelessness, and behavior problems. *Journal of Child and Family Studies, 28*(2), 370–386. https://doi.org/10.1007/s10826-018-1265-3.

Muentner, L., Kapoor, A., Weymouth, L., & Poehlmann-Tynan, J. (2021). Getting under the skin: Physiological stress and witnessing paternal arrest in young children with incarcerated fathers. *Developmental Psychobiology, 63*(5), 1568–1582. https://doi.org/10.1002/dev.22113.

Muentner, L., Pritzl, K., Shlafer, R., & Poehlmann, J. (2022). Using a brief multimedia educational intervention to strengthen young children's feelings while visiting jailed parents. Manuscript submitted for publication.

Murphey, D., Bandy, T., & Moore, K. A. (2012). *Frequent residential mobility and young children's well-being* (pp. 1-9). Washington, DC: Child Trends.

Murphey, D., & Cooper, P. M. (2015). Parents behind bars: What happens to their children. *Child Trends, 42,* 1–22. https://www.childtrends.org/wp-content/uploads/2015/10/2015-42ParentsBehindBars.pdf.

Murray, J., & Farrington, D. P. (2008). Parental imprisonment: Long-lasting effects on boys' internalizing problems through the life course. *Development and Psychopathology, 20*(1), 273–290. https://doi.org/10.1017/S0954579408000138.

Murray, J., Farrington, D. P., & Sekol, I. (2012). Children's antisocial behavior, mental health, drug use, and educational performance after parental incarceration: A systematic review and meta-analysis. *Psychological Bulletin, 138*(2), 175–210. https://doi.org/10.1037/a0026407.

Murray, J., Loeber, R., & Pardini, D. (2012). Parental involvement in the criminal justice system and the development of youth theft, marijuana use, depression, and poor academic performance. *Criminology, 50*(1), 255–302. https://doi.org/10.1111/j.1745-9125.2011.00257.x.

Murray, J., & Murray, L. (2010). Parental incarceration, attachment and child psychopathology. *Attachment & Human Development, 12*(4), 289–309. https://doi.org/10.1080/14751790903416889.

National Research Council. (2014). *The growth of incarceration in the United States: Exploring causes and consequences.* National Academies Press. https://doi.org/10.17226/18613.

Noyes, J. L., Paul, J. C., & Berger, L. M. (2018). Should we be intervening solely (or even mostly) on the basis of parental incarceration? In C. Wildeman, A. R. Haskins, & J. Poehlmann-Tynan (Eds.), *When parents are incarcerated: Interdisciplinary research and interventions to support children* (pp. 173–193). American Psychological Association. https://doi.org/10.1037/0000062-009.

Pace, C. S., Muzi, S., Madera, F., Sansò, A., & Zavattini, G. C. (2021). Can the family drawing be a useful tool for assessing attachment representations in children? A systematic review and meta-analysis. *Attachment & Human Development,* 1–26. https://doi.org/10.1080/14616734.2021.1991664.

Palmer, F. B., Anand, K. J., Graff, J. C., Murphy, L. E., Qu, Y., Völgyi, E., Rovnaghi, C. R., Moore, A., Tran, Q. T., & Tylavsky, F. A. (2013). Early adversity, socioemotional development, and stress in urban 1-year-old children. *Journal of Pediatrics, 163*(6), 1733–1739. https://doi.org/10.1016/j.jpeds.2013.08.030.

Penn, A., author; Harper, R. E., & Leak, N. M., illustrators. (1993). *The Kissing Hand.* New York: Simon & Schuster.

Perry, A. R., & Bright, M. (2012). African American fathers and incarceration: Paternal involvement and child outcomes. *Social Work in Public Health*, 27(1–2), 187–203. https://doi.org/10.1080/19371918.2011.629856.

Pesonen, A. K., Räikkönen, K., Feldt, K., Heinonen, K., Osmond, C., Phillips, D.I.W., Barker, D.J.P., Eriksson, J. G., & Kajantie, E. (2010). Childhood separation experience predicts HPA axis hormonal responses in late adulthood: A natural experiment of World War II. *Psychoneuroendocrinology*, 35(5), 758–767. https://doi.org/10.1016/j.psyneuen.2009.10.017.

Pesonen, A. K., Räikkönen, K., Heinonen, K., Kajantie, E., Forsén, T., & Eriksson, J. G. (2008). Reproductive traits following a parent–child separation trauma during childhood: A natural experiment during World War II. *American Journal of Human Biology*, 20(3), 345–351. https://doi.org/10.1002/ajhb.20735.

Phillips, S. D., & Zhao, J. (2010). The relationship between witnessing arrests and elevated symptoms of posttraumatic stress: Findings from a national study of children involved in the child welfare system. *Children and Youth Services Review*, 32(10), 1246–1254. https://doi.org/10.1016/j.childyouth.2010.04.015.

Poehlmann, J. (2005a). Children's family environments and intellectual outcomes during maternal incarceration. *Journal of Marriage and Family*, 67(5), 1275–1285. https://doi.org/10.1111/j.1741-3737.2005.00216.x.

Poehlmann, J. (2005b). Incarcerated mothers' contact with children, perceived family relationships, and depressive symptoms. *Journal of Family Psychology*, 19(3), 350–357. https://doi.org/10.1037/0893-3200.19.3.350.

Poehlmann, J. (2005c). Representations of attachment relationships in children of incarcerated mothers. *Child Development*, 76(3), 679–696. https://doi.org/10.1111/j.1467-8624.2005.00871.x.

Poehlmann, J. (2012). Jail-prison observation checklist. Unpublished manuscript, University of Wisconsin–Madison.

Poehlmann, J., Dallaire, D., Loper, A. B., & Shear, L. D. (2010). Children's contact with their incarcerated parents: Research findings and recommendations. *American Psychologist*, 65(6), 575–598. https://doi.org/10.1037/a0020279.

Poehlmann, J., Park, J., Bouffiou, L., Abrahams, J., Shlafer, R., & Hahn, E. (2008). Representations of family relationships in children living with custodial grandparents. *Attachment & Human Development*, 10(2), 165–188. https://doi.org/10.1080/14616730802113695.

Poehlmann, J., Shlafer, R. J., Maes, E., & Hanneman, A. (2008). Factors associated with young children's opportunities for maintaining family relationships during maternal incarceration. *Family Relations*, 57(3), 267–280. https://doi.org/10.1111/j.1741-3729.2008.00499.x.

Poehlmann-Tynan, J., & Arditti, J. A. (2018). Developmental and family perspectives on parental incarceration. In C. Wildeman, A. R. Haskins, & J. Poehlmann-Tynan (Eds.), *When parents are incarcerated: Interdisciplinary research and interventions to support children* (pp. 53–81). American Psychological Association. https://doi.org/10.1037/0000062-004.

Poehlmann-Tynan, J., Burnson, C., Runion, H., & Weymouth, L. A. (2017). Attachment in young children with incarcerated fathers. *Development and Psychopathology*, 29(2), 389–404. https://doi.org/10.1017/s0954579417000062.

Poehlmann-Tynan, J., Cuthrell, H., Weymouth, L., & Burnson, C. (2018). Incarcerated parents. In B. H. Fiese, M. Celano, K. Deater-Deckard, E. N. Jouriles, & M. A. Whisman (Eds.), *APA handbook of contemporary family psychology: Applications and broad impact of family psychology* (pp. 503–521). American Psychological Association. https://doi.org/10.1037/0000100-031.

Poehlmann-Tynan, J., Cuthrell, H., Weymouth, L., Burnson, C., Frerks, L., Muentner, L., Holder, N., Milavetz, Z., Lauter, L., Hindt, L., Davis, L., Schubert, E., & Shlafer, R. (2020). Multisite randomized efficacy trial of educational materials for young children with incarcerated parents. *Development and Psychopathology, 33*(1), 1–17. https://doi.org/10.1017/s0954579419001792.

Poehlmann-Tynan, J., & Dallaire, D. H. (2021). Incarcerated mothers and their children: Implications for policy and practice. In J. Poehlmann-Tynan & D. H. Dallaire (Eds.), *Children with incarcerated mothers* (pp. 121–150). https://doi.org/10.1007/978-3-030-67599-8_8.

Poehlmann-Tynan, J., & Eddy, J. M. (2019). A research and intervention agenda for children with incarcerated parents and their families. In J. M. Eddy & J. Poehlmann-Tynan (Eds.), *Handbook on children with incarcerated parents* (2nd ed., pp. 353–371). Springer. https://doi.org/10.1007/978-3-030-16707-3_24.

Poehlmann-Tynan, J., Engbretson, A., Vigna, A. B., Weymouth, L. A., Burnson, C., Zahn-Waxler, C., Kapoor, A., Gerstein, E. D., Fanning, K. A., & Raison, C. L. (2019). Cognitively-based compassion training for parents reduces cortisol in infants and young children. *Infant Mental Health Journal, 41*(1), 126–144. https://doi.org/10.1002/imhj.21831.

Poehlmann-Tynan, J., Muentner, L., Pritzl, K., Cuthrell, H., Davis, L., Hindt, L., & Shlafer, R. (2021). The health and development of young children who witnessed their parent's arrest prior to parental jail incarceration. *International Journal of Environmental Research and Public Health, 18*(9), 4512. https://doi.org/10.3390/ijerph18094512.

Poehlmann-Tynan, J., & Pritzl, K. (2019). Parent–child visits when parents are incarcerated in prison or jail. In J. M. Eddy & J. Poehlmann-Tynan (Eds.), *Handbook on children with incarcerated parents* (2nd ed., pp. 131–147). Springer. https://doi.org/10.1007/978-3-030-16707-3_10.

Poehlmann-Tynan, J., Runion, H., Burnson, C., Maleck, S., Weymouth, L., Pettit, K., & Huser, M. (2015). Young children's behavioral and emotional reactions to Plexiglas and video visits with jailed parents. In J. Poehlmann-Tynan (Ed.), *Children's contact with incarcerated parents: Implications for policy and intervention* (pp. 39–58). Springer International Publishing. https://doi.org/10.1007/978-3-319-16625-4_3.

Poehlmann-Tynan, J., Runion, H., Weymouth, L. A., & Burnson, C. (2018). Children with incarcerated parents. In T. H. Ollendick, S. W. White, & B. A. White (Eds.), *The Oxford handbook of clinical child and adolescent psychology.* Oxford University Press. https://doi.org/10.1093/oxfordhb/9780190634841.013.33.

Poehlmann-Tynan, J., & Turney, K. (2021). A developmental perspective on children with incarcerated parents. *Child Development Perspectives, 15*(1), 3–11. https://doi.org/10.1111/cdep.12392.

Powell, B., Cooper, G., Hoffman, K., & Marvin, B. (2013). The Circle of Security intervention: Enhancing attachment in early parent-child relationships. Guilford Publications.

Pragst, F., & Balikova, M. A. (2006). State of the art in hair analysis for detection of drug and alcohol abuse. *Clinica Chimica Acta, 370*(1–2), 17–49. https://doi.org/10.1016/j.cca.2006.02.019.

Pritzl, K., Milavetz, Z., Cuthrell, H., Muentner, L., & Poehlmann-Tynan, J. (2022). Young children's contact with their parents in jail and child behavior problems. *Journal of Offender Rehabilitation, 61*(2), 88–105. https://doi.org/10.1080/10509674.2021.2018381.

Putnam, S. P., & Rothbart, M. K. (2006). Development of short and very short forms of the Children's Behavior Questionnaire. *Journal of Personality Assessment, 87*(1), 102–112. https://doi.org/10.1207/s15327752jpa8701_09.

Radloff, L. S. (1977). The CES-D scale: A self-report depression scale for research in the general population. *Applied Psychological Measurement, 1*(3), 385–401. https://doi.org/10.1177/014662167700100306.

Ranabir, S., & Reetu, K. (2011). Stress and hormones. *Indian Journal of Endocrinology and Metabolism, 15*(1), 18–22. https://doi.org/10.4103/2230-8210.77573.

Raul, J. S., Cirimele, V., Ludes, B., & Kintz, P. (2004). Detection of physiological concentrations of cortisol and cortisone in human hair. *Clinical Biochemistry, 37*(12), 1105–1111. https://doi.org/10.1016/j.clinbiochem.2004.02.010.

Reichman, N. E., Teitler, J. O., Garfinkel, I., & McLanahan, S. S. (2001). Fragile families: Sample and design. *Children and Youth Services Review, 23*(4–5), 303–326. https://doi.org/10.1016/S0190-7409(01)00141-4.

Rescorla, L. A., & Achenbach, T. M. (2004). The Achenbach System of Empirically Based Assessment (ASEBA) for ages 18 to 90 years. In M. E. Maruish (Ed.), *The use of psychological testing for treatment planning and outcomes assessment: Instruments for adults* (pp. 115–152). Lawrence Erlbaum Associates.

Rodriguez, N. (2016). Bridging the gap between research and practice: The role of science in addressing the effects of incarceration on family life. *Annals of the American Academy of Political and Social Science, 665*(1), 231–240. https://doi.org/10.1177/0002716216633404.

Roid, G. H., & Barram, R. A. (2004). *Essentials of Stanford-Binet intelligence scales (SB5) assessment.* John Wiley & Sons.

Roid, G. H., & Pomplun, M. (2012). *The Stanford-Binet Intelligence Scales.* Guilford Press.

Roisman, G. I., & Cicchetti, D. (2017). Attachment in the context of atypical caregiving. *Development and Psychopathology, 29*(2), 331–335. https://doi.org/10.1017/s0954579417000013.

Rothbart, M. K., Ahadi, S. A., & Hershey, K. L. (1994). Temperament and social behavior in childhood. *Merrill-Palmer Quarterly*, 21–39.

Rothbart, M. K., Ahadi, S. A., Hershey, K. L., & Fisher, P. (2001). Investigations of temperament at three to seven years: The Children's Behavior Questionnaire. *Child Development, 72*(5), 1394–1408. https://doi.org/10.1111/1467-8624.00355.

Rubenstein, B. Y., Toman, E. L., & Cochran, J. C. (2021). Socioeconomic barriers to child contact with incarcerated parents. *Justice Quarterly, 38*(4), 725–751. https://doi.org/10.1080/07418825.2019.1606270.

Ruhland, E. L., Davis, L., Atella, J., & Shlafer, R. J. (2020). Externalizing behavior among youth with a current or formerly incarcerated parent. *International Journal of Offender Therapy and Comparative Criminology, 64*(1), 3–21. https://doi.org/10.1177/0306624X19855317.

Ruiz, D. S., & Kopak, A. (2014). The consequences of parental incarceration for African American mothers, children, and grandparent caregivers. *Journal of Pan African Studies, 7*(6), 9–25. http://www.jpanafrican.org/docs/vol7no6/7.6-4-Ruitz-Oct26.pdf.

Russell, E., Koren, G., Rieder, M., & Van Uum, S. (2012). Hair cortisol as a biological marker of chronic stress: Current status, future directions and unanswered questions. *Psychoneuroendocrinology, 37*(5), 589–601. https://doi.org/10.1016/j.psyneuen.2011.09.009.

Sanders, M. R. (2008). Triple P-Positive Parenting Program as a public health approach to strengthening parenting. *Journal of Family Psychology, 22*(4), 506–517. https://doi.org/10.1037/0893-3200.22.3.506.

Sawyer, W., & Bertram, W. (2018, May 13). *Jail will separate 2.3 million mothers from their children this year.* Prison Policy Initiative. https://www.prisonpolicy.org/blog/2018/05/13/mothers-day-2018/.

Sawyer, W., & Wagner, P. (2019). *Mass incarceration: The whole pie 2019*. Prison Policy Initiative. https://www.prisonpolicy.org/reports/pie2019.html.

Sawyer, W., & Wagner, P. (2020). *Mass incarceration: The whole pie 2020*. Prison Policy Initiative. https://www.prisonpolicy.org/factsheets/pie2020_allimages.pdf.

Schmeer, K. K., Guardino, C., Irwin, J. L., Ramey, S., Shalowitz, M., & Dunkel Schetter, C. (2020). Maternal postpartum stress and toddler developmental delays: Results from a multisite study of racially diverse families. *Developmental Psychobiology, 62*(1), 62–76. https://doi.org/10.1002/dev.21871.

Senghor, S. (2016). *Writing my wrongs: Life, death, and redemption in an American prison.* Convergent Books.

Shanahan, R., & Agudelo, S. V. (2012). The family and recidivism. *American Jails, 26*(4), 17–24. https://www.prisonpolicy.org/scans/vera/the-family-and-recidivism.pdf.

Shlafer, R. J., Davis, L., Hindt, L., Weymouth, L., Cuthrell, H., Burnson, C., & Poehlmann-Tynan, J. (2020). Fathers in jail and their minor children: Paternal characteristics and associations with father-child contact. *Journal of Child and Family Studies, 29*(3), 791–801. https://doi.org/10.1007/s10826-020-01696-3.

Shlafer, R., Duwe, G., & Hindt, L. (2019). Parents in prison and their minor children: Comparisons between state and national estimates. *The Prison Journal, 99*(3), 310–328. https://doi.org/10.1177/0032885519836996.

Shlafer, R. J., Loper, A. B., & Schillmoeller, L. (2015). Introduction and literature review: Is parent-child contact during parental incarceration beneficial? In J. Poehlmann-Tynan (Ed.), *Children's contact with incarcerated parents: Implications for policy and intervention* (pp. 1–21). Springer International Publishing. https://doi.org/10.1007/978-3-319-16625-4_1.

Shlafer, R. J., & Poehlmann, J. (2010). Attachment and caregiving relationships in families affected by parental incarceration. *Attachment & Human Development, 12*(4), 395–415. https://doi.org/10.1080/14616730903417052.

Shonkoff, J. P., Garner, A. S., Siegel, B. S., Dobbins, M. I., Earls, M. F., McGuinn, L., Pascoe, J., Wood, D. L., & Committee on Early Childhood, Adoption, and Dependent Care. (2012). The lifelong effects of early childhood adversity and toxic stress. *Pediatrics, 129*(1), e232–e246. https://doi.org/10.1542/peds.2011-2663.

Shulman, H. B., D'Angelo, D. V., Harrison, L., Smith, R. A., & Warner, L. (2018). The Pregnancy Risk Assessment Monitoring System (PRAMS): Overview of design and methodology. *American Journal of Public Health, 108*(10), 1305–1313. https://doi.org/10.2105/AJPH.2018.304563.

Siegel, J. A. (2011). *Disrupted childhoods: Children of women in prison.* Rutgers University Press.

Skora Horgan, E., & Poehlmann-Tynan, J. (2020). In-home video chat between young children and their incarcerated parents. *Journal of Children and Media, 14*(3), 400–406. https://doi.org/10.1080/17482798.2020.1792082.

Smith, C. J., & Young, D. S. (2017). A retrospective look at the experience of parental incarceration and family reentry during adolescence. *Social Work in Public Health, 32*(8), 475–488. https://doi.org/10.1080/19371918.2017.1360819.

Stalder, T., Kirschbaum, C., Heinze, K., Steudte, S., Foley, P., Tietze, A., & Dettenborn, L. (2010). Use of hair cortisol analysis to detect hypercortisolism during active drinking phases in alcohol-dependent individuals. *Biological Psychology, 85*(3), 357–360. https://doi.org/10.1016/j.biopsycho.2010.08.005.

Stalder, T., & Kirschbaum, C. (2012). Analysis of cortisol in hair—state of the art and future directions. *Brain, Behavior, and Immunity, 26*(7), 1019–1029. https://doi.org/10.1016/j.bbi.2012.02.002.

Stalder, T., Steudte, S., Miller, R., Skoluda, N., Dettenborn, L., & Kirschbaum, C. (2012). Intraindividual stability of hair cortisol concentrations. *Psychoneuroendocrinology*, *37*(5), 602–610. https://doi.org/10.1016/j.psyneuen.2011.08.007.

Staufenbiel, S. M., Penninx, B. W., Spijker, A. T., Elzinga, B. M., & van Rossum, E. F. (2013). Hair cortisol, stress exposure, and mental health in humans: a systematic review. *Psychoneuroendocrinology*, *38*(8), 1220–1235. https://doi.org/10.1016/j.psyneuen.2012.11.015.

Swavola, E., Riley, K., & Subramanian, R. (2016) Overlooked: Women and jails in an era of reform (pp. 1–48). New York: Vera Institute of Justice. https://www.vera.org/downloads/publications/overlooked-women-and-jails-report/legacy_downloads/overlooked-women-and-jails-report.pdf.

Sykes, B. L., & Pettit, B. (2019). Measuring the exposure of parents and children to incarceration. In J. M. Eddy & J. Poehlmann-Tynan (Eds.), *Handbook on children with incarcerated parents* (2nd ed., pp. 11–23). Springer. https://doi.org/10.1007/978-3-030-16707-3_2.

Tadros, E., Fanning, K., Jensen, S., & Poehlmann-Tynan, J. (2021). Coparenting and mental health in families with jailed parents. *International Journal of Environmental Research and Public Health*, *18*(16), 8705. https://doi.org/10.3390/ijerph18168705.

Tasca, M. (2014). "It's not all cupcakes and lollipops": An investigation of the predictors and effects of prison visitation for children during maternal and paternal incarceration [Unpublished doctoral dissertation]. Arizona State University.

Tasca, M. (2016). The gatekeepers of contact: Child–caregiver dyads and parental prison visitation. *Criminal Justice and Behavior*, *43*(6), 739–758. https://doi.org/10.1177/0093854815613528.

Tasca, M., Rodriguez, N., & Zatz, M. S. (2011). Family and residential instability in the context of paternal and maternal incarceration. *Criminal justice and behavior*, *38*(3), 231–247. doi:10.1177/0093854810391632.

Teicher, M. H. (2018). Childhood trauma and the enduring consequences of forcibly separating children from parents at the United States border. *BMC Medicine*, *16*(1), 1–3. https://doi.org/10.1186/s12916-018-1147-y.

Testa, A., & Jackson, D. B. (2021). Parental incarceration and school readiness: Findings from the 2016 to 2018 National Survey of Children's Health. *Academic Pediatrics*, *21*(3), 534–541. https://doi.org/10.1016/j.acap.2020.08.016.

Teti, D. M., & Ablard, K. E. (1989). Security of attachment and infant-sibling relationships: A laboratory study. *Child Development*, 1519–1528. https://doi.org/10.2307/1130940.

Teti, D. M., Nakagawa, M., Das, R., & Wirth, O. (1991). Security of attachment between preschoolers and their mothers: Relations among social interaction, parenting stress, and mother's sorts of the Attachment Q-Set. *Developmental Psychology*, *27*(3), 440–447. https://doi.org/10.1037/0012-1649.27.3.440.

Thomas, A., Wirth, J. C., Poehlmann-Tynan, J., & Pate Jr, D. J. (2022). "When She Says Daddy": Black fathers' recidivism following reentry from Jail. *International Journal of Environmental Research and Public Health*, *19*(6), 3518. https://doi.org/10.3390/ijerph19063518.

Thomas, K. A., & So, M. (2016). Lost in limbo: An exploratory study of homeless mothers' experiences and needs at Emergency Assistance Hotels. *Families in Society*, *97*(2), 120–131. doi:10.1606/1044-3894.2016.97.15.

Thomas, R., & Zimmer-Gembeck, M. J. (2007). Behavioral outcomes of parent-child interaction therapy and Triple P-Positive Parenting Program: A review and meta-analysis. *Journal of Abnormal Child Psychology*, *35*(3), 475–495. https://doi.org/10.1007/s10802-007-9104-9.

Thomson, S., Koren, G., Fraser, L. A., Rieder, M., Friedman, T. C., & Van Uum, S.H.M. (2010). Hair analysis provides a historical record of cortisol levels in Cushing's syndrome. *Experimental and Clinical Endocrinology & Diabetes, 118*(02), 133–138. https://doi.org/10.1055/s-0029-1220771.

Thurau, L. H. (2015). *First, do no harm: Model practices for law enforcement agencies when arresting parents in the presence of children* [White paper]. http://strategiesforyouth.org /sfysite/wpcontent/uploads/2012/09/First_Do_No_Harm_Report.pdf.

Tsemberis, S., McHugo, G., Williams, V., Hanrahan, P., & Stefancic, A. (2007). Measuring homelessness and residential stability: The residential time-line follow-back inventory. *Journal of Community Psychology, 35*(1), 29–42. https://doi.org/10 .1002/jcop.20132.

Tuerk, E. H., & Loper, A. B. (2006). Contact between incarcerated mothers and their children: Assessing parenting stress. *Journal of Offender Rehabilitation, 43*(1), 23–43. https://doi.org/10.1300/J076v43n01_02.

Turner, J. J., Bradford, K., Higginbotham, B. J., & Coppin, A. (2021). Examining the outcomes of the InsideOut dad fatherhood education program for incarcerated minority fathers. *Family Journal, 29*(3), 305–315. https://doi.org/10.1177/1066480 72097854.

Turney, K. (2014a). The consequences of paternal incarceration for maternal neglect and harsh parenting. *Social Forces, 92*(4), 1607–1636. https://doi.org/10.1093/sf/sot160.

Turney, K. (2014b). Stress proliferation across generations? Examining the relationship between parental incarceration and childhood health. *Journal of Health and Social Behavior, 55*(3), 302–319. https://doi.org/10.1177/0022146514544173.

Turney, K. (2018). Adverse childhood experiences among children of incarcerated parents. *Children and Youth Services Review, 89*, 218–225. https://doi.org/10.1016/j .childyouth.2018.04.033.

Turney, K. (2021). Family member incarceration and mental health: Results from a nationally representative survey. *SSM—Mental Health, 1*, 100002. https://doi.org /10.1016/j.ssmmh.2021.100002.

Turney, K., & Conner, E. (2019). Jail incarceration: A common and consequential form of criminal justice contact. *Annual Review of Criminology, 2*(1), 265–290. https://doi.org/10.1146/annurev-criminol-011518-024601.

Turney, K., & Haskins, A. R. (2014). Falling behind? Children's early grade retention after paternal incarceration. *Sociology of Education, 87*(4), 241–258. https://doi.org /10.1177/0038040714547086.

Turney, K., & Haskins, A. R. (2019). Parental incarceration and children's well-being: Findings from the fragile families and child well-being study. In J. M. Eddy & J. Poehlmann-Tynan (Eds.), *Handbook on children with incarcerated parents* (2nd ed., pp. 53–64). Springer. https://doi.org/10.1007/978-3-030-16707-3_5.

Turney, K., & Wildeman, C. (2015). Detrimental for some? Heterogeneous effects of maternal incarceration on child wellbeing. *Criminology & Public Policy, 14*(1), 125–156. https://doi.org/10.1111/1745-9133.12109.

Ullmann, E., Perry, S. W., Licinio, J., Wong, M. L., Dremencov, E., Zavjalov, E. L., & Tseilikman, V. (2019). From allostatic load to allostatic state  an endogenous sympathetic strategy to deal with chronic anxiety and stress?. *Frontiers in Behavioral Neuroscience, 13*, 47. https://doi.org/10.3389/fnbeh.2019.00047.

Vaghri, Z., Guhn, M., Weinberg, J., Grunau, R. E., Yu, W., & Hertzman, C. (2013). Hair cortisol reflects socio-economic factors and hair zinc in preschoolers. *Psychoneuroendocrinology, 38*(3), 331–340. https://doi.org/10.1016/j.psyneuen.2012.06.009.

Valenzuela, M. J., & Sachdev, P. (2007). *Life Experiences Questionnaire (LEQ)* [Database record]. APA PsycTests. https://doi.org/10.1037/t71113-000.

Valiente, C., Lemery-Chalfant, K., Swanson, J., & Reiser, M. (2008). Prediction of children's academic competence from their effortful control, relationships, and classroom participation. *Journal of Educational Psychology, 100*(1), 67. https://doi.org/10.1037/0022-0663.100.1.67.

Van Holland, B. J., Frings-Dresen, M. H., & Sluiter, J. K. (2012). Measuring short-term and long-term physiological stress effects by cortisol reactivity in saliva and hair. *International Archives of Occupational and Environmental Health, 85*(8), 849–852. https://doi.org/10.1007/s00420-011-0727-3.

Van IJzendoorn, M. H., Vereijken, C.M.J.L., Bakermans-Kranenburg, M. J., & Marianne Riksen-Walraven, J. (2004). Assessing attachment security with the Attachment Q Sort: Meta-analytic evidence for the validity of the observer AQS. *Child Development, 75*(4), 1188–1213. https://doi.org/10.1111/j.1467-8624.2004.00733.x.

Vaughn, B. E., & Waters, E. (1990). Attachment behavior at home and in the laboratory: Q-sort observations and strange situation classifications of one-year-olds. *Child Development, 61*(6), 1965–1973. https://doi.org/10.2307/1130850.

Vernon-Feagans, L., Garrett-Peters, P., Willoughby, M., Mills-Koonce, R., & Family Life Project Key Investigators. (2012). Chaos, poverty, and parenting: Predictors of early language development. *Early Childhood Research Quarterly, 27*(3), 339–351. https://doi.org/10.1016/j.ecresq.2011.11.001.

Visher, C. A. (2007). Returning home: Emerging findings and policy lessons about prisoner reentry. *Federal Sentencing Reporter, 20*(1), 93–102. doi:10.1525/fsr.2007.20.2.93.

Visher, C. A. (2013). Incarcerated fathers: Pathways from prison to home. *Criminal Justice Policy Review, 24*(1), 9–26. doi:10.1177/0887403411418105.

Visher, C., & Courtney, S. M. (2007). *One year out: Experiences of prisoners returning to Cleveland*. Urban Institute Justice Policy Center.

Wagner, P., & Jones, A. (2019). State of phone justice: Local jails, state prisons and private phone providers. Prison Policy Initiative. https://www.prisonpolicy.org/phones/state_of_phone_justice.html.

Wakefield, S., Lee, H., & Wildeman, C. (2016). Tough on crime, tough on families? Criminal justice and family life in America. *Annals of the American Academy of Political and Social Science, 665*(1), 8–21. https://doi.org/10.1177/0002716216637048.

Wakefield, S., & Powell, K. (2016). Distinguishing petty offenders from serious criminals in the estimation of family life effects. *Annals of the American Academy of Political and Social Science, 665*(1), 195–212. https://doi.org/10.1177/0002716216633078.

Wakefield, S., & Uggen, C. (2010). Incarceration and stratification. *Annual Review of Sociology, 36*(1), 387–406. https://doi.org/10.1146/annurev.soc.012809.102551.

Wakefield, S., & Wildeman, C. (2013). *Children of the prison boom: Mass incarceration and the future of American inequality*. Oxford University Press. https://doi.org/10.1093/acprof:oso/9780199989225.001.0001.

Wakefield, S., & Wildeman, C. (2018). How parental incarceration harms children and what to do about it. *National Council on Family Relations, 3*(1), 1–6.

Washington State Department of Corrections. (n.d.). *Community Parenting Alternative (CPA)*. Retrieved from: https://www.doc.wa.gov/corrections/justice/sentencing/community-parenting.htm.

Waters, E. (1995). Appendix A: The Attachment Q-Set (version 3.0). *Monographs of the Society for Research in Child Development, 60*(2–3), 234–246. https://doi.org/10.1111/j.1540-5834.1995.tb00214.x.

Waters, E., & Deane, K. E. (1985). Defining and assessing individual differences in attachment relationships: Q-methodology and the organization of behavior in infancy and early childhood. *Monographs of the Society for Research in Child Development, 50*(1–2), 41–65. https://doi.org/10.2307/3333826.

Western, B. (2018). *Homeward: Life in the year after prison.* Russell Sage Foundation.

Western, B., Lopoo, L., & McLanahan, S. (2004). Incarceration and the bonds among parents in fragile families. In M. Pattillo, D. Weiman, & B. Western (Eds.), *Imprisoning America: The social effects of mass incarceration* (pp. 21–45). Russell Sage Foundation.

Western, B., & Wildeman, C. (2008). Punishment, inequality, and the future of mass incarceration. *Kansas Law Review, 57*(4), 851–877. https://doi.org/10.17161/1808 .20098.

Weymouth, L. A. (2016). *Family chaos, caregiving quality and stress among children of jailed parents: A pilot study* [Unpublished doctoral dissertation]. University of Wisconsin -Madison.

White, B. A., West, K. J., & Fuller-Thomson, E. (2020). Is exposure to family member incarceration during childhood linked to diabetes in adulthood? Findings from a representative community sample. *SAGE Open Medicine, 8.* https://doi.org /10.1177/2050312120905165.

Wildeman, C. (2010). Paternal incarceration and children's physically aggressive behaviors: Evidence from the fragile families and Child Wellbeing Study. *Social Forces, 89*(1), 285–309. https://doi.org/10.1353/sof.2010.0055.

Wildeman, C., Haskins, A. R., & Poehlmann-Tynan, J. (2018). Conclusion: Steps for future interdisciplinary research and interventions for children with incarcerated parents. In C. Wildeman, A. R. Haskins, & J. Poehlmann-Tynan (Eds.), *When parents are incarcerated: Interdisciplinary research and interventions to support children* (pp. 195–199). American Psychological Association. https://doi.org/10.1037/0000062-010.

Wildeman, C., Schnittker, J., & Turney, K. (2012). Despair by association? The mental health of mothers with children by recently incarcerated fathers. *American Sociological Review, 77*(2), 216–243. https://doi.org/10.1177/0003122411436234.

Wildeman, C., & Turney, K. (2014). Positive, negative, or null? the effects of maternal incarceration on children's behavioral problems. *Demography, 51*(3), 1041–1068. https://doi.org/10.1007/s13524-014-0291-z.

Xie, Q., Gao, W., Li, J., Qiao, T., Jin, J., Deng, H., & Lu, Z. (2011). Correlation of cortisol in 1cm hair segment with salivary cortisol in human: Hair cortisol as an endogenous biomarker. *Clinical Chemistry and Laboratory Medicine, 49*(12), 2013–2019. https://doi.org/10.1515/CCLM.2011.706.

Yaros, A., Ramirez, D., Tueller, S., McKay, T., Lindquist, C. H., Helburn, A., Feinberg, R., & Bir, A. (2018). Child well-being when fathers return from prison. *Journal of Offender Rehabilitation, 57*(2), 144–161. https://doi.org/10.1080/10509674 .2018.1441204.

Yi, Y., Turney, K., & Wildeman, C. (2017). Mental health among jail and prison inmates. *American Journal of Men's Health, 11*(4), 900–909. https://doi.org/10.1177 /1557988316681339.

Yocum, A., & Nath, S. (2011). Anticipating father reentry: A qualitative study of children's and mothers' experiences. *Journal of Offender Rehabilitation, 50*(5), 286–304.

Young, D. S., & Smith, C. J. (2019). Young adult reflections on the impact of parental incarceration and reentry. *Journal of Offender Rehabilitation, 58*(5), 421–443. https:// doi.org/10.1080/10509674.2019.1615596.

Young, D. S., & Smith, C. J. (2000). When moms are incarcerated: The needs of children, mothers, and caregivers. *Families in Society, 81*(2), 130–141. https://doi .org/10.1606/1044-3894.1007.

Zahn-Waxler, C., Shirtcliff, E. A., & Marceau, K. (2008). Disorders of childhood and adolescence: Gender and psychopathology. *Annual Review of Clinical Psychology, 4*, 275–303. https://doi.org/10.1146/annurev.clinpsy.3.022806.091358.

Zeng, Z. (2020). *Jail inmates in 2018*. NCJ 253044. U.S. Department of Justice, Office of Justice Programs, Bureau of Justice Statistics. https://bjs.ojp.gov/content/pub/pdf/ji18.pdf.

Zeng, Z., & Minton, T. D. (2021). *Jail inmates in 2019*. NCJ 255608. U.S. Department of Justice, Office of Justice Programs, Bureau of Justice Statistics. https://bjs.ojp.gov/content/pub/pdf/ji19.pdf.

Zhang, J., & Flynn, C. (2020). University students/graduates who have experienced parental incarceration: A qualitative exploratory study of protective processes. *Qualitative Social Work, 19*(5–6), 882–900. https://doi.org/10.1177/1473325019888007.

# Notes on Contributors

Hilary Cuthrell began working with individuals involved in the criminal legal system in 2009, while earning an undergraduate degree at DePaul University in Chicago, Illinois. She then earned her MS and PhD from the School of Human Ecology-Human Development and Family Studies program at the University of Wisconsin-Madison in 2016. While enrolled at the University of Wisconsin-Madison, she spent several years working on research centered on children with incarcerated parents while in Dr. Julie Poehlmann's Parent-Child Interaction Lab. She acted as an affiliate of the University of Wisconsin-Madison's Center for Child and Family Well-Being, where she served for four years under the U.S. federal government's Intergovernmental Personnel Act program with the National Institute of Corrections in Washington, DC. As a correctional program specialist, she primarily works on programs designed to enhance visits between children and their incarcerated parents in jails and prisons throughout the United States. Throughout her work, she continues to search for innovative ways to document and share lived experiences by individuals and families entangled in the criminal legal system.

Luke Muentner is a postdoctoral research associate in the University of Minnesota's Department of Pediatrics, Division of General Pediatrics and Adolescent Health. His research investigates the collateral consequences of parental incarceration and community reentry for children and families. He received his PhD and MSW from the University of Wisconsin-Madison's Sandra Rosenbaum School of Social Work, where he was also a graduate research fellow with the Institute for Research on Poverty. In addition to his academic work, he has social work practice experience supporting men reintegrating into the community after jail and prison, designing and implementing community interventions for families following parental incarceration, as well as engaging with grassroots organizing efforts for criminal legal reform and prison abolition. Throughout his work, he advocates for the expansion of evidence-based rehabilitative programming and community-based alternatives to incarceration that meet individuals' needs while simultaneously emphasizing and amplifying aspects of individual, family, and community resilience.

JULIE POEHLMANN is a professor in Human Development and Family Studies and the Dorothy A. O'Brien Professor of Human Ecology at the University of Wisconsin-Madison. She is also an affiliate of the Institute for Research on Poverty and the Center for Healthy Minds, and a licensed psychologist. Through publications and outreach efforts during the past 25 years, she has brought the attention of the child development community and the public to children with incarcerated parents and their families, with more than 100 publications, including editing two books and three monographs focusing on children with incarcerated parents. Her research has been funded by the National Institutes of Health, the Institute for Clinical and Translational Research, the Department of Justice, and the Mind and Life Institute. She has served as an advisor to Sesame Workshop to help develop, disseminate, and evaluate their Emmy-nominated initiative for young children with incarcerated parents called Little Children, Big Challenges: Incarceration, in addition to consulting on multiple initiatives in Wisconsin, across the United States, and internationally.

HILARY, LUKE, and JULIE love working together and they contributed equally to this book.

# Index

**Available titles in the Critical Issues in Crime and Society series:**

Michael J. Lynch, *Big Prisons, Big Dreams: Crime and the Failure of America's Penal System*

Liam Martin, *The Social Logic of Recidivism: Cultural Capital from Prisons to the Streets*

Allison McKim, *Addicted to Rehab: Race, Gender, and Drugs in the Era of Mass Incarceration*

Raymond J. Michalowski and Ronald C. Kramer, eds., *State-Corporate Crime: Wrongdoing at the Intersection of Business and Government*

Susan L. Miller, *Victims as Offenders: The Paradox of Women's Violence in Relationships*

Torin Monahan, *Surveillance in the Time of Insecurity*

Torin Monahan and Rodolfo D. Torres, eds., *Schools under Surveillance: Cultures of Control in Public Education*

Ana Muñiz, *Police, Power, and the Production of Racial Boundaries*

Marianne O. Nielsen and Linda M. Robyn, *Colonialism Is Crime*

Leslie Paik, *Discretionary Justice: Looking Inside a Juvenile Drug Court*

Anthony M. Platt, *The Child Savers: The Invention of Delinquency*, 40th anniversary edition with an introduction and critical commentaries compiled by Miroslava Chávez-García

Lois Presser, *Why We Harm*

Joshua M. Price, *Prison and Social Death*

Heidi Reynolds-Stenson, *Cultures of Resistance: Collective Action and Rationality in the Anti-Terror Age*

Diana Rickard, *Sex Offenders, Stigma, and Social Control*

Jeffrey Ian Ross, ed., *The Globalization of Supermax Prisons*

Dawn L. Rothe and Christopher W. Mullins, eds., *State Crime, Current Perspectives*

Jodi Schorb, *Reading Prisoners: Literature, Literacy, and the Transformation of American Punishment, 1700–1845*

Susan F. Sharp, *Hidden Victims: The Effects of the Death Penalty on Families of the Accused*

Susan F. Sharp, *Mean Lives, Mean Laws: Oklahoma's Women Prisoners*

Robert H. Tillman and Michael L. Indergaard, *Pump and Dump: The Rancid Rules of the New Economy*

Mariana Valverde, *Law and Order: Images, Meanings, Myths*

Michael Welch, *Crimes of Power and States of Impunity: The U.S. Response to Terror*

Michael Welch, *Scapegoats of September 11th: Hate Crimes and State Crimes in the War on Terror*

Saundra D. Westervelt and Kimberly J. Cook, *Life after Death Row: Exonerees' Search for Community and Identity*